Confessions from Correspondentland

"Nick uses words like a musician uses notes... He was my inspiration when I was first trying to break into foreign correspondent reporting."

Alex Crawford OBE
Sky News Special Correspondent

"Nick Bryant is everything a foreign correspondent should be: fair-minded, humane, witty, and warm."

Justin Webb
BBC Radio 4's *Today* programme

Nick Bryant is the New York correspondent for the BBC. He served as the BBC Washington correspondent during the Bush and Clinton presidencies, and was also based in South Asia, where he reported from Afghanistan, India and Pakistan. He has written for *The Times*, *Economist*, *Independent*, and *Australian*. Nick studied history at the University of Cambridge and has a doctorate in American politics from the University of Oxford.

NICK BRYANT

CONFESSIONS FROM CORRESPONDENT-LAND

THE DANGERS & DELIGHTS OF LIFE AS A FOREIGN CORRESPONDENT

ONEWORLD

A Oneworld Book

Published by Oneworld Publications 2012
Originally published in Australia by William Heinemann,
an imprint of Random House Australia Pty Ltd,
Level 3, 100 Pacific Highway,
North Sydney NSW 2060

This edition published in 2013

ISBN 978-1-85168-933-0
eBook ISBN 978-1-78074-101-7

Internal design by Xou, Australia
Typeset in Sabon by Xou, Australia
Cover design by Kirk DouPonce, DogEared Design
Printed and bound by CPI Group (UK) Ltd, Croydon, CR0 4YY

Oneworld Publications
10 Bloomsbury Street, London WC1B 3SR

To my darling Fleur, who has brought
me on the happiest of detours

Contents

Introduction

Hotel Kabul

The laundry list at the Kabul Intercontinental spoke of the sudden changes that had overtaken my life: shirts, $1; trousers, $3; commando suits, $15. In the lobby down below, chipboard hoardings covered a row of shattered windows, destroyed the week before when Taliban insurgents launched a rocket attack that showered glass on new arrivals checking in at reception and knocked diners in the restaurant off their chairs. Prostrate at my feet was our translator, a Kandahari man with rotting teeth, two wives, extravagantly applied black eyeliner and a vaguely flirtatious stare, who was kneeling towards Mecca in readiness for sundown prayers. Just over the way was a huge white marquee, a gift from Germany, where it had previously been used to host Rhineland beer festivals. Now, two years on from the attacks of 9/11, it played host to tribal leaders, returned refugees and even women's rights activists who had gathered for a *loya jirga*, a grand council, convened to pave the way for elections now that the Taliban had fled the capital. Outside the window, howling manically, was a pack of feral dogs tearing apart a defenceless goat, which was usefully metaphoric for the power struggles about to be unleashed next door.

Cast in the role of founding fathers was a disreputable

collection of unreformed warlords, who arrived at the opening ceremony of the *loya jirga* in brand-new SUVs, with smoke-glassed windows and Kalashnikov-toting bodyguards at front and rear. Slaloming through the thigh-high concrete blast walls past policemen wearing heavy, Stalin-style overcoats and soldiers sitting atop rusting Soviet-era tanks, the length of their motorcades was a measure of their power.

Following in their wake came a mud-splattered white minibus carrying a children's choir dressed in traditional costumes representing every ethnic tribe. Picked as much for their cuteness as for their musicianship, these infants had spent weeks rehearsing a special Afghan peace song. Presumably, the American and United Nations image-makers who had choreographed this pageant intended the cameras to focus on these beatific youngsters. Alas, when the choir drew up to the convention site, the children had to sprint from their minibus to the safety of the marquee with the scrambling urgency of pupils escaping a Columbine-style shooting, such was the fear that Taliban snipers could take potshots from the mountains high above. Since the grammar of television news demands that reports begin with an exclamation mark, the pictures were irresistible and ideal for an opening montage of shots.

Kabul felt different. Momentous. Thrilling. After spending much of the previous five years perched inside a backless tent on a rooftop high above the White House, providing a galloping commentary on the presidencies of Bill Clinton and George W. Bush, I had made it back to that kingdom of the journalistic mind that perhaps we should call 'Correspondentland'. That place of boundless adventure, breathless reportage and ill-fitting flak jackets, of khaki waistcoats with a ridiculous surfeit of pockets, often exaggerated tales of derring-do and occasional moments of extreme personal recklessness, which we preferred to call bravery.

In Washington, my colleagues in the West Wing press pack were a clean-cut bunch with near-perfect teeth, hurricane-proof hair and the kind of smiles that did not quite say 'Have a nice day' but were buoyant nonetheless. In Kabul, the conflict-frazzled journalists looked like extras from the set of an Indiana Jones remake after months of on-location filming. That simple difference in clothing spoke of the frontier I had crossed: I had gone from being a suits correspondent to rejoining the fraternity of boots.

Travelling the world with the White House press corps, we used to grumble that the seats in business class on the press charter did not fully recline, or that the souvenir stands outside our hotel filing centres had only a narrow range of carved African tribal decorations (Abuja), babushka dolls (Moscow) or Imodium (Delhi). Here at Hotel Kabul, however, the phrase 'occupational hazards' truly meant just that, from the plug-less heaters in our ice-cold rooms, which could only be activated by jamming two frayed wires into a live power socket, to the outdoor pool, which was shamrock green. As for the chipboard hoardings in the foyer, they were a complete conversational taboo. Even to mention them was a sign that you did not belong, and no one would admit to that.

At a time when Iraq was in virtual lockdown, with many international journalists wary of leaving their bureaux or hotels out of fear of being kidnapped and then beheaded, Afghanistan was not only a must-see destination on the post-9/11 beat but also a can-see destination. For foreign correspondents, it had long been viewed as a kind of adult theme park, divided, Disney-like, into a hotchpotch of different realms. There was Warlordland: the personal fiefdoms of vying chieftains – hard men with heavily armed private armies, homicidal tendencies and ludicrously gauche mansions with pink stucco facades funded from the proceeds of black-tar heroin. Warlordland, as often as not, occupied the same turf as Opiumland, the vast swathes of countryside planted with poppy flowers that continued to be the source of ninety per cent of the world's heroin. Even then, two years after the 'liberation' of Kabul, it was possible to speak of a Talibanland: the pockets of obdurate resistance in the south and east of the country, where black-turban-clad Talibs imposed their murderous reading of sharia law.

More familiar to a recent transplant from Washington was a kind of Main Street, USA, located at Bagram Air Base, a sprawling military complex 40 minutes from Kabul. In observance of the rule that wherever American soldiers tread fast food must quickly follow, there was a Burger King, Pizza Hut, Popeyes Chicken and a number of Seattle-style coffee bars – food and drink intended as much for its comfort as its speed. Just about the only thing that was not super-sized about the American presence was its fighting contingent, for the simple reason that so many soldiers had been diverted to Iraq.

Though the men and women who remained behind sported T-shirts decorated with the slogan 'Get Osama for Mama' – gone now was the Cold War chic of 'Kill a Commie for Mommy' – it was proving infuriatingly difficult to establish the precise whereabouts of Osama bin Laden. He was thought to be somewhere over the Pakistan border in lawless Waziristan, hunkered down in some cave or secret compound, but the search for Saddam Hussein's latest bolt-hole, along with those elusive weapons of mass destruction, had now taken precedence.

Like all good theme parks, this new Afghanistan was based to a large extent on pretence and unreality, and, as was often the way in the post-9/11 world, few things were quite as they seemed. Consider the road from Kabul to Kandahar. Long stretches had been recently covered with asphalt in what was now being touted as a monument to post-war reconstruction. Yet when a section of the highway was opened on the eve of the *loya jirga*, VIPs had to be helicoptered to the site of the ceremony because it was too hazardous to drive. The Taliban regularly killed and kidnapped the construction workers who had built it, and now threatened to turn their guns on the visiting dignitaries. That day, the country's interim leader, and future president, Hamid Karzai, who arrived wearing his trademark Karakul hat made from the downy fur of lamb foetuses, performed the ribbon-cutting duties. Yet Karzai only rarely ventured beyond the city limits of the capital, and thus the de facto president of Afghanistan was commonly known as 'the Mayor of Kabul' – a lesser title that tidily captured his powerlessness.

Likewise, the *loya jirga* was presented as a cradle of democracy, even though the presence of so many warlords, and their involvement in the national government, implied that any form of parliamentary government would be dead at birth. With these militia commanders sitting threateningly at the front of the stage, like an identity parade of suspected war criminals, free speech and debate were impaired severely, if not virtually impossible. When a brave young female delegate, an émigré recently returned from the United States, rose to her feet to harangue the warlords for their barbarous ways, she had to be closeted away for weeks at a United Nations compound, Kabul's impromptu version of the witness-protection programme. After that, there were not many dissenting voices, since so few people could muster the courage to speak out. Rendered mute, their reticence offered the most eloquent statement on the true state of Afghanistan.

Unspeaking or not, the Afghans themselves were notoriously hard to read. In a country where the life expectancy was then just 42, most of the men looked prematurely old, sometimes by as much as a decade or even more. The ravages of 30 years of almost continual state of war had not so much been written on their faces as carved with a blunt chisel. Some of the most macho militiamen were unabashed paedophiles, who routinely buggered the beardless young dancing boys who dressed in women's clothes with bells strapped to their feet in a custom known as *bacha bazi*.

Still more impenetrable were the country's mothers and daughters. Even in Kabul, a large proportion of them continued to don pale-blue burqas, despite the abolition of the Taliban decrees that threatened public stonings if they appeared outside without them. But how many women continued to wear these sun-bleached gowns out of choice, in observance of their faith, and how many wore them out of compulsion, in fear of their husbands and imams? Only a small number would speak, making it almost impossible to tell. And we urgently needed their testimony to get a handle on Realityland.

Unable to assemble a collage made up of individual stories, we tended to peddle grand narratives instead, with all the exaggerations and simplifications that went with them. At the very moment that nuance and complexity were demanded of reporters covering the post-9/11 world, all too often we succumbed to the Bush administration's insistence on clarity and certainty. Good versus evil; for us or against us; New Europe as opposed to Old Europe; democracy against totalitarianism; modernity against nihilism; and all the Manichean variations. We also adopted its nomenclature. What truly should have been called 'the Bush administration's war on terror' came to be known, more simply and lazily, as 'the war on terror', as if it had our endorsement. It was only much later that we added the qualifier.

Nowhere was this sense of alignment stronger than in Washington. When first I started reporting from the American capital, at the height of the Monica Lewinsky scandal in 1998, I quickly got used to the sight of members of the White House press corps rising to their feet even when the president came into their presence. Soiled blue dress or not, he was, after all, their head of state. In the aftermath of 9/11, however, too many reporters dropped to bended knee. Polished enamel flag-pins started appearing on the suit lapels just as quickly as scepticism started disappearing from their copy.

Few were as brazen as Geraldo Rivera of Fox News, who bought a pistol and vowed to gun down Osama bin Laden, but by the same token few wanted to be labelled as unpatriotic. On overseas trips with the president, one of the chief wire reporters, whose copy commonly set the tone of the overall coverage, took to wearing an NYPD baseball cap to display his fealty. It did not mean necessarily that he agreed with the Bush administration, but it hinted at a 'Don't fuck with America' bunker mentality that the White House tended to take on the road. It was a climate in which half-truths and half-baked theories, especially about the stockpiling of weapons of mass destruction in Iraq, were often accepted unquestioningly as gospel. Why, faulty intelligence even made regular appearances on the front page of the *New York Times*, that one-time haven of reportorial infallibility, which gave it the stamp of truth.

Even before 9/11, George W. Bush had mastered the art of flattering the White House press corps – a technique that, paradoxically, centred on their belittlement. Favoured reporters were given playful nicknames, which some interpreted as an attempt to create the sophomoric bonhomie and occasional cruelty of a college frat-house, but which felt more like a final club at Harvard because of its exclusive membership. The tallest reporter in the press pool was christened 'Super-stretch', while the next in Bush's vertiginous ranking system became known as 'Stretch' and then 'Little Stretch'. The reporter for the wire service The Associated Press was known always as 'the AP person', while a partially blind reporter who then worked for the *Los Angeles Times* was called 'Shades'.

A nickname not only conferred insider status, and admitted selected reporters into a kind of West Wing brotherhood, but also changed the character of presidential press conferences and the more regular question-and-answer sessions in the Oval Office. Ideally, they should have been combative, like a martial art where the skirmish was bookended with protocols of respect. But the genius of Bush's bantering style was that it disarmed so many of his potential critics.

During the period of ultra-patriotism that followed the attacks, when home-grown journalists could perhaps be forgiven for their lapses, the foreign press should have filled the void. But most of us had ended up in America precisely because we loved America, so we, too, often equated scepticism with disloyalty. In the months and years after the attacks of 9/11, we should have been solely dedicated to the quest for understanding, but frequently we were sidetracked, along with our American colleagues, by a desire for revenge. We, too, had been caught in the clutch of circumstance, and it made some of us temporarily lose our grip.

Perhaps my reassignment to South Asia, where it was easier to take a more dispassionate look at the Bush administration's war on terrorism, was an attempt to balance the ledger. Perhaps I was living out a personal variant of what the then secretary of state Colin Powell described as the 'Pottery Barn rule', his unheeded warning to President Bush on the eve of the Iraq war: you break it, you buy it. Perhaps I was simply more interested in America's original post-9/11 mission, the hunt for Osama bin Laden.

Yet I am in danger of sounding maudlin, when my real intention is to convey the fun and white-knuckle thrills of Correspondentland, along with my good fortune in ending up there. Certainly, it seemed a distant prospect on the morning I sat my university entrance exam, when my history teacher swung by to tell me that the examiners would look upon my application with hilarity, which he later claimed was a textbook example of successful reverse psychology but at the time seemed rather callous. Fortunately, the dons at Cambridge were gentler and offered me a place based on a few semi-coherent essays on the economic impact of proportional reputation, of all things, that vexed historical perennial the Irish question, and the societal scourge 'known as football hooliganism', in the cultivated wording of the examination paper.

Had I been more philosophically minded, I might have been tempted to answer the 'Is this a question?' teaser, which now sounds like the sort of thing Bill Clinton might have said under oath during a deposition. Yet I played it safe and was offered a place conditional on me passing my A-levels, which was a formality, and demonstrating a rudimentary knowledge of a foreign language, which was anything but. Shamefaced as I am to admit this, languages have never been my forte, and it required the combined forces of a French teacher, the head of modern languages and even one-on-one sessions with the headmaster to pass muster. Unused to getting pupils into Oxbridge, my comprehensive school on the outskirts of Bristol went all out, and lavished upon me the kind of attention now reserved for contestants on an extreme-makeover show.

Perhaps it was the panic of being compelled to learn French in the space of a few months that made me forget it almost as quickly, which helps explain what to this day remains my most embarrassing moment on air. It came in Paris during the 1997 French elections, when I launched into a live interview with a guest who had arrived just as the presenter in London crossed to me and who did not speak a word of English. This became apparent immediately when he stared at me blankly at the end of my first question – my second, too – and responded with a baffled 'pardon?'. Just about all that my surviving French vocabulary would facilitate was the daily procurement of coffees and pastries in the patisserie next to our Paris bureau. Needless to say, my most awkward interview doubled as my shortest, and I handed back to London more quickly than my guest could say *'je ne comprends pas'*.

I had gone up to Cambridge to read architecture, that most multidimensional of subjects, and floundered from the outset. Judged solely on their aesthetics, my proposed buildings were rather eye-catching. At least, I thought so at the time. Structurally, however, they were calamitous. Like foreign languages, maths and physics were weak subjects for me at school, but they were twin disciplines that any budding architect needed to master. Fearing I would never do so, I sought refuge in the history faculty, which was housed in a startling modern building designed by Britain's most celebrated architect, which was continually being plugged for leaks.

My new history tutor, who regarded me as an academic

dilettante, was not particularly welcoming and often started supervisions by looking me up and down with utter disdain. 'Nicholas,' he would say sternly, 'you look like you have come straight from the sports field.' Here, however, he was only half-right, for I had often stopped off on the way back from a football or cricket match via the offices of the university newspaper, where I had handed in my latest copy or picked up my next assignment.

Promiscuous as a student journalist, I covered everything from the usual undergraduate rent strikes to a crazed boffin, never to be heard of again, who believed he had come up with a cosmological construct rivalling Einstein's theory of relativity; and from visiting politicians at the fag end of the Thatcher years to the KGB's recruitment of Cambridge undergraduates in the dying days of the Cold War. With the Berlin Wall about to tumble, along with the statues of various eastern European tyrants – and at a time when post-war history dons started lectures by brandishing their now redundant study notes and theatrically tearing them into pieces – these were thrilling days for the news business. Yet, however much I would like to claim the 1989 revolutions as the crucible moment in my professional life – my very own perestroika moment, if you like – the move towards journalism was more gradual and less epiphanic. Perhaps after years spent poring over newspapers, drinking coffee, propping up bars and occasionally having to write something, it seemed as good a way as any of prolonging my student life.

For now, though, I had come up with a simpler strategy for remaining a student, which was to remain a student. Much to the surprise of my history tutor, for whom I was always something of a backslider, I became a born-again academic: a Damascene conversion that set me on the road to Oxford, where I enrolled as a PhD student in American politics.

Studying President John F. Kennedy's record as an undergraduate, I had started to suspect that my childhood hero was not quite as heroic as history had cast him, particularly when it came to dismantling segregation in the American south. So, as a postgraduate, I set about trying to debunk the myth that Kennedy should be spoken of in the same breath as Abraham Lincoln, as the second Great Emancipator. JFK's response to the March on Washington, where King successfully subpoenaed the conscience of white America with his 'I have a dream' speech, was a case in point. Fearing its violent potential, the Kennedy administration first tried to persuade King and his cohorts to cancel the protest. When that failed, it ordered up one of the biggest peacetime military mobilisations in American history to ensure that it did not degenerate into a mass brawl.

On the 30th anniversary of King's speech, a newspaper column on 'The Race Riot That Never Was', as the subeditors headlined the piece, gave me my first byline in a national broadsheet. By now, however, I was making regular trips up the motorway to London, where I had been given my first part-time job in what was still known as Fleet Street, even though all the newspapers had moved out.

Bizarrely, and for reasons that we will touch briefly upon later, it came at a high-society gossip column in London, for the *Evening Standard*. Here, the idea of a scoop was to reveal that the Duchess of Devonshire's crocuses had bloomed unseasonably early or that some doddery viscount had tripped on the steps of The Athenaeum Club, sprained his wrist and discovered that he could not lift a shotgun for at least three weeks, thus ruling him out of the start of the grouse season.

Since the sparse details of these stories could usually be recounted in the space of the opening paragraph, or often the opening sentence, the skill was to pad them out with reaction from other toffs, who would provide quotes that were sympathetic, incredulous or, best of all, witheringly snotty. Then the prominence attached to each story would be determined by either the rank of those involved or the standing of those who volunteered quotes – where they fitted within what I suppose could be described as a sliding scale of social hierarchy, so long as it is understood that the slides took place, like slowly shifting tectonic plates, over many hundreds of years.

With British celebrity culture now in full flower, other parts of the paper focused on A-, B- or C-list celebs. Maintaining a quaint fastidiousness, 'The Londoner's Diary' was obsessed instead with the title that preceded the name – unless, of course, the letters spelt out HRH. It was a recondite world in which dukes would always lord it over a marquess, a viscount would always trump a baron and a royal, however minor, would always be guaranteed the banner headline. With no contacts within the upper echelons of high society, and little chance of making any, I came brandishing high-table tittle-tattle from Oxford. I also had nuggets of gossip ground from the rumour mill of Westminster, much of which started out as pillow talk courtesy of my girlfriend at the time, who worked as a parliamentary researcher and ended up in the Cabinet.

The diary's ruddy-faced editor, who was charming to the point of unctuousness in the company of the aristocrats who appeared in his pages, was a tyrant towards those who worked for him – or under him, as he preferred to think of it. His great early-morning ritual, which was conducted in courtly silence, saw him move from one desk to the other, listening to each frail-voiced reporter as they opened up their notebooks and sketched out their freshest yarn. Then, after a sometimes interminable pause, the editor would deliver his verdict: a cackle of high-pitched delight that sounded like an orgasmic hyena, or a violent tantrum in which his complexion changed from red to beetroot to rosewood. Then, he would move to the next desk, the blood having drained from his face, and repeat the entire spectacle again. Needless to say, the punishment meted out to new recruits was always especially cruel, particularly those who failed to arrive with any gossip worth publishing – an egregious lapse that automatically disqualified them from ever being invited back again. Withering scoldings were the norm. Tears were not uncommon. Once, an empty-handed new recruit was dispatched to the basement, mop in hand, where he was instructed to wash the editor's car, still caked in mud after a weekend hunting trip.

Happily, I never became the target of his tyrannical rants, nor the victim of a management technique modelled on the public-school fagging system. On reflection, I think it helped that the editor, who had always struggled to locate my classless accent, thought I was Australian, which granted me a kind of diplomatic immunity. By the time that I corrected him, classlessness had become so fashionable in modern Britain that he considered me a useful addition to his stable, which at that point only included thoroughbreds with pukka bloodlines.

Despite being made to feel unexpectedly welcome, then, I was determined to bid farewell to the world of high-society gossip before the Duchess of Devonshire's crocuses could bloom again. After finishing my PhD and moving permanently up to London, I started to plot my next upward move.

It came via an escalator that took me to the tabloid newspaper on the floor above, the *Daily Mail*, a still more brutal environment where the editor was so profligate with his use of a certain swearword that his mid-morning conference became known as 'The Vagina Monologue'.

Thankfully, I found refuge opposite the paper's industrial correspondent, a castaway from Fleet Street who smoked so many cigarettes that he produced almost as many emissions as the few surviving industries left for him to cover. When I arrived, just about his most glamorous assignment was a week in Blackpool covering the Trades Union Congress annual conference, but in years gone by he had navigated much more exotic and turbulent waters. Not only had he been one of the first British journalists to yomp into Port Stanley to see the Union Flag hoisted again over a newly liberated Falkland Islands, but he had also been imprisoned in Tehran during the Iranian Revolution and was rumoured still to be living off the overtime. Folklore had it that when finally he made it back to London he could empty any pub in Fleet Street by wailing the Islamic call to prayer that used to wake him in the morning and prevent him sleeping at night.

The man was a tabloid genius, his fingers dancing over his ash-specked keyboard, a cigarette always dangling from his mouth, as he produced near flawless copy on virtually any given subject. One day, he was instructed to produce a colour piece on the plight of a Cornish fishing village labouring under some new missive from Brussels, an assignment completed by early in the afternoon with aplomb. The smell of fish was the smell of life itself, according to his first paragraph, in a piece rich with character and local colour. However, his evocative opening had been filed, like the rest of the story, not from the quayside in Cornwall but from his desk in Kensington High Street. For months afterwards, colleagues pinched their noses as they walked past our desk, complaining about the stench of rotting mackerel. 'They asked me to be creative with my copy,' the industrial correspondent would harrumph, in his thick Lancastrian burr, 'so I hope they won't mind me being creative with my expenses.'

For all the tabloid tomfoolery, there were few better places to learn the rudiments of journalism. To begin with, the editors and subs were absolute sticklers for accuracy. Consider the night that a Conservative member of parliament was found dead at his home in Chiswick, trussed up in a complex series of wires, levers and pulleys, dressed in stockings and suspenders and with his teeth clenching a citrus fruit. Was it a tangerine, a nectarine or a satsuma that had contributed to his autoerotic asphyxiation? It was the job of the paper's squadron of crime reporters to find out definitively, having been told that 'a small orange' simply would not suffice.

There was the single-minded pursuit of the stories, fuelled by the career-enhancing hope of front-page glory and the career-ending fear of returning empty-handed to the newsroom. Then there was the assiduous cultivation of contacts. The crime boys regularly went on after-work benders with officers from Scotland Yard, the cantankerous motoring correspondent was clearly a buddy of Stirling Moss's – the only time his face showed anything resembling a smile was when his hard-pressed secretary announced that Stirling was on line one – and the royal correspondent was a close personal confidant of Princess Diana. One lunchtime, I watched in admiration from a local coffee shop as he descended into an underground car park near Kensington Palace for what I assumed must be a Deep Throat-style rendezvous with Her Royal

Highness. When the paper hit the news-stands the following morning, he was the author of the front-page splash, yet another of his Diana exclusives.

Though I had the lowliest of jobs at the paper, there were odd occasions when I could cause a flurry of mild excitement on the newsdesk. While the England cricket team was on tour in the West Indies, I discovered that the captain's then girlfriend might also be playing away – a story that wound up on page three. It meant that at the very moment a menacing quartet of West Indian fast bowlers were aiming bouncers at Mike Atherton's head, a home-town tabloid had aimed a beamer squarely at his heart.

But my biggest scoop belonged on the front page: the tale of how a Labour Party frontbencher, a household name to boot, was regularly bonking his secretary. Impeccably sourced and legally watertight, the story could have made my tabloid name. Alas, I could never bring myself to share the details with the news editor. Working on the Street of Shame had already aroused feelings of uneasiness, and to have done the dirty would have brought on an even worse bout of existential torment.

Years later, the *News of the World* revealed that the new foreign secretary Robin Cook was leaving his wife to be with his long-time Westminster mistress. Yet, in common with a surprising number of tabloid hacks, who regularly withhold embarrassing secrets out of compassion for their prospective victims, I opted for valour over glory. From that moment on, in the time-honoured custom of British tabloids, I realised that I would have to make my excuses and leave.

All along, the BBC had been the target of my ambitions. Arriving late one afternoon at JFK airport in New York at the end of a trip to the Galapagos Islands, I heard from my flatmate back home that the corporation wanted me to sit a written examination in London the very next morning. With only an overnight flight's worth of time to prepare, I did what any self-respecting British journalist would do: buy a copy of *The Economist* and read it forensically from cover to cover. It was exactly the kind of 'cuts job', in fact, that I would routinely perform as a foreign correspondent.

By the time I touched down at Heathrow, I was not only fluent in the gross domestic product of all the Benelux countries, but I could also quote their seasonally adjusted rates of inflation – factoids that proved to be entirely superfluous when I sat my test but served the useful purpose of giving me almost bullet-proof self-confidence. Fortunately, the examiners looked kindly on my answers, as did a 'board' of interviewers drawn from the upper reaches of BBC management who cross-examined me the following week. My curriculum vitae, no doubt like theirs, was embellished with degrees from the usual suspects, along with the names of some illustrious academic referees: precisely the kinds of adornments that the BBC always favoured. However, the clincher for my new employer was unquestionably my sojourn with a tabloid.

If my time at the *Evening Standard* and *Daily Mail* sharpened my news senses, my first months at the BBC were spent straightening out my syntax and grammar. I, like my seven fellow trainees, came under the tutelage of an old hand from the radio newsroom, renowned throughout the correspondent corps for his grammatical punctiliousness. War reporters filing from the most perilous of hotspots were regularly stopped in mid-flow at the mention of a split infinitive or dangling participle, even if it meant the hurried refile was punctuated instead by the sound of ricocheting bullets. Clamouring for a slice of this kind of action, we, too, hoped soon to be shouting into microphones over the din of exploding ordnance, but for now we were held captive in a first-floor classroom at Broadcasting House in London, the inspiration for Orwell's Ministry of Truth, grappling with the basics of the English language in our own version of Room 101.

Our escape came when we were dispatched, like fresh-faced subalterns, to the regional outposts of the BBC empire for a week in local radio. I opted for Liverpool, partly because the city had become something of a production line for improbable stories and partly because BBC Radio Merseyside had such a strong reputation for packaging and distributing them. Its office was also located on the dreamy-sounding Paradise Street, which seemed in my mind at least to rival other great Liverpudlian landmarks such as Strawberry Field and Penny Lane, and thus sounded vaguely providential.

Old Radio Merseyside hands who had graduated to The Network, as London was reverently known, warned me to expect a tough, hard-hitting newsroom full of jaundiced old hacks who despised London and looked upon news trainees from the capital in much the same way that Romans used to watch Christians sent up from the dungeons of the Colosseum. But whereas I arrived expecting the *Boys from the Blackstuff*, I was greeted instead by Carry on Broadcasting.

As I walked through the doors on Paradise Street and took my seat in reception, a chirpy disc jockey, aided by his fabulously camp sidekick, was halfway through his daily general-knowledge quiz in which the good people of Merseyside were invited to hold their plums. Later, I learnt that 'Hold Your Plums' – a double entendre plucked from the fruit machines – was as much a Scouser institution as The Cavern Club or the Mersey ferry, and that one listener had enshrined herself in local folklore by replying 'Heil' when asked to provide Hitler's first name. But for now, as I waited to be introduced to the news editor, 'Hold Your Plums' served the useful purpose of vastly inflating my own testicular fortitude. If Radio Merseyside could hold its plums, then perhaps it might even take a nervous young trainee to its heart.

Certainly, they were kind enough to give me a slice of some of the best stories, the first of which more than adequately met the description 'Only in Merseyside'. It was week two of the national lottery, and a local teenager had come up with the brilliant ruse of buying a new ticket featuring last week's winning numbers and splicing it together with an old ticket featuring last week's date. Joyous that the city had produced one of the first lottery millionaires, the local paper splashed a photo of the photocopied ticket, being brandished proudly by its newly minted owner, across its front page. Alas, lottery officials in London quickly detected the stench of a giant-sized rat and revealed the next morning that, of the handful of winning tickets, none had been purchased anywhere near the north-west. With the paper now demanding to see the original ticket, and with the teenager unable to provide it, he did a runner, and Liverpool was left to ruminate, as Liverpool so often does, on how it had produced the first lottery fraudster rather than one of its inaugural millionaires.

By now, the youngster had been missing a few days, and I was dispatched to interview his anguished mother in a lace-curtain bungalow on the fringes of town. Still in the overly diligent phase of my career, my notepad was filled with an exhaustive list of questions, but the interview required only one. 'What would you say to Jonny,' I asked in a voice of faux concern that I would come to perfect over the years, 'if he's listening to this broadcast?'

'Come home, Jonny, come home!' came her howling reply.

'COME HOME!'

Fortunately, Jonny did come home shortly afterwards, just in time for tea – or, for the purposes of Radio Merseyside, just in time for its drive-time programme, where he was given a stiff on-air reprimand from the presenter, who placed him in the radio equivalent of the public stocks.

By the end of our training, we were equipped with all manner of skills and expertise, which seem antique now and seemed antique back then. In the days of reel-to-reel recorders, the tools of our trade were white chinagraph pencils, razor blades and thin reels of sticky tape, with which we marked, slashed and then spliced together the soundbites making up our reports. A hesitant interviewee, with a bad 'um' and 'ah' habit, could take hours to edit, or 'de-um', in editing parlance.

Still more frustrating was the time we consumed foraging under edit machines among discarded piles of magnetic tape, in the hope of finding a now-needed thought or abandoned consonant or vowel that had been rashly thrown onto the cutting-room floor. On occasions, it could be hazardous work as well, especially when deadlines pressed in and the required blade-work was undertaken at a furious pace. To this day, my body bears just two scars from my years as a correspondent: a wound on the crown of my head sustained on the subcontinent, which we will come to in due course, and a diagonal disfigurement at the top of one of my fingers, when my razor blade missed the editing block and de-ummed my flesh.

To save my body from further impairment, I learnt the trick of alternating the shoulder on which I carried my German-made reel-to-reel tape recorder, a device called a Uher that felt like it had been minted out of lead. It rescued me from a handicap common among radio journalists of a certain vintage: the Uher droop.

As our training progressed, we worked on our correspondent voices mainly by ventriloquising the correspondent voices of others. We learnt that good television was bereft of adjectival padding, that the trick always was to look for small, humanising details and that the great BBC fallback line of enquiry if, in a live interview, all your pre-prepared questions have been exhausted with two minutes left to run is 'How will this news be received in the south of the country?'. It works virtually every time.

But after our training was complete, I remember being left with a needling sense of the limitations of our new mediums. Most of us had come from newspapers, the purest form of journalism, where stories were usually long enough to accommodate the twin luxuries of explication and complication. By contrast, television news rewarded brevity and simplicity, and reduced multifaceted stories to their most elemental parts. It did to news what Hollywood movies routinely do to the works of great fiction: plotlines that could not easily be retold were simply discarded; peripheral characters were banished from view; and the temptation was not just to simplify but to exaggerate. Much like a reader would barely recognise a much-loved novel after it was put through the cinematic wringer, the characters in our news reports would often identify only with the shadowy outline of their story.

The cadetship finished as it had started, with a written test, and then we were absorbed, like low-grade motor oil, into the BBC news machine. I ended up at our rolling news channel, Radio Five Live, which had so many hours of airtime to fill that even new arrivals were allowed to plug the gaps.

Sure enough, by day two I had been handed my first assignment. That morning, the *Daily Mirror* had managed to expose the cracks in Downing Street security by squirrelling a reporter into the prime minister's office. As the latest recruit, I was tasked with revealing the fissures in *Daily Mirror* security by squirrelling myself into the editor's office high above Canary Wharf.

From getting lost on the Docklands Light Railway to finding myself temporarily imprisoned in the stairwell of a 230-metre skyscraper, my first forays could hardly be described as auspicious. But the fear of returning to the newsroom empty-handed pushed me on, and I eventually managed to sneak past the security guards at reception, locate the executive floor and get within metres of the editor's office. All the way, I had been faithfully capturing every moment of haplessness, and now my tape recorder was in record mode as I took my final steps towards glory.

With the spires of the City in the near distance and the arc of the Thames below, the view from Piers Morgan's office was magnificent, and I took great delight in describing the panorama to our listeners. Soon, my commentary was interrupted, as obviously I hoped it would be, by a fretful secretary mortified that I was reclining in her boss's executive leather chair. Then came Piers Morgan himself, who was happy to play along in this pantomime by delivering a gentle scolding and describing me as a journalistic low-life.

By now, the main challenge was to make it back to Broadcasting House in central London, and to brandish my razor blade with sufficient speed to deliver the report for the late-afternoon show. With the deadline bearing down on me, I pulled it off with the help of an industrious sound engineer, who underlaid the piece with that most hackneyed of musical clichés, the pounding theme tune from *Mission Impossible*. Over consecutive hours, we ran

Confessions from Correspondentland

the story in two parts: the first ending with your correspondent banging helplessly on the door of some random office 43 floors up as I tried to escape from the fire escape; the second ending with the self-congratulatory words 'Mission accomplished', a phrase that would feature in very different circumstances much later in my career.

For now, though, as the music died away and the presenter guffawed with delight, I basked in something that I have never managed to replicate: a ripple of applause that spread throughout the newsroom. I had delivered a piece of light entertainment rather than hard-hitting journalism, but it mattered not. After two days spent on the nursery slopes of my career, I had been earmarked as a black-run reporter. So much so that when the news came through from Jerusalem 48 hours later, the newsdesk rang to tell me that I had been booked on a plane at dawn the following morning. It was 4 November 1995, and the Israeli prime minister, Yitzhak Rabin, had just been assassinated. My journeys as a foreign correspondent were about to begin.

As for the *loya jirga* in Kabul, the children's choir eventually made it through the security checks and barbed wire to perform on stage before the delegates. Their song was of a land tired of suffering and unfaithfulness, of a country lonely and unhealed, of stars and moons, of poetry and song, and of saddened and weary hearts. As no doubt intended, it provided the ideal coda for our report, but now we feared it might never even be aired. A giant red banner had just appeared on the bottom of the television screen in our hotel room, pulsating with the words 'BREAKING NEWS'.

Moments later, America's top official in Iraq, 'the American Viceroy' L. Paul Bremer, stepped beaming before the cameras (prematurely, the Bush White House would later complain) to deliver a six-word announcement: 'Ladies and gentlemen, we got him!' All that night, and well into the next week, the bulletins would be dominated by the extraordinary sight of a one-time dictator with a ragged grey beard having a swab of DNA taken by a US military doctor wearing white rubber gloves and wielding a wooden spatula. Saddam Hussein had been captured, and the headlines belonged to another corner of Correspondentland.

Chapter 1

Two Bad Saturdays and a Very Good Friday

Even for a novice, it was easy to see how the details of Yitzhak Rabin's assassination would lend themselves to immediate legend and nourish the belief that his death was somehow preordained. On that balmy November night in 1995, the Israeli prime minister had attended a peace rally in front of the City Hall in Tel Aviv, where 100,000 people had gathered in placid rebuttal to the Jewish nationalists and extreme right-wing Zionists who in the weeks before had held a string of protests at which they brandished placards depicting Rabin wearing an Arab headdress and, worse still, a Nazi uniform.

'I have always believed that the majority of people want peace and are ready to take the chance for peace,' said the former general, who two years earlier had shaken the hand of the then Palestinian leader, Yasser Arafat, on the South Lawn of the White House.

As they stood together on stage, looking out over the largest rally that Tel Aviv had witnessed for more than a decade, the Israeli foreign minister Shimon Peres raised the possibility of an assassin lurking in the crowd. Ever the soldier, Rabin did not seem perturbed. Nor did his wife, Leah, who was asked by a radio reporter if her husband had taken the precaution of wearing a bullet-proof vest. 'Have you gone crazy?' she scoffed. 'What are we – in Africa?'

The rally reached its climax with Rabin mumbling his way through an unfamiliar peace song, the words and music of which had been handed to him beforehand by a diligent aide. Then, as he got down from the stage and walked towards his prime-ministerial limousine, he spoke briefly to a radio reporter, not knowing that this would become his valedictory interview: 'I always believed that the majority of the people are against violence.'

Moments later, a young assassin stepped forward and fired four times from a Beretta semi-automatic pistol. By the time the 73-year-old reached the hospital, the doctors could not detect any blood pressure or heart beat. Still inside his jacket pocket was the music of the peace song, now spattered with his blood.

When work called late that Saturday night, I did not even bother asking who was the assassin. Here, I repeated the same mistake as Rabin's Shin Bet bodyguards, who had not been prepared psychologically for anyone other than an Arab gunman carrying out the killing. Yet the murderer was a 25-year-old student named Yigal Amir, a former Israeli soldier who lived with his strictly Orthodox parents and claimed to be acting 'on God's orders'.

Later, the Israeli police discovered that he had been ejected from a Rabin rally in September for screaming about the abandonment of over a hundred thousand West Bank settlers. They found on his bookshelf at home a copy of *The Day of the Jackal*. Proudly, Amir told police that he had tried on two previous occasions to get close enough to the prime minister to kill him, and now, unlike Frederick Forsyth's failed assassin, he had finally achieved his goal. Israel's favourite son, the great hero of the Six Day War, had been slain by a fellow Jew – an act of fratricide immediately comprehensible in the frenzied aftermath, given the fury aroused by the peace process, but unthinkable just a few seconds earlier.

By now, our Jerusalem bureau had been fully mobilised, and, as ever in these circumstances, the BBC newsdesk at base bolstered its numbers with fly-ins from London. By happy chance, I was fully sober and, in the days before mobile phones were standard issue, close to an old-fashioned landline. It helped, too, that more senior colleagues with mobile phones were too drunk to notice their phones were ringing and vibrating, then ringing and vibrating again. Hard though it is to recall in this age of hyper-connectivity, it was possible back then as a journalist to be spectacularly out of the loop, and to remain so for many hours. As a result, I suddenly found myself leapfrogging others on the call list who simply could not be raised, such was the rush to get anyone on a plane to the Middle East who could wield a microphone.

Violent deaths of beloved leaders always resonate in the national imagination, inviting not only mass mourning but also mass hysteria. Yet as soon as we touched down at Ben Gurion Airport in Tel Aviv, it became immediately clear that there was something very solid about the emotional response. It was almost as if the mourners themselves were aware that Rabin, the cranky chain-smoker, would have frowned upon any sentimental excess.

By far the biggest vigils were held outside Rabin's home, and at the Kings of Israel Square in Tel Aviv, where his final peace rally had been held. But all across Jewish Jerusalem, Israelis sat in small huddles, young people especially, clutching peace candles, praying and intoning psalms so quietly that our intruding microphones struggled to register any sound. The lines outside the Knesset, where Rabin's body lay in rest in a simple coffin draped with the Israeli flag, stretched for miles down a road lined with Cypress trees and pines, and within 36 hours a million Israelis had filed solemnly past. When his remains were borne on a military command vehicle through the streets to the burial site, again tens of thousands stood weeping.

Breaking with the Jewish tradition of burial before sundown the day after death, the funeral had been pushed back until Monday so that international leaders could make the journey to Jerusalem, and not since the funeral of the Japanese emperor Hirohito had so many gathered in one place. Heading a delegation that included two former presidents, Jimmy Carter and George Herbert Walker Bush, and 40 members of Congress, Bill Clinton traced a line back to the assassinations of Lincoln, the Kennedy brothers and Martin Luther King, who in Memphis also appeared to have a rendezvous with death. He characterised Rabin as a 'martyr for peace'.

For once, the American president was completely upstaged by Arab leaders, who were making their first visit to Jerusalem since it had been conquered by Israeli forces in 1967. King Hussein of Jordan, wearing his red-and-white-checked headdress and regularly wiping away tears, called Rabin a 'friend' and 'brother', and sighed, 'You lived as a soldier. You died as a soldier for peace.' The Egyptian president Hosni Mubarak, who had shunned Israel since taking office, was less generous, but prepared still to don a blue baseball cap handed to him by Israeli officials when Rabin was laid to rest, in deference to the Jewish tradition of covering the scalp at religious ceremonies.

The emotional punch, meanwhile, came from Rabin's 17-year-old granddaughter, Noa Ben-Artzi, whose freckled beauty and fierce determination that this solemn national occasion should also have the character of a more intimate family farewell made her its unlikely star. 'Forgive me, for I do not want to talk about peace,' she said. 'I want to talk about my grandfather.'

Alas, everyone else *did* want to talk about peace, and the possibility that Yigal Amir had succeeded in his aim of sabotaging the Oslo Accords. Rabin was not just a central character but also its indispensable character. The standard cliché that week was also a truism: only the man who won the West Bank could hand it back.

But the fact that Rabin had been the chief of staff of the Israeli Defence Forces who orchestrated victory over Egypt, Syria and Jordan in the Six Day War only partly explained his towering authority. Nor did it stem from the accident of birth that made him Israel's first native-born prime minister. Just as important was the simple fact that Rabin was so gruff, irritable and of his generation. So it was not just as an Israeli soldier that he could stand before his nation, in defiance of the Jewish nationalists, to make the case for a historic compromise trading land for security. It was, as his friend the *New York Times* columnist Thomas Friedman pointed out at the time, as an Israeli Sabra.

As the years progressed, I covered various peace initiatives involving the Palestinians and a succession of Israeli prime ministers, from Shimon Peres to Ehud Barak, from Ariel Sharon to Ehud Olmert, but Rabin was matchless. It is tempting to think he could have delivered lasting peace to the region, but that is to tread territory usually best avoided: the land of might-have-been.

As a cub reporter on my first foreign assignment, that week in the Middle East felt like correspondent boot camp. It was the first time I ever had a loaded weapon cocked towards me, when a Palestinian policeman took umbrage at me for wandering onto a prohibited section of the beach next to Yasser Arafat's shoreline headquarters in Gaza. Holding me at gunpoint in a briefly threatening manner, he suggested I should leave with a couple of twitches and flicks of his AK-47.

That same day, I also had my first encounter with an Islamic militant, when a bearded 20-something slipped, almost unnoticed, into the back seat of our car, in true cloak-and-dagger fashion, to outline in more detail how Hamas had reacted to Rabin's assassination. Needless to say, Hamas was delighted, because the killing had the twin benefits of eliminating such a long-time opponent of Palestinian nationalism and of undercutting Arafat, whom it cast as a traitor for dealing with the Israelis.

Nor had I visited the Gaza Strip, the slum-like slither of land that hugged a 25-mile stretch of Mediterranean coastline, where Arafat had made his triumphant return from exile the previous year in the hope that a scruffy fiefdom, over which he enjoyed only partial control, could blossom into a fully functional Palestinian state. And never before had I cast eyes on the Palestinian leader himself. Fearing it would inflame passions on both sides, he had avoided Rabin's funeral, but in the days afterwards he welcomed a string of Western diplomats to the one-time beach club that was now the headquarters of the newly established Palestinian National Authority.

For all the trappings of pseudo-statehood, and for all his dressy flourishes – he reportedly spent an hour each morning sculpting his black-and-white-checked kafiya into something closely resembling the map of Palestine and then fastening it with a brooch in the shape of a phoenix – Arafat already looked a lesser figure. His bulbous lips trembled, his hands shook, as if an ice chill were coming off the Mediterranean, and in his shaky pronouncements he displayed precisely the kind of hesitancy that would encumber the peace process for years to come. Even then, there was a feeling that he preferred the pretence of an ongoing peace process rather than ever reaching its endpoint: a fully negotiated settlement. Better to remain a victim, the theory went, than sue for a peace deal that would never fully satisfy his Palestinian followers.

Back in Jerusalem, as Israeli politicians shuttled between television studios offering on-air assessments of Rabin's legacy, I also came into contact with many of the leaders who over the coming years would face Arafat across the negotiating table – or not, as the case may be. There was the Likud leader Benjamin Netanyahu, proud, angry and touchy, who throughout the week ran the gauntlet of reporters asking him if his rhetoric in support of the Jewish settlers had contributed to the venomous climate in which Rabin was killed. There was the mayor of Jerusalem, Ehud Olmert, another future prime minister, and a hate-figure among Palestinians for advancing the Judaisation of a city whose eastern half they viewed still as their capital.

With Olmert, I thought myself fiendishly clever at scoring a one-on-one interview by persuading him to let me dive into the back of his armour-plated limousine as he sped to his next engagement across town. Unfortunately, I rather dumped on my own scoop, by constantly putting my Olmerts before my Ehuds. Perhaps sensing I was a novice, he was generous enough to overlook being called 'Mr Ehud' the first three times, but not the fourth. 'It's Ehud Olmert,' he snapped, as the car drew to the side of the road, and I was cast out onto the gravel verge like a hostage who had suddenly outlived his usefulness. Then, having wound up on Jerusalem's desert fringes, I had to figure out how to get back in time to edit – heavily edit – my botched report.

Throughout the week, my fumbling efforts seemed even more pathetic when compared with those of the BBC's foreign-correspondent corps, the elite of the elite. But at least there were occasional morale-lifting moments, when I realised that this illustrious band of brothers, as it largely was in those days, could stumble too.

Early one morning, a correspondent drafted in from a neighbouring bureau was slated to perform what is called a two-way, a straightforward question-and-answer session involving a reporter on the ground and a presenter in London designed to provide a quick update of any overnight developments. In this instance, there had been a crucial development: an arrest in the assassination investigation pointing towards a more elaborate right-wing conspiracy. The problem was that the correspondent, who had not yet cast his eyes over the early-morning news wires, was completely in the dark. The general rule of thumb in two-ways is for the correspondent to inform the presenter what is happening. Here, the roles were inadvertently reversed. What followed, then, was a masterclass in the art of generic correspondent doggerel.

Was this a significant development, asked the presenter, having laid out the bare details of the overnight arrest in the introduction. Indeed it was, replied the panicky correspondent as his eyes searched for the nearest computer screen. It was clearly a major development in the investigation, and the police would be treating it as a significant breakthrough. Follow-up questions yielded more answers completely devoid of enlightening information. The suspect would be held in custody under tight security, the correspondent ventured. The police would look to glean as much information as possible in the hope of furthering their inquiry. Then they would decide whether or not to mount a prosecution.

Nothing about the two-way was factually incorrect, but neither, in all its non-specific artfulness, could any of it have been described as being of factual use. Declaring himself 'a complete pilchard', the correspondent left the radio booth and hunted down the latest piece of Reuters copy, knowing that another two-way loomed at the top of the next hour.

In his defence, at least he had the bravado to battle on. Years earlier, a correspondent dispatched at late notice to Moscow at a particularly chilly phase of the Cold War was bowled such a tricky googly from a presenter in London on the latest machinations at the Kremlin that he remained completely silent, gently took off his headphones, placed them down on the desk in front of him and tiptoed out of the radio studio. The presenter explained the dead air by saying there was a problem with the line, but the problem was with the correspondent, who had simply done a runner.

On other occasions that week, correspondents ran into difficulty through no fault of their own, entirely innocent victims of the broadcasting equivalent of friendly fire. To provide a radio commentary of Rabin's funeral, we naturally called on the resident Jerusalem correspondent, a reporter blessed with such a booming voice that it was often said he could broadcast to London merely by opening the nearest window. Unfortunately, the studio crossed to him just as the wail of sirens that marked the beginning of the funeral started to fade and mourners began to observe a two-minute silence. First, his boom was reduced to an uncharacteristic whisper, and then to silence as those around him threatened to carry out a lynching.

I made so many stuff-ups on that first foreign assignment that, were there a penalty-points system for errant correspondents, I probably would not have been allowed back out onto the road. Fortunately, however, none of them made it to air, which is the broadcasting equivalent of a tree falling in an empty forest.

As we gathered for a celebratory meal at the end of the week, I felt that I could at least sit at the same table as the other correspondents, even if I was a long way from ordering the wine. That privilege went to our most senior man in the Middle East, a moustachioed correspondent with the debonair looks of a Spitfire pilot and the same raffish air, whom I would meet a few years hence in another corner of Correspondentland. We were both live on air from our studio in Washington on election night in 2000 when Al Gore first threw in the towel and then suddenly wrenched it back. Our friend the self-styled 'complete pilchard' was at the restaurant as well, proving that he could also drink like a fish. So, too, was the correspondent who came with his own sonic boom, who would later become one of my dearest colleagues. Six years later, after becoming Washington correspondents, we both suffered the most exasperating day of our careers on what should have been our finest hour. That was 9/11, a story for later on, and perhaps the only time I have covered a more consequential story than Rabin's assassination.

As the Israeli Merlot started to work its magic, I smugly congratulated myself on the rapid progress of my career. In the space of less than a week, I had gone from Piers Morgan's office to Yasser Arafat's beachside compound, and from the Docklands Light Railway to the Temple Mount. Sunni Muslims believed this to be the place where the prophet Muhammad ascended into heaven. I, too, left Jerusalem feeling things were on the up.

—

Such was the state of dazed disbelief, so overindulgent was the emotional excess, that my homeland felt more like a foreign country in the seven days after the death of Diana in 1997. It was a strange and unrecognisable place. Just about the only thing that seemed instantly familiar to reporters was the orderliness of the queue outside St James's Palace, where mourners lined up uncomplainingly, sometimes for as long as 12 hours, to sign the book of condolence.

Though late-twentieth-century Britain could hardly be described as a place of unfeeling stoicism or wholly constipated sentiment – a *Guardian* headline that week, 'Nation Learns to Grieve', implied some kind of congenital defect that had previously barred Britons from any form of public lamentation or private tenderness – it did exercise a certain emotional control that was now, in the wake of the news from Paris, almost completely absent. The normal, unwritten protocols of grief, founded on restraint and reserve, had been entirely disregarded.

Planeloads of flowers had to be flown in from as far as Thailand and South Africa. An extra five million red roses were imported from Israel alone. Churches observed record attendances. Helplines run by groups such as the Samaritans reported much heavier than usual call-loads.

Though Australians could normally be relied upon to bring a sense of proportion on such occasions, the country's finest wordsmith, Clive James, came close to completely losing it. 'No,' he shrieked at the start of every one of his 24 paragraphs in a eulogy penned for the *New Yorker*.

Neither could we rely on members of the Scotland football team, not normally the most tender-hearted of men, who threatened to strike unless their Saturday-afternoon World Cup qualifier with Belarus was moved to the Sunday to avoid a clash with Diana's funeral.

Even the *Daily Telegraph*, whose reporters were usually recruited because they represented the quintessence of old-style Britishness, had the wobbles. Dispatched to provide a colour piece on the crowds of mourners thronging The Mall, Tom Utley, a *Telegraph* traditionalist, reported instead from within himself. 'Quite a few people, and I must include myself, thought her pretty awful at times – and many have been amazed, as I have, to discover how terribly we miss her now.'

As journalists pondered what had happened to their country, the country could just as reasonably have asked what had happened to its journalists. Nobody wanted to be out of sync with the emotional zeitgeist, which amplified things even more. It took Boris Johnson, then one of its scribes, to resume normal *Telegraph* service, by accusing Britain of 'undergoing a Latin American carnival of grief'.

As with the assassination of Rabin, the first, patchy reports came through late on a Saturday night, and even though I was now sufficiently senior to have been issued with my very own bleeper, I was at a wedding in Dorset and did not at that point of the evening possess the necessary sobriety to make full use of it.

Oddly, I happened to be surrounded by Parisians, many of whom were catching a flight back to the French capital early the next morning. But by the time I responded to the bleep, the news was that the car crash was nowhere near as bad as first feared and there was now no need to make a dash over the Channel.

In the scramble for information, CNN had put to air an interview with an eyewitness, an American in Paris, no less, who said he had been driving in the opposite direction along the Pont de l'Alma tunnel in Paris when the Mercedes had ploughed into the concrete pylon. For ten minutes, he provided what must have been riveting testimony, then ended his account with the words 'Baba Booey'. The BBC, when it started replaying this account, simply edited out the mystifying pay-off. Unknown to any of the production team in London, Baba Booey was the nickname of a producer working for Howard Stern, the American shock jock, who encouraged listeners to play hoaxes at moments of breaking news. Everything he had said was complete fiction, the cruellest one at that.

With the hoaxer finally rumbled, the tone of the coverage changed in an instant. Our Paris correspondent was picking up dark rumblings from his local contacts. Even bleaker news came from the Philippines, where the British foreign secretary Robin Cook was on tour. He told the BBC's diplomatic correspondent that Diana had been killed, but he placed the interview under strict embargo so the news would come first from the French Government.

For years, the BBC had been planning for the death of the queen mother, with regular royal-death rehearsals and a thumping great compendium of guidelines that editors were expected to memorise. Now, though, it was overtaken by a much larger and wholly unexpected drama, which the normal set of rules found hard to accommodate fully. Under their strict letter, the BBC could not report the death of a member of the royal family without the news first having been officially confirmed by Buckingham Palace, whose on-duty press officer that weekend had left the office on Friday night without a mobile phone. However, although the news from the Philippines had been handed to our correspondent under embargo, it was inevitable that someone would soon break it.

Sky News, often the nippy speedboat up against our hulking carrier fleet, was already reporting rumours that Diana was dead. Not only were there now competitive pressures to weigh but also a moral dilemma. The BBC was wilfully reporting something that we knew to be untrue: that Diana was alive.

This point was made most forcefully by our distinguished royal correspondent, Paul Reynolds, who found himself fighting a behind-the-scenes battle in between long stints live on air. The author of one of the most searing lines of that troubled decade for the British royals, 'the knives are out for Fergie at the Palace', Paul was simply too honourable a journalist to continue with this charade. Finally, the Press Association broke the embargo and announced at 4.44 am on Sunday 31 August that Diana had died. Eventually, we followed suit and marked Diana's passing, as the guidelines decreed, with the playing of 'God Save the Queen' – a gesture that would seem ridiculously incongruous by the middle of the following week.

Like many of my compatriots, I had gone to bed thinking that Diana was still alive and awoke to the jolting news of her death. Unlike many of my compatriots and colleagues, I failed completely to grasp its magnitude, and I compounded this lapse by not even bothering to rush back to London. Returning much later along the motorway, again with little haste, we listened to the stream of interviews with Aids patients, landmine specialists and the homeless, which did so much in those early hours to produce the instant revisionism on Diana's contribution to national life. Still, it was only when we reached Kensington and saw for ourselves the police outriders blocking the traffic so that the black hearse carrying her coffin could continue unimpeded that its impact started to register more fully Even then, however, there was little hint of the unreality about to unfold.

Arriving home, I retrieved from the wardrobe my most sombre dark suit and headed immediately for Buckingham Palace. Mourners had already made a start on one of the many carpets of flowers that would appear at the royal hubs of grieving. As I watched them descend on the palace late into the night, I remember thinking that the first waves were made up of the types of people you would have expected to make the journey: Elizabethans and arch-monarchists – the sort who would line The Mall for the trooping of the colour and purchase small Royal Doulton tea sets to mark the great regal jubilees – and a sprinkling of American tourists, who found themselves eavesdropping on Britain's day of mourning.

As the vigil went on, however, and journalists were confronted by this great 'outpouring of grief', to redeploy the overworked phrase of the week, the character of the crowd changed. Multi-generational, multi-faith and fabulously multi-ethnic, this polyglot patchwork of people looked much more like modern Britain. It helped explain why emotional gears that had been hitherto held in check were raced through so very quickly. More than that, it reminded us that those dog-eared national stereotypes were woefully out of date.

For me, two encounters with members of the public linger still in the mind. One afternoon in the middle of that week, as I was driven the short distance from Buckingham Palace to Kensington Palace in the back of a black cab, the taxi driver started telling me about the death of his own mother, a bereavement that had been dragged back to the forefront of his mind. By the time we reached the Royal Albert Hall, he was in tears. A few hundred metres later, as he set me down opposite the flower-bedecked gates, he could hardly read the meter.

Odder still was a conversation with a local parish vicar in north London on the morning of Diana's funeral. I asked him to sum up the mood of his parishioners, which I thought was a fairly perfunctory line of questioning, but it unleashed a stream of comic-strip tears. Nothing more aptly illustrated the weirdness of that week than to have a 60-something parish priest crying on the shoulder of a 20-something journalist.

By now, of course, Diana had been appropriated by the masses, who had taken their cue from the then prime minister, Tony Blair. Casting himself as the country's grief counsellor, he had described her – touchingly, haltingly and with great theatricality – as 'The People's Princess'.

Whereas Blair grasped immediately the public mood and started to tap the well of hyper-emotion, the royal family followed so far behind that they appeared to inhabit not so much a parallel universe as an entirely different epoch. That morning, when the queen, Prince Charles and the royal princes gathered for morning service at Crathie Kirk parish church near Balmoral, Diana's name was not even mentioned, and the tragedy was dealt with in an oblique reference during one of the prayers. Then there was the cold grammar of the Court Circular, which dealt matter-of-factly with her death: '. . . the royal family learnt this morning with great sadness of the death of Diana, Princess of Wales. Divine service was later held . . .'

At the start of the week, there was a fierce backlash against the press, the supposed accomplices of the Paris paparazzi. By Wednesday, however, the anger had been redirected towards the royal family. Britons remained sufficiently deferential to put up with the social exclusivity of the monarchy but not its emotional aloofness. Scapegoated to begin with, the tabloids could hardly believe their luck and now started to harness the mood of rebelliousness against the monarchy.

'Where Is the Queen When the Country Needs Her?' asked *The Sun*. 'Why Can't the Royal Family Show its Grief?' blasted the *Daily Mail*. 'Your People Are Suffering. Speak to Us Ma'am,' screamed the *Daily Mirror*. Speak to us she did. Breaking with the usual rules of British deference, a monarch bowed before public opinion – even going so far as to deliver her live speech to the nation in a room overlooking the Victoria Memorial, so that she could co-opt the mourners as her backdrop.

The next morning, the BBC launched a massive outside broadcast, which brought together on the radio its two main networks, the venerable Radio Four and its adolescent upstart Radio Five Live, the news and sports channel. One offered the traditional voice of measured authority; the other was edgy, estuarial and classless. With the joint broadcast bringing together the stars from both networks, veteran presenters from Radio Four's flagship news programme suddenly found themselves rostered alongside sports correspondents who normally commentated on the football or cricket. The results were inadvertently hilarious.

As the funeral cortège made its way down Whitehall, one of Radio Four's most plummy presenters handed the commentary baton over to one of the football correspondents, who felt compelled to quote from another Diana. Should we not remember the words of the American songstress Diana Ross, he suggested, before quoting the first two lines of 'Reach Out and Touch (Somebody's Hand)'. Then, presumably hoping to make the world an even better place, he reprised it again.

As he, in turn, handed over to another pukka presenter, listeners must have thought the BBC was suffering some terrible identity crisis. But it perfectly captured the confused national mood, where populist and emotive forms of expression had crowded out more traditional ideas about decorum and self-control. A nostalgic imperial culture was vying with a celebrity culture and even a football culture, that other great outlet for mass emotionalism. It seemed at times that we were witnessing a nationwide rendering of the Liverpudlian response to the Hillsborough disaster eight years earlier, with its flowers, anthems and mass ceremonials. Our coverage merely reflected this messy incoherence.

The assignment of reporters and presenters that day could be read like an unofficial ranking of BBC talent – a global one at that, since some of the finest international reporters had been flown home especially for the occasion and stationed at key landmarks along the funeral route: Kensington Palace, Hyde Park Corner, Buckingham Palace, Clarence House.

Lesser lights, like me, were pushed to the suburban fringes of north London, where Diana's hearse would travel on the way to her final resting place at Althorp, her ancestral home in Northamptonshire. I found myself on the upper reaches of Finsbury Road, an arterial route lined with fried-chicken joints and bargain-basement travel agents, which locals had tried to spruce up by tying purple bows to the lamp posts and traffic bollards. The prose that I had prepared for my commentary was an even deeper shade of purple, but the words never made it beyond my notepad.

As the hearse moved out of central London, it travelled at such a hurtling pace that it flashed by in a matter of seconds. Reporters had been spaced out at 500-metre intervals to commentate in relay, but hardly anyone got to utter a single word. Rendered mute, all we passed up the route was gossip: the news of a string of meltdowns, full-on hissy fits, from senior correspondents closer to central London who had been denied the chance to grieve on air.

At that stage of my career, I was way too junior to have yet achieved tantrum status, although it was something I clearly aspired to in the future. And, if anything, I packed away my microphone that morning thinking it was probably just as well that I never got to broadcast my sentimental mush to the rest of the world. In any case, the rhetorical bar had been raised so very high so very early in the week that by the day of the funeral there was simply nowhere left to go. It had become like listening to an athletics commentator covering the latter stages of a middle-distance race, who had reached the uppermost pitch of his voice with 400 metres still remaining.

All that week, I had struggled to get into the full emotional swing – I had even gone to watch a romantic comedy at the cinema and, about 40 minutes into the film, breached the prohibition on laughing out loud in public – but I would hate to make it sound as if I were completely immune to the feelings of my compatriots. I even admit to a few moments of moistness. Rather embarrassingly, my very own outpouring of grief came when Elton John started singing 'Goodbye, England's Rose'. By the end of the first line, I was a quivering wreck, although on air, at least, I managed to keep any stray feelings in check.

Just as Britain changed that week, so, too, did British journalism. Still novel then, the internet firmly established itself as the home of far-fetched conspiracy theories, offering crackpot counter-narratives to official versions of events. The tabloids reconsidered their use of telephoto journalism, though the paparazzi were not banished for long. We also saw the first full flowering of what might be called 'How do you feel?' reportage, where feelings were harvested almost as assiduously as facts. Even within venerable journalistic institutions such as the BBC and *Daily Telegraph*, a new premium was attached to tears and watery secretions. On stories that involved death or any form of loss, no longer was it acceptable merely to get a quote. The words had to come with sentiment. We not only took the pulse of the public but also felt their pain.

The vocabulary of news started to change as well. Words such as 'cathartic', 'epiphany' and 'closure' began to litter our coverage. The mental distance between interviewer and interviewee also got narrower, and sometimes even vanished. As well as deploying the language of therapeutic care, some reporters started to dabble in pop psychology, while others assumed the air of full-blown psychotherapists. Through this couchification of journalism, the aim was not merely to elicit emotional reactions but also to probe the psyche.

Charles and Diana were again integral to this process, especially when their disintegrating marriage started being retrospectively viewed more as a psychodrama than a news story. Over at Westminster, as well, some of the same techniques came to be applied to help make sense of the tortured relationship between Tony Blair and Gordon Brown. Call it what you will – the couchification or the Oprafication of news – but journalism was starting to reward emotion-gatherers as well as news-gatherers.

As a postscript to Diana's death, it is worth recalling the mood the following year, when an embarrassed reticence hung over the anniversary commemorations. They ended up being a lot more emotionally subdued than most commentators expected.

Noticeably more self-conscious, it was almost as if Britons now felt ill at ease, ashamed even, with the binge-grieving of 12 months earlier. Yet it could hardly be described as a return to pre-Diana normalcy, for the Britain of the past has never since managed to reassert itself.

—

'Comfort has come to the streets of Belfast.' The words were lyrical enough to have come from the lips of one of Northern Ireland's great poets, a Seamus Heaney, say, or perhaps Van Morrison, Belfast's most celebrated balladeer. But they were uttered by a kindly landlady as she showed me to my room in a bed and breakfast three weeks after the IRA had announced its first ceasefire in August 1994.

I was just about to join the BBC and had travelled to Belfast partly out of curiosity and partly because I thought, precociously, that I would soon end up being assigned there. Back then, Northern Ireland was the nursery of Correspondentland, and most of the reporters who had gone on to cover wars abroad had started by covering our very own war at home. So this had the feel of pre-school.

By day, I would do the sights: the Belfast terror tour, making sure to swap taxis from a Catholic firm to the Protestant one as I went between the Falls Road and Shankill Road. In the evenings, I would drink pints of Guinness in a bar near Queen's University and read Tim Pat Coogan's monumental history *The Troubles*. In the morning, my landlady would cook me an Ulster fry, with bacon, eggs, sausages, white pudding and soda bread – one of the world's great breakfasts.

There would be a neatness in the narrative had I recalled that gentle woman 17 months later as I dashed out of the pub, leapt into the taxi, shouted at the driver to head towards Canary Wharf and sprinted the last mile through the cordoned-off streets of London's Docklands. Alas, an IRA bomb had just shattered the comfort she had spoken of so expectantly. At 5.28 pm on Friday 9 February 1996, a man using the well-known *nom de guerre* 'P. O'Neill' had dictated a message from the IRA Army Council to a reporter from the Irish national broadcaster, RTÉ, announcing that its ceasefire would end at six o'clock. Then, at 5.54 pm, another man using the IRA codeword 'Kerrygold' rang the switchboard of the *Irish News* in Belfast to warn that a 'massive bomb' was about to go off beside South Quay tube station in Docklands. Did the man say Kerrygold, the woman asked. Just like butter, came the blank reply.

Shortly after seven o'clock, the IRA detonated a half-tonne bomb that killed two people and turned a corner of London's new financial hub into a scene of ruin. Mirror-glass office buildings were completely gutted, standing like giant filing cabinets that had been ransacked in a robbery. The streets were strewn with rubble, broken glass, fragments of office furniture and once neatly filed papers. Then there was the usual posse of reporters that had converged on the scene like a flash mob. Never before had I witnessed first-hand the destructive power of explosives – in this case a blend of ammonium-nitrate fertiliser and fuel oil. Nor had I experienced that peculiar feeling, at once thrilling and unnerving, of running towards danger when virtually everyone else was heading fast in the opposite direction.

Soon, I was heading over to Ireland. Nine days after the Docklands bomb, a 21-year-old Irishman blew himself up on a double-decker bus on the Strand when the bomb he was transporting across London exploded prematurely. The dead bomber, Edward O'Brien, had grown up in Gorey, a prosperous market town south of Dublin in County Wexford, and I travelled there, along with an Irish colleague, to find out why he had signed up as an IRA volunteer.

The clues were easy enough to find. The site during the 1798 uprising of an attack by rebels on British Crown forces, Gorey was steeped in Republican mythology. The insurrection had been memorialised in stone. Rebel songs were sung still in the pubs. Nobody wanted to speak, however, about why O'Brien felt motivated to continue waging a fight that the vast majority of people in Gorey had relegated to the past.

Faced with this wall of silence, my Irish colleague knew precisely what to do. First making sure we had a hefty supply of cigarettes, he arranged for us to meet the local priest. A gaunt, fidgety chain-smoker, with small flints of dandruff dotted on the shoulders of his black suit, the priest came straight from central casting. But he listened sympathetically as we made our pitch, and he signalled, through a fug of cigarette smoke, that he would help.

Instantly, Gorey opened up for us, and my colleague even managed to speak to the elderly IRA veteran who used to stand outside chapel on a Sunday morning, with young O'Brien at his side, selling copies of *An Phoblacht*, the Republican movement's propaganda sheet. Back then, the lame joke whenever coming in to land at an Irish airport was to make sure that you readjusted your watch by at least 200 years, but occasionally it doubled as useful advice. As we soon discovered, young Edward O'Brien's imagination had indeed been fired by an insurrection that had unfolded nearly two centuries before his birth. From the 1798 uprising to a botched bombing on the Strand, the historical thread was unbroken.

More happily, many of my journeys over the Irish Sea in the coming years were to cover fresh rounds of political talks rather than fresh bouts of violence. Then there was the marching season, which fell somewhere between the two. Once a two-month festival of noisy though largely trouble-free parades, it had become a proxy battleground for the venting of sectarian tensions.

As in Gorey, it was like disappearing through a wormhole of time. Covering it could be a thoroughly dispiriting experience, but there was also a certain charm in driving through some of the most beautiful countryside that the British Isles have to offer, en route to towns and villages that for most of the year were tranquil and obscure.

By the time we would arrive, the opposing sides had usually taken up their positions, like medieval armies in observance of ancient rites. The Orangemen would be gathered at one end of town, with their bowler hats, tangerine V-shaped collarettes, folded umbrellas, white gloves, dark suits (acrylic in the main), Union Flags, Boyne Standards and wall-sized Lodge banners emblazoned with images of William of Orange. The fife and drum bands would be warming up with scales and arpeggios, their tunics decorated with epaulets, ribbonry, badges and insignia bearing grand, if self-protective, names: Red Hand Defenders, Pride of the Hill, Mourne Young Defenders. Even babies were adorned with Loyalist paraphernalia, such as bibs reading 'Born on the Twelfth of July'.

Catholic protesters, carrying placards featuring the silhouette of an Orangeman with a no-entry sign superimposed, would have assembled at the other end of the main street, or have been hemmed in on side roads so they could not assault the marchers.

Playing their own part in this pageantry, the police would be occupying the middle ground, clad in black riot gear and standing alongside their battleship-grey Land Rovers parked bumper to bumper to form a barrier. Then, at the appointed hour, the bands would strike up to the pounding beat of a huge Lambeg drum, while the protesters would hurl abuse and missiles. In one country village, it was Lucozade bottles. In another, at the sound of a high-pitched whistle, protesters hurled hundreds of golf balls, most of which were eagerly scooped up by the policemen, who presumably planned to tee off with them as soon as the marching season was over, and with it their ban on leave. Along the most contentious parade routes, it was Molotov cocktails and occasionally gunfire.

Of all the sectarian interfaces, none was angrier than Drumcree. Contentious parade routes normally skirted predominantly Catholic neighbourhoods, but here it passed right through the middle. Held on the Sunday before the traditional 12 July celebrations, which marked King William's victory at the Battle of the Boyne, Orangemen set out from their fortress-like lodge in the centre of nearby Portadown. Then they marched out of town to the steepled church at Drumcree set in rolling hills that evoked the music of Elgar and Vaughan Williams rather than the high-pitched squeal of the piccolos and flutes.

After holding a service to commemorate the Battle of the Somme, the Orangemen returned to the centre of town via the Garvaghy Road, which was lined on either side by Catholic housing estates. It was there that trouble usually flared, and by the mid-1990s the Garvaghy Road had become Northern Ireland's most active sectarian fault line. In 1995, the police banned the parade, only to back down when thousands of Orangemen amassed on the hills around Drumcree and threatened to hammer through the army barricades using a bulldozer and petrol tankers.

My own Drumcree initiation came two years later, in 1997, shortly after Tony Blair had taken office, when the new Labour government indicated to the local Catholic residents' group that the parade would again be banned. With another stand-off certain to ensue, BBC safety advisers issued us with hard-hats, protective goggles, fire extinguishers and even flameproof underwear. For fear of identifying any of our Irish colleagues as Protestant or Catholic, we were also warned not to use their Christian names. A careless 'Seamus' or 'Billy' uttered on the wrong side of the battlelines could put them in real danger.

That weekend, we all expected serious trouble, but there was still something shocking about the outburst of violent fury from local residents when police Land Rovers screamed onto the Garvaghy Road in the pre-dawn hours to pave the way for Orangemen and formed an impregnable phalanx of armoured vehicles on either side of the parade route. Calling it the 'least worst option', the government and security forces had decided the Portadown Orangemen should be allowed to march, whatever the backlash from the local Catholic community.

It was fearsome. After the parade passed by, and the police and soldiers beat a hurried retreat, they were chased down the Garvaghy Road by hundreds of youths hurling rocks, petrol bombs and what we later found out were bottles filled with sulphuric acid. One of our cameramen thought he was standing in a puddle of water. Then his shoes started to melt. Through the melee of exploding Molotov cocktails and fizzing baton rounds, the Orangemen could be seen in the mid-distance marching beneath a ceremonial archway bedecked with Loyalist colours that marked the line of demarcation between Catholic Portadown and Protestant Portadown. The raucous cheers that greeted them could just be heard above the din.

True to the fault-line effect of Drumcree, aftershocks spread throughout the province. Still wearing our flameproof undies, we headed to Londonderry – in keeping with the BBC rule, I will call it Londonderry first, then Derry thereafter – where trouble was sure to flare. Parking a short walk from the Bogside, so as to avoid having our car hijacked by rioters, we walked down to a patch of land near the famed 'Free Derry' sign, where Martin McGuinness, Sinn Féin's chief negotiator and an IRA leader in Derry on Bloody Sunday, was addressing a crowd of supporters. 'The place to be demanding justice is on the streets confronting your opponents,' he yelled, which was an invitation for absolute mayhem. A new Battle of the Bogside erupted soon after and raged through the night.

At the front, teenagers sprinted down the street like javelin throwers, straining for every extra yard, and hurled petrol bombs at the police and army. In the rear, small boys, some as young as nine or ten, carried milk crates full of ready-made Molotov cocktails up to the main battlelines. But the ringmasters were the IRA men disguised in woollen ski masks, with holes for the eyes and mouths, who turned the violence on and off like a stopcock.

Away from all the rioting, there was fun to be had during the marching season and especially at Drumcree. At times, it took on the feel of a journalistic folk festival, a sort of Glastonbury for trouble-seeking correspondents, who set up camp on the nationalist side of the barbed-wire fences erected by the Royal Engineers, close to the local Gaelic football club. Knowing they could end up there for a week or so, news teams arrived in campervans or pulling caravans, well stocked with beer, whisky and other, more illicit, forms of recreational entertainment. Though Portadown became for weeks the focus of a massive security clampdown, from the journalists' mobile homes it was common to hear the sound of laughter and sniff the faint whiff of hash.

Long into the night, reporters would trade marching-season war stories. The Northern Ireland veterans had the best yarns and were also gifted anecdotalists. But at least I could tell of once being confronted by an irate Orangeman who threatened to spear me with a ceremonial pike, and also of coming close to having my posterior peppered with bullets. We had been filming a paramilitary show of force on a Loyalist estate off the Shankill Road, another ritual of the marching season, where a teenage honour guard fired a volley into the air to the delight of a baying crowd. On this occasion, however, the sub-machine gun proved way too heavy for the young Loyalist doing the firing, and, rather like a weightlifter struggling under the load of a giant barbell, his knees started to buckle. With each stumble and stagger, the trajectory of the bullets got lower and lower, and we got closer and closer to the ground, rueing our decision to film from directly in front of the firing squad.

Then part of the global conflict circuit, Drumcree attracted the world's big-name, international war correspondents, such as Christiane Amanpour of CNN, which added a certain frisson. But by far my favourite international blow-in was an Australian reporter who worked for Downtown Radio, one of the commercial stations in Belfast. His hourly updates, delivered in a thick Waltzing Matilda twang, made the Garvaghy Road sound like a side street in Broken Hill. What else could we call him but 'Crocodile Drumcree'?

However violent, what was always remarkable about the marching season was how quickly Northern Ireland rebounded.

Although many journalists saw in the rubble of burnt-out buildings and the charred carcasses of hijacked buses images that illustrated perfectly the sorry state of the peace process, it was another overused cliché, 'It's always darkest before the dawn', that often had the ring of truth. Just 15 days after my first Drumcree in 1997, the IRA announced its second ceasefire. Soon after, Sinn Féin entered a fresh round of peace talks.

In October, politicians of all shades, from the representatives of the IRA to the spokesmen of the Loyalist paramilitaries, from Ian Paisley's Democratic Unionist Party to John Hume's nationalist Social Democratic and Labour Party (SDLP), met at Stormont for the first all-party talks in 25 years. Then, in November, Gerry Adams led a Sinn Féin delegation to Downing Street, the first time that a Republican leader had gone through the door of Number 10 since the days of Michael Collins and David Lloyd George. Just six years earlier, the IRA had fired mortar bombs that exploded in the back garden. Now, Gerry Adams, who was still a member of the IRA's Army Council, entered in a tie, a suit and a dark woollen overcoat, the bland attire that a visiting Belgian finance minister might wear.

By the following Easter, 1998, a peace deal had been hammered out, and in a corner of Britain where dark adjectives such as 'black' or 'bloody' had attached themselves to the gloomiest days of the Troubles, there was finally a Friday that could truly be described as 'good'. On the night of the Good Friday Agreement, few things were more touching than the sight of a long line of swooning journalists, men as well as women, waiting for Senator George Mitchell, Bill Clinton's peace envoy and the chairman of the talks, to autograph copies of the peace deal. The most self-effacing of men, Mitchell was embarrassed by the fuss and wanted nothing more, after months of fraught negotiations, than to head back to America to see his young son. But his fingerprints were all over Northern Ireland's historic compromise, and before he could make a dash for the airport everybody wanted his signature on it, too.

Normally at Easter, the darkness of Christ's crucifixion on the Friday gives way to the celebration of his resurrection on the Sunday, but in parts of Northern Ireland that weekend this holy liturgy was turned on its head. The optimism of Friday was followed by uncertainty and resentment. On Easter morning in Crossmaglen, in the heart of IRA bandit country, the talk was of betrayal, with Gerry Adams cast as Judas.

Hundreds of dissident Republicans, many of them active IRA volunteers from the feared County Armagh Brigade, gathered in St Patrick's churchyard for their annual commemoration of the 1916 Easter Rising. There, amidst tombstones etched with the names of dead IRA men, they vowed to continue their armed struggle. Marching briskly to the centre of the graveyard, a man dressed in a combat jacket, balaclava and black beret appeared out of nowhere to address the crowd. 'There will be no settlement,' he shouted into a microphone as a British Army Lynx helicopter circled overhead. 'There'll be no peace for this country until those people up there leave this country.'

Another dissident Republican put it even more bluntly: 'To say this deal is transitional towards a united Ireland is bollocks.'

The British Army watchtowers of County Armagh; the IRA warning signs at the side of the country roads reading 'Sniper at Work'; newly painted murals on the gables in the Loyalist areas of Belfast that now included slogans such as 'Compromise and conflict' alongside the usual imagery of gun-toting paramilitaries;

former prisoners who spoke eloquently of 'new paradigms' and genuinely seemed to mean it: all this formed the backdrop to the referendum on the Good Friday Agreement, which would essentially decide the question asked intermittently since Partition in 1921 – could the people of Northern Ireland ever peacefully co-exist, and was that truly their desire?

The temptation was to cover the referendum campaign as if it were a straightforward choice between the future and the past, of reformers against rejectionists. However, in a country where history was ever present, it was far more convoluted. As one would expect, the high priest of the 'No' campaign was the Reverend Ian Paisley, whose most famous political catchphrase, delivered in a thunderous voice at maximum volume, was 'ULSTER SAYS NO'. (At a press conference in the lead-up to the vote, I asked the Big Man, as Reverend Paisley was known, some smart-arse question. 'Where are you from?' he bellowed. 'The BBC,' I timidly replied. 'I THOUGHT SO,' he roared back.) Yet it also included more quietly spoken victims of the Troubles – mothers, fathers, brothers and sisters – who detested the idea of watching the murderers of their relatives released from prison under the terms of the peace deal.

The 'Yes' campaign, meanwhile, was run with the help of Saatchi & Saatchi advertising executives dressed in Paul Smith suits, although its strongest advocates included some of Northern Ireland's most psychotic murderers and thugs. The poster boy for former Loyalist paramilitaries, for instance, was Michael Stone, a Charles Manson lookalike and notorious assassin. The last time most people in Northern Ireland had seen him was in some of the most infamous television footage from the Troubles, which showed him mounting a lone gun and grenade attack at the funeral in Milltown cemetery of three IRA members shot dead by the SAS in Gibraltar.

In the final week of campaigning, however, Stone was allowed out on day release from Maze Prison to appear at a 'Yes' rally organised by former paramilitaries at the Ulster Hall. To cries of 'We want Michael! We want Michael!' and with a banner draped from the balcony declaring that 'Michael Says Yes', Stone was greeted with such rapture that it made a mockery of the claim that a 'Yes' vote equated automatically with progress.

Days before the Good Friday Agreement, Tony Blair had declared it was no time for soundbites, then revealed that he could feel the 'hand of history' virtually massaging his shoulders. But although a prime architect of the agreement, his 'Hi, guys' trendy vicar routine always grated on the unionist leaders, who were men of Victorian manners and sensibilities. A member of the band Ugly Rumours at university, who strummed on his electric guitar in his upstairs flat in Downing Street, Blair may have thought of himself as a politician with rock-star charisma. But in the final days of campaigning, he was completely blown away by a rock star with rock-star charisma.

Bono arrived in Belfast, with The Edge by his side, to perform at a concert intended to arrest a last-minute slump in support for the 'Yes' campaign. Somehow, he also managed to persuade David Trimble, the buttoned-down leader of the Ulster Unionist Party, and John Hume of the SDLP to appear with him on stage. In choosing what to sing, Bono had considered the merits of John Lennon's 'Give Peace a Chance' (too obvious), Bob Marley's 'One Love' (too obscure), The Beatles' 'We Can Work it Out' (too corny) and even Rolf Harris's 'Two Little Boys' (too silly). Eventually, he settled on the 1969 love song that Lennon had written for Yoko

Ono, 'Don't Let Me Down', with the lines of the chorus changed so they now read 'All we are saying is give peace a chance'.

Before an ecumenical crowd of some 2000 sixth-formers drawn from Protestant and Catholic schools, Bono belted out the song with marvellous passion. (My most treasured souvenir from my time in Northern Ireland is a bootleg recording of his performance.) Then he introduced the bespectacled middle-aged politicians who had done more than any others to bring Northern Ireland to this point – of 'taking a leap of faith out of the past and into the future', as Bono put it.

Two more unfashionable politicians it was hard to imagine than the highly strung David Trimble or the podgy John Hume, but they made their awkward entrances from either side of the stage and then clasped hands in the middle. To appear more up-to-the-minute, both men had discarded their suit jackets, though not their ties, while David Trimble even cracked a smile. Bono had also made his own sartorial adjustment. Normally, he appeared in rose-tinted spectacles, but this time he came on stage without any sunglasses. Predicting a bright and brilliant future, he presumably wanted everyone to see his eyes.

The 'No' campaign was quick to condemn the concert, complaining that U2 was trying to buy the votes of young people with a free concert. Ian Paisley also claimed that, during one concert in America, Bono had set fire to the Union Flag – an accusation that the singer rejected vehemently. Yet, at a time when the late momentum was with opponents of the Good Friday Agreement, this south-of-the-border superstar gave the 'Yes' campaign the fillip it desperately needed: a late reminder that peace was hip and trendy, and that it meant Bono more than Michael Stone.

Just three days later, in the highest attended poll since

partition, 71 per cent of people in Northern Ireland voted 'Yes' to the Good Friday Agreement. In the Irish Republic, where the country's constitution penned by Éamon De Valera would soon be rewritten to drop its claim on the north, over 94 per cent voted in favour. When Ian Paisley arrived at the King's Hall in Belfast – the agricultural showground where the result was announced – he was met by Loyalist chants of 'Cheerio, cheerio, cheerio'. Paisley represented the sectarian politics of 'No'. For once, Ulster had said 'Yes'.

Later that night, the 'Yes' campaign hosted a strangely lifeless victory party in a rooftop bar with mauve lighting, panoramic views of the city and lukewarm Pinot Gris. But there was much better *craic* to be had at the BBC Club, just over the way from the newsroom, which was the scene of an almighty booze-up. Whatever they thought of the agreement, journalists celebrated the simple joy of having, for the first time in 30 years, a much more hopeful storyline to impart.

With Guinness, Harp lager and whisky – Bushmills for the Protestants and Jameson for the Catholics, not that it seemed to matter so much any more – we partied all night, and then, when dawn came, partied some more. Less than three months later, these same journalists would cover the massacre at Omagh, when dissident Republicans killed 29 people, many of them Catholic, after detonating a car bomb in a street packed with shoppers. It was Northern Ireland's worst single atrocity. Yet so strong was the sense of public revulsion that the hope also was that Omagh would become the last. For once, the Real IRA was even humiliated into an apology.

In the BBC Club, perhaps the home-town journalists had another cause for celebration: their newsroom would no longer have to accommodate over-ambitious blow-ins from London who had been heading to Belfast since the late 1960s in the hope of making a name for themselves. One of the biggest changes during my time in the BBC is also one of the most welcome: young tyro reporters are no longer blooded in Northern Ireland. Admittedly, it had taken longer than that gentle landlady had predicted, but comfort had come, by and large, to the streets of Belfast.

The end of the Troubles; the sudden death of England's most glorious rose; the assassination of Israel's favourite son: at a time when the requirements of continuous news turned big stories into mega-stories, I had the good fortune to cover three of them very early on. And, as if in a game of consequences, my luck held. On the return flight to Washington, after attending Rabin's state funeral, the then house speaker Newt Gingrich was so enraged that President Clinton declined to speak to him aboard Air Force One on the flight back from Israel that it contributed to his decision to starve the federal bureaucracy of congressional funding. This led directly to the government shutdown in late 1995 and early 1996, which in turn meant that Clinton came to rely more heavily on the team of White House interns, since regular staffers were not allowed to show up for work. One in particular caught his eye. She was a 21-year-old from Beverly Hills. Her name was Monica Samille Lewinsky.

Chapter 2

Dear Bill

What luck in those early years of my nascent career to have a guardian angel with lax morals, a chaotic personality, an appetite for everything and, better still, presidential ambitions. As a student journalist, the first story I ever managed to get published by a newspaper in London was about Governor Bill Clinton. It was a trifling diary item about a bar in Little Rock called Slick Willie, his then nickname, which had come up with a range of cocktails to mark his run for the White House – although even then the press was showing more interest in his penchant for Arkansas cocktail waitresses.

Six years later, as a young BBC reporter, President William Jefferson Clinton landed me my first permanent foreign posting, when scandal once more engulfed him, and we discovered that his taste in women now extended to voluptuous White House interns.

During the impeachment saga, it was often said that cameramen who had amassed vast sums of overtime pay splurged it on motor cruisers and small yachts on the Potomac or at Chesapeake Bay, which they inevitably christened *Monica*. Had the BBC paid its correspondents piece rates, I would have hurled the champagne towards the hull of a vessel named *Bill* or, perhaps, *Just William*. That diary story not only gave me the pleasure of seeing my work appear for the first time in print but also got me my start as a high-society gossip columnist. The Lewinsky scandal – though it should truly have been called the Bill Clinton scandal – made me a Washington correspondent. It was a job I had coveted from the time I realised I was not about to become the next Le Corbusier, turned my back on architecture and switched instead to studying American political history.

To meet him, of course, is to be exposed immediately to the Clinton Treatment: the mauling handshake; the empathetic nod; the piercing stare, fixed and admiring; the instant intimacy; a gravitational pull with the power to suck people into his orbit. Often, it is said that Clinton comes not only with his own force field but also his own personal weather system, and that he's so expert at the art of seduction that he can make even the most fleeting acquaintance feel as if he or she is the single most important person in the room. Still, when I first encountered him during the 1992 New Hampshire primary campaign I came away thinking there was something much more transactional about his celebrated interpersonal skills. The feeling was of being the most important voter in the room, or, in my case, the most important journalist.

I was over from Oxford at the time conducting research for my thesis on Jack Kennedy, a leader with whom Clinton was intermittently compared. I was trying to persuade him to agree to a short interview for his old university rag. Always obliging, the one-time Rhodes Scholar did not need much cajoling and suggested I contact his chief of staff in Little Rock, Betsey Wright, the sorter of his details, the keeper of his secrets and the freewheeling aide immortalised by the actress Kathy Bates in the movie *Primary Colors*. For a top-ranking aide in the midst of a presidential campaign, Wright could hardly have been more helpful. However, a candidate's time is not only donor money but also votes, and it was impossible for her to find a gap in his schedule, since there weren't any gaps in the first place.

So when next I ran into Clinton, I tried once again. This time, he was outside the John F. Kennedy Presidential Library in south Boston, where I spent my days poring over yellowing presidential papers in an archive that assassination-conspiracy theorists were convinced was bugged, and where the governor had gone for a posthumous character reference. Already, his campaign had published a black-and-white photograph taken when he was 17, looking preternaturally self-possessed as he shook the hand of JFK on the South Lawn of the White House – the Clinton handshake was a marvel even then – and took command of the small talk, as if Kennedy was merely house-sitting.

Before Clinton levered himself into his people mover, which in those early days could comfortably accommodate both his campaign staff and travelling press corps, he once again agreed in principle to the interview and suggested I badger Wright. As before, the governor seemed genuinely enthusiastic about the idea, although I had seen enough of him by now to recognise that this was his stock response to any idea put to him while trying to harvest votes.

Nothing if not persistent, I made my third approach at a campaign rally in a downtown Boston hotel, when I tried to corner Clinton in one of those narrow, back-of-house corridors favoured by presidential candidates needing to make a fast escape from the balloon-strewn ballroom, via the kitchen, to their waiting limousine. This time, I had even brought a snapper, a university friend studying photography who was happy to play the role of paparazzo. Perhaps Clinton felt he was being ambushed, since gone now was the easy charm of our first two encounters, and absent was his outstretched hand. Instead, the mere mention of the word 'Oxford', which had always been my best calling card, seemed to instil a sense of near panic in both him and his handlers.

As the governor was bundled out of a back entrance, it seemed my chances of landing an interview had vanished as well, and I left thinking the presence of the photographer had blown my chances. Yet, a few days later, the headlines offered a very different explanation. As a student at University College, Oxford, Clinton had managed to avoid being conscripted for Vietnam, through a combination of political contacts and the luck of drawing a high lottery number in the draft. Now that reporters had caught a whiff of the story, he no longer wanted his varsity days revisited.

With the then New York governor Mario Cuomo having declared himself a non-runner, Clinton had started the year well out in front in the race for the Democratic presidential nomination. Already, he had won the money primary by attracting the wealthiest donors. He had also achieved something of a landslide victory in the media primary, by winning over opinion-forming writers, such as Joe Klein of *New York* magazine, who wrote the first draft of the invented narrative of the campaign. But then came the moral primary, after the first bimbo eruptions started to explode on the front pages of the supermarket tabloids. They arrived not with pyrotechnics but peroxide, for the allegations of infidelity centred on Gennifer Flowers, the bottle-blonde cocktail waitress who claimed to have had a 12-year romance with Clinton. At her kiss-and-tell-all press conference, Flowers played a recording of a phone conversation with the governor in which he purportedly urged her to deny their affair. But her appearance that day lives in the memory for her embarrassed reticence in response to what is possibly the most tacky question ever uttered during a presidential campaign: 'Did Mr Clinton use a condom?'

With even papers like the *New York Times* and the *Washington Post* lapsing into British-tabloid-style sensationalism, the governor took an immediate hit in the polls. Then he managed to right himself temporarily by appearing in his famed *Sixty Minutes* interview on Super Bowl Sunday, when, with Hillary sitting dutifully by his side, he implicitly acknowledged his infidelity. The draft-dodging story, however, threatened to be terminal, since, with seven out of the past eight US presidents having served in the Second World War, Americans still expected their commanders-in-chief to have worn dog tags. Even more worrying for the scandal-prone Clinton was that the aura of inevitability around his candidacy had evaporated. His response was the melancholic cry 'I'm electable', though a dwindling number of reporters believed him.

On the plus side, the scandal led to the publication of an anguished 1400-word letter which the then 23-year-old Clinton had written from Oxford to a colonel in Arkansas explaining his opposition to the Vietnam War. It had plumbed 'a depth of feeling I had reserved solely for racism in America', he said, and fuelled a belief that no government 'rooted in limited, parliamentary democracy should have the power to make its citizens fight and kill in a war they may oppose'.

For his admirers, the letter demonstrated not only a powerful intellect but also his skill at elucidating the most complicated of issues. On the negative side of the ledger, however, it provided damning clues about the extent to which his character was so completely riven with politics even in his youth. 'I decided to accept the draft in spite of my beliefs for one reason,' Clinton offered as the sole explanation for finally putting his name forward, 'to maintain my political viability within the system.'

In those final manic weeks of the New Hampshire primary, I had actually signed up as a volunteer for the Clinton campaign, though I suspect it was less out of admiration for the governor and more because his bus left for Nashua, New Hampshire, on Saturday mornings an hour after those laid on by his main rivals, Paul Tsongas and Bob Kerrey. For my then girlfriend, who also made the trip north from Boston, it was the start of a celebrated career in the Clinton campaign, which took her all the way to a desk in the policy-shop just down the corridor from the famed War Room in Little Rock, Arkansas, where James Carville, the 'ragin' cajun', barked out orders and refused to change his lucky underwear. Alas, my involvement started and ended on the same day, after withdrawing my services in a fit of self-righteous pique.

At that stage, the draft-dodging allegations had not yet come to the fore, but they were of little concern. After all, the national obsession with Vietnam, like the fixation with student pot smoking, was discouraging some of America's most talented baby boomers from seeking high office – especially when combined with the puritanical streak of American journalists and their refusal to impose any statute of limitation on scandal. Nor was I concerned with Clinton's mutually consensual infidelities (back then, the allegations of non-mutually-consensual infidelities with Juanita Broaddrick and Kathleen Willey had not yet surfaced). Again, I was a student of Jack Kennedy, whose presidency had come to be called 'The Thousand Days' but was almost as noteworthy for its Thousand Nights – or, for that matter, its Thousand Afternoons, given the hours wiled away after lunch frolicking in the White

House pool, often with his secretaries 'Fiddle' and 'Faddle'. Neither was it his New Democrat politics, which, with its blend of public compassion and personal responsibility, was considered a little too conservative by many Cambridge liberals, who lamented Mario Cuomo's withdrawal.

Rather, my problem with Clinton stemmed from his handling of the case of Ricky Ray Rector, a black man whose party in 1981 had been denied entry at a dance hall at Tommy's Old-Fashioned Home-Style Restaurant in Conway, Arkansas. Rector had responded by killing one man and then, three days later, murdering a police officer. Guilty of a double homicide, he could hardly be described as a sympathetic figure. But he was also mentally retarded, chronically so, having destroyed his frontal lobe when he raised the gun to his temple and shot himself through the forehead. Now half-lobotomised and a colossal 298 lb, Rector waited on death row in Cummins Prison, Arkansas, howling, barking like a dog and, according to his guards, laughing uncontrollably.

Adding to his misfortune, his execution coincided with the lead-up to the New Hampshire vote, at the very moment when Gennifer Flowers was hogging the headlines. For Clinton, this presented an opening. Having insisted during a candidates' debate in New Hampshire that Democrats should 'no longer feel guilty about protecting the innocent', he left the campaign trail to oversee the execution. So, on 24 January 1992, after eating a last supper of fried chicken, steak and gravy, Rector was put to death by lethal injection. Famously, he had asked for his dessert, a plate of pecan pie, to be set aside for later. In the retelling of this story, however, another salient fact is commonly overlooked. Two hours before his execution, as he watched television news reports on how his final pleas for clemency had been rejected by the Arkansas governor, he announced to his attorney, 'Gonna vote Clinton.'

For the governor, the politics of the execution were uncomplicated. As for the ethics, they did not appear to trouble him. During the 1988 presidential election, he had watched George Herbert Walker Bush bludgeon Michael Dukakis over the release on weekend furlough from a Massachusetts prison of Willie Horton, a black convicted murderer, who then raped a woman. Early in his career, during the 1980 gubernatorial election, he himself had faced the same accusations of being too liberal, when the voters of Arkansas sacked him as governor – the crucible moment in his political career. Still traumatised by that defeat, Clinton needed to protect himself against the Republican charge that he was the 'Dukakis of the South'. The execution of Ricky Ray Rector provided the perfect rebuttal.

When the voters of New Hampshire went to the polls in their first-in-the-nation primary on 18 February 1992, Clinton placed second, which was just enough to validate his ringing boast of being 'The Comeback Kid'. Now, the kingmakers in the Democratic Party marvelled not at his invincibility but at his survivability. With the primary season heading south, Clinton triumphed in nearly all the Super Tuesday contests, which enabled him to lock up the Democratic presidential nomination.

With Fleetwood Mac's 'Don't Stop (Thinking About Tomorrow)' blaring in the background, he then took aim at George Bush Snr, the hero of the first Gulf War, who was a second-term shoe-in when I arrived in America at the back end of 1991. Over the coming year, however, Bush became the target of a pincer movement involving Clinton and his own guardian angel, Ross Perot, the fiery Texan independent who arguably contributed more to the president's eventual defeat. Clinton gleaned just 43 per cent of the popular vote, one of the lowest shares for a winning candidate, but Perot's presence in a rare triangular presidential contest meant that it was enough.

As a reward for her efforts in Little Rock, my girlfriend snagged us tickets to the inaugural festivities, that great Arkansan carnival of big hair, Ferrari-red lipstick and ballooning evening gowns, and we jetted off to Washington to witness the commencement of the Clinton era. From his bullet-proof pulpit on the western terrace of the Capitol, Clinton tried once more to evoke Kennedy, with talk of a New Covenant modelled on the New Frontier, but he had no rhetorical answer for Kennedy's 'Ask what' riff.

Instead, the most memorable moment of the day came when he let rip on his saxophone with B. B. King, which my girlfriend and I watched from the mosh pit of Clintonistas down below. On the night of Kennedy's inauguration, after Jackie had gone to bed, JFK went on to a party thrown by the Washington columnist Joe Alsop at his Georgetown home, where he committed his first adulterous act as president with the actress Angie Dickinson. (Shamefacedly, one of my research highs as a doctoral student was to dine at the Alsop residence and be shown the very bedroom where all this unfolded.) For Clinton, that kind of presidential peccadillo was still some way off.

—

Five years on, it looked as if the Clinton era was about to come to an abrupt end. At 1.11 am on 18 January 1998, the Drudge Report raised the curtain on the first presidential scandal of the online age by revealing that *Newsweek* was sitting on a scoop exposing the president's affair with a young White House intern barely older than his daughter, Chelsea.

Nothing gets Washington more excited than a rumoured resignation, and the Beltway commentariat was agog. Alarmed by the president's cradle-snatching, George Will, the effete conservative columnist, spoke of a 'yuck factor', while the ABC commentator Cokie Roberts complained that he had crossed a behavioural threshold. 'With an *intern*?' she harrumphed.

On 21 January, after the story had been confirmed in the mainstream press, Tim Russert, the ever-jovial host of NBC's *Meet the Press*, was unusually unsmiling: 'The next forty-eight to seventy-two hours are going to be critical.'

The legendary White House correspondent Sam Donaldson had made up his mind already: 'I think his presidency is numbered in days.'

Amidst the flow of other bodily secretions, the White House press corps smelt blood.

The news was jaw-dropping, though I watched it all unfold through gritted teeth, in the most literal sense of all. Just before Christmas, my dentist had noticed an ominous formation of billowing grey clouds on an X-ray of my lower-right mandible, and the removal of the tumour meant that my mouth had to be wired together for more than six weeks. *Newsweek* was reporting at the time that the scandal had 'made it virtually impossible to talk to your kids about the American presidency or let them watch the news'. My problem was that I could not speak, with any fluency, to anyone.

Still, during my weeks of muzzled convalescence, the Lewinsky scandal was one of the few things that I could actually digest. By the time that I had regained the use of my mouth, I had become such an aficionado that when the Washington bureau sought to beef up its numbers I was recruited to help. Initially, I went thinking I would be there a matter of months, until Clinton was either out of trouble or out of office. Five years later, I was still covering the White House beat.

Even now, in this era of unshockability, the details of the affair have the capacity for surprise. Not so much because of the sex but because of the intimacy. No doubt Ms Lewinsky was a little brazen on the night of their first sexual encounter in November 1995 when, after enjoying some flirtatious eye contact with the president, she showed him the straps of her G-string underwear. No doubt the president was a little reckless when, later that night, he groped her in his private study, above and below her waistband, and then watched her perform oral sex while he was on the phone to a Congressman.

But for all the lurid details relayed in the 453-page Starr Report – the world's most extensively researched and expensively produced work of pornography – it is their close rapport that continually comes through. Consider their pet names. Clinton called her 'Sweetie' and 'Baby', which admittedly sounded vaguely pornographic, but also the word 'Dear', which implied something altogether more tender. Lewinsky called him 'Handsome'. Conversations extended long into the night, where they talked about their childhoods, which again spoke of emotional intimacy. Investigators counted some 50 phone conversations, not all of them for the purposes of late-night masturbation, while Clinton also left four answer-machine messages at her home, which spoke, on his part, of incautious abandon. There was even a softness about the hurried sex, with Monica Lewinsky describing how the president would lean against the door, with the cushion just above his tailbone, to relieve his aching back.

The Starr Report, under the headings 'Emotional Attachment', 'Conversations and Phone Messages', 'Initial Sexual Encounters' and 'Continued Sexual Encounters', chronicled all the particulars. But it is the sub-section on 'Gifts' that truly lives up to its billing, for it provides the texture of their relationship. Of 30 or so presents, Monica Lewinsky gave him 'six neckties, an antique paperweight showing the White House, a silver tabletop holder for cigars or cigarettes, a pair of sunglasses, a casual shirt, a mug emblazoned "Santa Monica", a frog figurine, a letter-opener depicting a frog, several novels, a humorous book of quotations and several antique books.'

The president responded with a marble bear figurine, a hatpin, two brooches (one of them gold), a throw blanket, a souvenir from Radio City Music Hall in New York, where he had celebrated his 50th birthday, a signed copy of his State of the Union address, and, most famously, a special edition of Walt Whitman's *Leaves of Grass*, with its celebration of frowned-upon sensuality. Other than his gift of a box of chocolates, perhaps, these were not the accoutrements of a boss who looked upon his buxom young secretary solely for the purposes of physical relief. Certainly, they convinced Monica that there was something very solid about their relationship. Why, she even told a friend that the president implied they might one day be married after his term in office was over. Were Ken Starr to have granted himself a measure of poetic licence in the preparation of his report, he might even have gathered all these things together under a sub-section entitled 'Expressions of Love'.

Later, Clinton tried to put one of his presents to good use. In a note accompanying her gift of a $100 silk Zegna tie emblazoned with gold and navy-blue patterns, Monica had written, 'When I see you wearing this tie, I'll know that I am close to your heart.' The president wore it at a Rose Garden gun-control rally on the very morning that Monica Lewinsky appeared before the grand jury with some potentially fatal ammunition of her own. Trading on their one-time closeness, he was trying to appeal for her discretion, if not her silence. Alas, she was too busy that day to turn on the television.

When the president himself appeared before that same grand jury, to quibble, among other things, about the meaning of the word 'is', his greatest lie was to claim that a warm friendship with the young intern had matured into a sexual relationship. The truth was a complete mirror image. It started with a flash of knicker elastic and ended with Whitman's song of the body electric.

By early January 1998, Monica Lewinsky had revealed all this to federal investigators – previously, she had confided in 11 people, effectively guaranteeing that it would not remain secret for long in gossip-obsessed Washington – but Clinton remained in complete outer denial. To nervous aides, he explained that the intern had a post-adolescent crush and had even tried to blackmail him into having sex. To the public, he also professed his innocence. 'Now, I have to go back to work on my State of the Union speech. And I worked on it until pretty late last night,' he said with the First Lady at his side five days after the scandal broke – or, more pertinently, 16 days after he had last spoken to his former lover. 'But I want to say one thing to the American people. I want you to listen to me. I'm going to say this again: I did not have sexual relations with that woman, Miss Lewinsky. I never told anybody to lie, not a single time; never. These allegations are false. And I need to go back to work for the American people. Thank you.'

Observing Clinton on the campaign trail in 1992, the writer Joan Didion noticed 'the reservoir of self-pity, the narrowing of the eyes, as in a wildlife documentary, when things did not go his way'. Now, this description even more perfectly captured Clinton, as he suddenly became Washington's latest president of prey.

Mainly for reasons of taste and decency, the scandal threw up some tricky editorial dilemmas for the BBC suits in London involving what we could say and when we could say it. Mindful of the sensibilities of our viewers and listeners, they eventually decided that the phrase 'performed a sex act' would have to suffice for our early-morning audiences, while 'oral sex' was permissible after the nine o'clock watershed. As for the famed blue dress, the unwashed garment that was the sole reason that Clinton ever confessed to the affair, our choice of wording was positively euphemistic: it had been soiled by 'the president's DNA'.

All of these issues were compounded by the immediacy of round-the-clock news. When the Starr Report was published in all its titillating minutiae, correspondents naturally wanted to relay its contents as quickly as possible. But briefly consider how you would respond to being confronted by the following sentences, with a live microphone capturing your every word and an audience of tens of thousands hanging on them at home:

> . . . [S]he performed oral sex on the president on nine occasions. On all nine of those occasions, the president fondled and kissed her bare breasts. He touched her genitals, both through her underwear and directly, bringing her to orgasm on two occasions. On one occasion, the president inserted a cigar into her vagina.

> On another occasion, she and the president had brief
> genital-to-genital contact.

Nothing in your BBC training quite prepares you for that –
although at least no macadamia nuts sprinkled Kenneth Starr's
account, the alleged presidential insertion of which became one of
the great urban myths of the entire scandal.

Of course, the public appeared a lot less shocked about the
scandal than Washington, which is the main reason why Clinton
survived. That and the fact that Kenneth Starr and his Republican
allies continually overplayed their hand. When a videotape
of Clinton's appearance before the grand jury was released in
September 1998, rumours abounded beforehand that it showed the
president erupting into a childlike tantrum – a display of petulance
sure to harden public opinion against him and heighten calls for
him to resign. (By now, 78 newspapers, including *USA Today*, the
Philadelphia Inquirer and the *Atlanta Journal-Constitution*, had
called for him to go.)

For the most part, however, this four-hour screening was
numbingly boring, and it lives in the memory for Clinton's
dissembling rather than his irritability. 'It depends on what the
meaning of the word "is" is,' he said at one point during his
testimony. On the question of whether they had shared 'sexual
relations', he explained that sex for him meant the giving of
oral sex rather than the receiving – an almost Yuletide-like
expression of sexual charity. What we did not yet know was
that Hillary Clinton had been informed of the affair just three
days before the president's video-testimony. Rather than tell
her himself, Clinton had reportedly dispatched his lawyer,
David Kendall, to do so.

Had this been more widely known at the time – this particularly juicy nugget came out in the reporter Peter Baker's book *The Breach* – Clinton, and the Democrats through association, might have fared much worse in the congressional mid-terms. As it was, Newt Gingrich's Republicans, the president's accusers, suffered a net loss of five seats. Politically embarrassed, and later personally embarrassed when revelations surfaced about his own marital infidelity, Newt Gingrich resigned his post.

We therefore witnessed a curious inversion of how scandals are supposed to play out in Washington: the Democratic president had admitted to an affair, but it was a Republican house speaker who lost his job. Throughout the whole scandal, however, there was always the feeling that the sound of shattering glass might come from the houses of those throwing the stones. Congressman Henry Hyde, the chairman of the House Judiciary Committee and the main prosecutor of impeachment, suffered the ignominy of seeing an affair from 40 years ago splashed across the front pages. Even on the day of Clinton's impeachment in the House of Representatives, another Republican speaker, Gingrich's successor, Bob Livingston, was lanced on his own erection, and was forced to resign when *Hustler* magazine caught wind of his own adulterous frolics.

What followed in the New Year was still more bizarre: the sight of Clinton being tried by the US Senate, a body whose membership included some of Washington's most celebrated philanderers. Peering down from the press gallery, it was rather like seeing teenagers watching a movie in the living-room with their parents and facing the squirming horror of knowing that a sex scene was about to unfold before them on screen. Never before had senators become so closely acquainted with the mouldings and paintings on the walls and ceilings above and around them.

That said, Strom Thurmond of South Carolina, the 100-something former Dixiecrat who had run for the presidency in 1948 as a white supremacist and then fathered a black love child, was the spriteliest I had seen him in years. The record holder for the longest solo filibuster in senate history – 24 hours and 18 minutes – he seemed to regard the presidential sex show about to unfold in the well of the chamber as his reward. Most of his 99 colleagues, however, had no appetite for such sordidness and made sure the trial was as brief as possible, apparently to save themselves from embarrassment as much as the president.

For me, the postscript to the impeachment saga came in March 1999, just six weeks after the end of the senate trial, when Clinton appeared at the Radio and Television Correspondents' Association dinner at the Washington Hilton. Like the Japanese cherry blossoms that start blooming on the Washington mall, these black-tie dinners are a rite of spring, a ritual that requires the president to submit himself to a gentle roasting and then to hit back with a stand-up routine of his own.

That night, with everyone still recovering from the exertions of the past 15 months, the simple fact that the Clintons had accepted the invitation earned them a good deal of warmth and protection, and when the MC Jay Leno cracked a lone Lewinsky gag there were boos from the floor. 'Just one?' pleaded Leno.

In his opening remarks, Clinton acknowledged the weirdness of turning up to a dinner attended by 2000 journalists. 'If this isn't contrition,' he said, 'I don't know what is.' Then he risked another post-impeachment quip: 'I know you can't really laugh about this. I mean, the events of the last year have been quite serious. If the senate vote had gone the other way, I wouldn't be here. I demand a recount.'

As the strained laughter evaporated, the president introduced onto the stage a surprise guest, the 'prime minister of the United Republic of Karjakador' – a play on his habit during the impeachment crisis of only appearing before the press when accompanied at the podium by a visiting international leader. Together, they performed a slapstick routine that was not only funny but, as ever at these dinners, impressively produced and well rehearsed.

What was most extraordinary about the evening, however, was not the president's self-deprecation but how he handled himself in another ceremony he was expected to perform. Every year, a journalist was honoured for their excellence in reporting 'Congressional and political affairs', a citation that took on an especially unfortunate connotation. And, sure enough, that year's recipient was the ABC's Jackie Judd, the correspondent who discovered the existence of the stained blue dress, 'apparently as a kind of souvenir', in the words of her award-winning report.

As her name was read out and she started on her journey to the stage, all eyes naturally fixed upon Clinton to see how he would react. Yet far from showing any hint of embarrassment or discomfort, he greeted her with his trademark handshake, a rosy smile and a look almost of parental pride. The First Lady, sat a few seats away on a top table that faced out over the audience, was nowhere near as good at political play-acting. Indeed, if the looks she darted towards her errant husband could have killed, a Secret Service agent would have been rugby-tackling the president.

Just as he survived the scandal, Bill Clinton got through the awkwardness of this encounter with his unique blend of theatricality, likeability, political smarts and sheer bravado. From years of covering him, it remains to this day my favourite Bill moment, and by far the most telling. In this glorious instance of maximum unauthenticity, we could see the real Clinton.

—

Devotees of *The West Wing* would be crushingly disappointed by the reality of Washington. White House counsels are rarely as beautiful as Rob Lowe, press secretaries are never as witty as C. J. Cregg, presidents rarely quote long passages from the scriptures to break the tension of policy meetings, and their aides stalk the corridors of power with noticeably less fleet of foot, speed of mind and swiftness of tongue.

Doubtless, there are high-powered, big-brain types who can neatly encapsulate the world's most complicated problems in five pithy bullet points, and all in the time that it takes to hightail it from the Oval Office to the Situation Room. But I have yet to meet them, and nor truly would I wish to. Rather, the real West Wing is unexpectedly stately, elegant and orderly. Its corridors are not clogged with harried young BlackBerry-wielding aides, nor are the offices strewn with flip charts, whiteboards, campaign paraphernalia, plastic basketball hoops or stacks of empty pizza boxes. The West Wing has the look more of an English country house – albeit one with a state-of-the-art security system and its own private army – than the boiler-room of American executive government.

All this is not to deny that *The West Wing* got a lot right. It captured the workaholic culture of official Washington, the perpetual politicking, the bristling egos, the obsession with the news cycle, and the Beltway patois of pinched abbreviations that turns the president of the United States into POTUS, the first lady into FLOTUS and the justices of the Supreme Court into SCOTUS. It accurately portrayed how most global problems end up in the Oval Office – although much of the president's daily work is conducted in an adjacent private study – and how the personality of the incumbent stamps itself so completely on the administration that bears his name.

As originally envisaged, *The West Wing* intended to make the president an invisible presence, rather like Marlon Brando in *The Godfather II: Part 2*. That, however, would have made it totally implausible. For no city in the world, not even the Vatican or Pyongyang, is quite so preoccupied with the thoughts, beliefs, statements, musings, body language, blood pressure, eating habits, moods, whims, idiosyncrasies and indiscretions of a single being. The West Wing, real and imagined, *is* the president.

As a place to work and live, Washington definitely has its limitations. The food, aside from its Frisbee-sized power steaks, is poor. The climate is horrible, especially in the swampy summer. On the style front, residents look like they have taken their fashion cues from watching reruns of *Dynasty*. It can be stultifyingly unimaginative, which partly explains why the suffix 'gate' is attached to every scandal, however big or small. It suffers from being overpopulated by lawyers, lobbyists, politicians, policy wonks, diplomats and, yes, even journalists. Nowhere in the world has a higher concentration of self-important narcissists – with the possible exception, I suppose, of Hollywood, that west-coast Washington for beautiful people. With the mainly white population congregated in the north-west quadrant and the mainly black population occupying the rest, it is one of America's most racially polarised cities. Ridiculously, it still suffers from the democratic deficit of not having any representation in the US Senate and of relying on a fairly powerless 'delegate' rather than a full-blown lawmaker in the House of Representatives, an example of how black disenfranchisement survives even today.

But it is *the* place to be. Washington 'dies at sundown, it is too hot in the summer, too damp in the winter, too dry on Sunday and more interested in politics than it is in sex,' observed the veteran reporter Russell Baker of the *New York Times*, 'but I like it.' Most correspondents are much more fulsome in their praise and admit to falling completely for its seductive charms.

On the reporting front, the set-piece staple of the day is the televised lunchtime White House briefing, where the president's press secretary stands behind the world's most closely watched podium, in front of the world's most familiar blue curtain, and tries to stonewall reporters. (Earlier in the morning, the press secretary takes questions in an off-camera briefing called 'the gaggle'.)

The correspondents hurling the questions sit in pre-assigned seats, marked with small brass nameplates, etched with the kind of inscription work that you would expect to find on a Little League championship shield or a spelling-bee trophy. The 49 seats are allocated, as you would expect in a city obsessed with seniority, by rank. The front row is occupied by the major television networks (ABC, NBC, CBS) and the key wire services (the Associated Press and Reuters), while CNN has also muscled its way onto it. Next come the major newspapers, such as the *New York Times*, the *Washington Post* and the *Wall Street Journal*. Then come some of the lesser lights, such as the *Chicago Tribune*, Voice of America and the *Christian Science Monitor*. These days, there is even a place, on the seventh row, for the Christian Broadcasting

Network, sandwiched between two once-great newspapers, the *Boston Globe* and the *Baltimore Sun*.

Some of the more venerable institutions, such as *Time*, have now been relegated. If memory serves, the demotion came about after a former *Time* correspondent by the name of Jay Carney could not see much point in turning up every day to the briefings, which is richly ironic because he has recently been appointed as the White House press secretary.

Alas, international news organisations, such as the BBC, have always struggled in the stamped-seats stakes, and we tended to jostle for standing room at the sides and back of the briefing room. To be honest, none of us ever really minded, because the *Time* guy had pretty much got it right: if the White House had anything useful to impart, it would have done so already with a leak to the *Times*, the *Post* or, as is increasingly the case, Politico, the online news-sheet. Similarly, if an errant administration official had something the White House didn't want you to know, it would already have appeared in the papers, and the morning briefing was unlikely to offer much in the way of elucidation.

After the briefings, correspondents would rush out to their live television positions on the gravel-strewn patch of land next to the North Lawn known as Pebble Beach, which has since been renamed Stonehenge after the crushed bluestone was replaced with concrete. With the alabaster columns of the North Portico over our shoulders, the shot was intended to convey the notion that we all had an inside track on the internal workings of the building behind, even though none of us could boast genuine access to the president.

In my day, the grand marquess of the White House press corps, the legendary Helen Thomas, still occupied pole position in the middle of the front row. Like some medieval gargoyle carved into the facade of a great cathedral, however, she was there largely for decorative purposes and did not perform a vital function. Her long-time employer, the wire service United Press International (UPI), had years ago fallen into a state of disrepair, and as UPI waned so too did its star correspondent. Now an octogenarian, Thomas rarely got to ask the first question at presidential press conferences but did maintain the tradition, which she herself had revived during the Kennedy administration, of ending them with a cheery 'Thank you, Mr President'.

But I honestly cannot remember ever reading a single word that Helen Thomas had written, and I dare say the same was true of many Washington-based reporters. For sure, there was a pantomime-like fun to be had watching her bully and badger White House press secretaries, especially the nervy debutants (in her later years, she even resembled a character from a pantomime). And, to her credit, in the aftermath of 9/11 she not only refused to succumb to the mood of ultra-patriotism but also railed against it.

Increasingly, however, her questions took on the feel of mini-monologues – Bush's first press secretary, Ari Fleischer, started referring to her lengthy interjections as 'advocacy hour' – and, like many of Washington's human landmarks, her reputation would have been better served by an earlier and more graceful exit.

As it was, she left under a cloud of her own making, when she barked that Israel should 'get the hell out of Palestine', and its citizens should return to Germany and Poland. President Barack Obama, who only a few months before had presented her with cupcakes to mark her 89th birthday, condemned this blast of anti-Semitism. So, too, did the White House Correspondent Association, the organisation she not only once headed but also came to personify. For those who maintained the view that Washington was Hollywood for ugly people, Thomas was like a faded silent-movie star: she had turned Pennsylvania Avenue into Sunset Boulevard and cast herself as Norma Desmond, the crazed idol who now lived in her own fantasy world.

By far the most fun to be had with the White House press corps was way beyond the Beltway – the multi-laned ring road that doubled as a great halo of power – on international trips with the president. Aside from a small complement of reporters who flew on Air Force One, we would travel on a press charter where the seating assignments copied those of the White House briefing room. En route, the White House media team handed out pocket-sized briefing books, embossed with the presidential seal, which contained useful – and US-friendly – factoids about the countries we were about to visit. There were potted biographies of everyone the president was likely to meet, the times of the baggage calls (always ludicrously early), and helpful cultural pointers, which had the unintended side effect when travelling with George W. Bush of highlighting his own cultural faux pas.

In the run-up to the trips, we happily surrendered our passports to a US immigration official and were not handed them back until we returned to Washington. It meant we enjoyed the bliss of passport-free travel, jetting from one country to the next unencumbered by customs, immigration or any brush with local officialdom and sometimes even the locals themselves.

From the moment we left Andrews Air Force Base, we were pretty much ensnared inside 'The Bubble', a mobile West Wing, near hermetically sealed, that would move from country to country, city to city, and from one windowless ballroom to the next. These bland, featureless digs served as our temporary filing centres, where the desks were laid out according to the usual ranking system. (The only time that I ever witnessed a departure from the rankings was when those champion bureaucrats at Vnukovo International Airport on the outskirts of Moscow refused to play ball with our usual passport-less travel ruse and demanded that we collect our documentation, one by one in alphabetical order. Being a 'B', I was one of the fluky ones. Pity poor *La Repubblica*'s White House correspondent, Arturo Zampaglione.)

Regardless of where we went, we were shuttled around town in buses that never stopped for traffic lights and were accompanied everywhere by motorcycle outriders wearing polished white leather gloves. The 'green corridor' it was called. Then we would faithfully record each of the president's intricately stage-managed appearances with his hosts. To help us keep track of what was said, the White House transcription service was always on hand, like a wandering band of courtroom stenographers, to provide us with a verbatim record of every utterance. To help us keep track of what was thought, White House aides would occasionally deliver background briefings, providing scraps of information that we gobbled up like performing seals being tossed small sardines by their handlers, an aquatic reworking of Pavlov's dogs.

Used to so much pampering, certain members of the White House press corps were prone to self-centredness. On a four-hour coach trip from Orly Airport in Paris to the Normandy beaches – 'Why couldn't we have flown?' – some complained of bad 'butt wear', which overlooked the meaning of the event we had travelled there to cover, a commemoration marking D-Day. Other correspondents, however, were a complete joy. By far my favourite was Mark Knoller of CBS News, a bearded radio correspondent who was a doppelganger for Pavarotti and had a voice that was arguably more thunderous.

As well as pumping out hourly radio dispatches that boomed off the walls of the filing centres like explosions in a quarry – the most startling thing I ever heard during a presidential trip was New York coming across the line to ask Knoller to refile, this time with further volume – he was a total White House trivia-hound, a fastidious gatherer of presidential facts, which he generously shared with colleagues. How many trips had the president taken? How many days had he spent on vacation? How many times had he used a teleprompter? How many times had he played golf, or, more recently, basketball? How many times had the president deployed the phrase 'I will not rest until . . .'? Long before Google or LexisNexis, Knoller had all the answers, having compiled all the data himself in his soundproof cubbyhole in the basement below the White House briefing room.

If this bearded wonder could be faulted in any way at all, it was for a slight hesitation on words that began with 'p', which had unfortunate occupational drawbacks, especially on trips to Russia in President Putin's day. If I were to be picky, he also overused the clatter of bongo drums as his opening sound effect in reports filed on one of Clinton's trips to Africa.

For all his foibles, Knoller remained one of the White House's greatest treasures – almost on a par with the Lincoln bed or Abigail Adams's silver-plated coffee urn.

Other Washington fixtures were far less appealing. I confess to never becoming a great fan of the bulk of the Beltway's pundocracy, a bunch of talking heads happy to pontificate whatever the subject, whatever the time of day, in a round-the-clock gush of uninformed verbiage. Here, being plugged into so many worldwide stories simultaneously was both Washington's greatest strength and its greatest weakness.

So many pundits with so little knowledge were expected to pass judgement on so many global issues with so little time to prepare. The cable networks, with the exception of certain programs on CNN, favoured pundits who spoke simply, loudly, ideologically, passionately and, best of all, ill-temperedly. Unfortunately, this meant that the voices of some of the finest brains in Washington, who could bring not only expertise but also nuance to studio discussions, regularly got ignored. Over the years, my general rule of thumb came to be that the more you saw a pundit the less you needed to listen. For some, their main qualification appeared to be that they lived within a short cab ride of a cable news studio and, thus, a live hook-up with New York. They were little more than dial-an-opinion postcode pundits.

The marvellous exception was the great Christopher Hitchens. Not only was he one of the few commentators to bother visiting the countries he pontificated about, but he could also speak with enviable erudition. His mind was like a literary and historical archive from which he could retrieve material in an instant. What made his contributions all the more remarkable was that whenever I met him I was sure he was pissed – or, if not, well on his way.

The author of a savage polemic on Bill Clinton, *No One Left To Lie To*, he was used a lot by the BBC during impeachment, and when he came to the studio a strong aroma of white wine or Johnnie Walker Black Label whisky usually paved the way. When the on-air light in the studio turned to lustrous red, however, Hitchens was a marvel, delivering soundbites as delicately crafted as sonnets.

Such was his output and vast accumulation of knowledge,

I was actually convinced for a time that there were three Christopher Hitchenses: one who did the speaking and writing, one who did all the required reading, and one who did the drinking. During those Washington years, I was writing my book on Kennedy and the civil-rights movement, and Hitchens very kindly gave it a generous review in his books column in the *Atlantic Monthly*. What quickly became evident from his depth of knowledge was that he had read not only my book but also most of its bibliography.

There were other things about Washington for which I did not much care. People living inside the Beltway had a vastly bloated view of their own importance and succumbed to an 'inside the Beltway' feeling of separateness and superiority. I know this to be true because I felt it very powerfully myself. 'Washington feels like a conspiracy we're all in together,' wrote Henry Allen, a long-time resident and scribe for the *Washington Post*, 'and nobody else in America quite understands.'

For all that, I absolutely adored the place, and I woke up each morning thinking there was no better place to be a correspondent. I loved its urgent pace, its obsession with politics, intrigue and palace gossip. A complete sucker for the majestic trappings of the modern presidency, I went all adolescent at the sight of a motorcade, was stirred by the thumping beat of 'Hail to the Chief' and felt a slight frisson whenever Marine One flew over the top of my Georgetown terrace on its way to Camp David.

Though I never got to fly on Air Force One, I hardly slept when I found myself catching a lift late one night on the back-up plane painted in the same livery on a red-eye flight from Dar es Salaam to Cairo. Truth be told, it was not much more comfortable than routine economy, but there was a certain pleasure in having drinks served on napkins with the presidential seal by air stewardesses who you sensed could probably break you in two with a couple of flicks of their beautifully manicured nails.

Back in Washington, I adored the monumentalism of the architecture and L'Enfant's grand layout. Many an evening I would saunter down to The Mall, sit on the steps of the Lincoln Memorial and imagine what it must have been like that sultry August afternoon in 1963 when a young preacher from Alabama cast aside his prepared remarks at the pleading of the singer Mahalia Jackson, who shouted, 'Tell them about the dream, Martin,' and launched into a rhetorical riff that became the crowning moment of the non-violent struggle. Peering down The Mall, past the shimmering spire of the Washington Monument to the US Capitol in the hazy distance, there were even times when I thought I could almost hear the stirring music of *The West Wing* building to a crescendo in the background.

—

Having fought so unrelentingly to remain its occupant, Bill Clinton's departure from the White House almost inevitably descended into an orgy of self-indulgence, self-justification and self-congratulation. (His one-time rival Bob Dole had joked it might take a SWAT team to evict him on inauguration day.)

His valedictory vanity tour began with his farewell speech at the 2000 Democratic convention in Los Angeles, an appearance preceded by an elongated solo walk-on, where he stalked vast tracts of backstage corridors at the Staples Center as delegates tracked his progress on giant screens, like athletics fans awaiting the arrival into the stadium of the winner in the marathon.

Taking presidential showboating to new highs, it was the

kind of entrance that would have made even the promoters of a Las Vegas world-title bout blush with embarrassment. In saluting the American people, 'who do the work, raise the kids, dream the dreams', he was essentially saluting himself for delivering what he claimed were new heights of prosperity, progress and peace. Almost pleading for a legacy, he was desperate that his presidency should be remembered for something other than cigars, interns and, more unfairly, macadamia nuts.

The tour continued with a return visit to Dover, New Hampshire, a personal landmark on his road to the White House, since it was there, in the darkest days of the 1992 primary, that he vowed to stick with the people 'until the last dog dies'. Now recalling one of his most folkloric quotes, I watched him tell an admiring crowd 'the last dog is still barking'. Sure enough, he continued yapping away, like a puppy desperate for attention, on inauguration day itself, 21 January 2001.

After he had handed over to George W. Bush and been choppered from Capitol Hill, Clinton decided to break with custom and deliver a departing speech to a campaign-style rally in a hangar at Andrews Air Force Base. Already that day, he had blotted the next chapter of his life by pardoning Marc Rich, a fugitive millionaire felon whose main claim to fame up until that moment had been his appearance on the FBI's 'Ten Most Wanted List'. Now, with this final indulgence at Andrews, he tested the forbearance of even his most devoted followers.

By the twilight of Clinton's presidency, it had become fashionable to talk of a Saturday-night Bill, inside which demons ran amok, and a Sunday-morning Bill, where his good angels reasserted themselves. It was the junk-food-guzzling, intern-squiring narcissist as opposed to the brilliant policy wonk, political strategist and communicator. In his rendering of Bill Clinton as Governor Jack Stanton in *Primary Colors*, Joe Klein captured the bad Bill more completely than any other author, just as his short biography, *The Natural*, summed up the frustrations of many one-time admirers angered that Clinton had self-sabotaged his presidency. 'A surplus of libido and a deficit of integrity' was Klein's snappy take.

Yet perhaps the most wistful appraisal came from Robert Reich, Clinton's former Labor secretary, who had first met him on a liner mid-Atlantic when they voyaged together as Rhodes Scholars to Oxford. 'On Mondays and Wednesdays and Fridays I say, "Thank God Bill Clinton was there," you know, to hold back the right-wing Republican tide, to preserve things that we believed in,' Reich reflected. 'And then on Tuesdays and Thursdays and Saturdays I say to myself, "What a waste. All that talent and all that ability, and he did not do what he intended to do and get accomplished. Maybe if he had been more disciplined, both in terms of his agenda, and also his personal life, more could have been done."' Then came the kicker. 'And then on Sundays I don't think about it.'

Alas, I could not claim Sunday as a Clinton day of rest. By strange coincidence, I happened to attend the same Methodist church, The Foundry, on Sixteenth Street, a few blocks up from the White House and just around the corner from the basement apartment that provided my first digs in Washington. Though I had no idea this was the First Couple's place of worship when I started attending, there was a voyeuristic fascination in sharing pews with the Clintons, even if it meant that the throne of grace was only accessible through airport-style metal detectors. Church became much more fun when there was the possibility of exchanging the peace with a Secret Service agent packing a semi-automatic machine gun. For years, I also suspected the lead bass in the choir was on the government payroll; perhaps the well-built head soprano as well. Throughout the impeachment crisis, it made for compelling Clinton-watching, and I was surprised that not more journalists had latched onto it.

A few weeks before he left office, as he attended The Foundry for the last time as president, Clinton even had the front to deliver the sermon, the unexpected announcement of which in the morning's order of service had me scrambling madly around for a pen and scraps of paper on which to transcribe. In full 'Sunday morning Bill' mode, Clinton was quite brilliant, the best I had seen him in years. He quoted John Quincy Adams: 'There is nothing quite so pathetic in life as an ex-president.' He bemoaned how his new-found reliance on commercial air travel would be a major test of his Christian bearing and confessed that he might well find it disorientating for a while to walk into a room without a band striking up 'Hail to the Chief'.

His sermon included an oblique reference to the Monica Lewinsky scandal – 'the storm and the sunshine of the last eight years', as he put it – and a brief rumination on the poison that had polluted Washington, which produced another allusion to impeachment: 'I have spent a lot of time, as you might have noticed, in a reasonably combative arena. I am not without competitive instincts. A lot of days, just showing up was an act of competition.'

He acknowledged the spiritual support of The Foundry's minister, the Reverend J. Philip Wogaman, who met Clinton for weekly one-on-one sessions, and who once described the president to me, with a wry smile and delightful ecclesiastical understatement, as 'a work in progress'.

Then, as he looked to the future, the self-styled architect of the 'bridge to the twenty-first century' did the vision thing anew. He described a world of greatly enhanced global interdependence, of new opportunities to relate to people across national, cultural and religious lines and of the breathtaking advances in biomedical sciences, which had the potential to dramatically lengthen and improve lives. Foreshadowing the mood of paranoia that followed 9/11, he warned that the biggest threat to humankind would be 'the fear of the other'. Finally, he thanked his fellow parishioners 'for your constant reminder in ways large and small that though we have all fallen short of the glory, we are all redeemed by faith in a loving God'.

Afterwards, as members of the congregation filed past the Clintons and performed various genuflections, I thrust out my own hand and thanked him for his work in Northern Ireland. (It would have been churlish in the circumstances to bring up Bosnia or Rwanda, I hope you will agree.) Clinton gave a slow, knowing nod and even managed to convey the sense that I had somehow managed to move him. No longer in need of votes, now he was in search of a legacy. As he gripped my hand, he gave me the distinct feeling of being the most important complimenter in the room.

Chapter 3

W

Just as Afghanistan conjured up adventure and romance for the boots wing of the foreign-correspondent corps, New Hampshire fired the imaginations of those who ploughed their trade in suits. For a White House correspondent especially, confined for years on end inside the presidential bubble, nothing was more professionally invigorating than being allowed out on the campaign trail on quadrennial political furlough.

The reporting life at 1600 Pennsylvania Avenue was nothing if not eventful – for three years out of every four, there were few better datelines than the White House – but the road that led there was more beguiling. In the theme park of Afghanistan, correspondents had to criss-cross the country to find the warlords, poppy fields or Taliban. In New Hampshire, everywhere was Candidateland: diners, truck-stops, ski-fields, high schools, hot-dog stands, veterans' halls, white clapboard churches, college campuses and even the frozen lakes that were dotted in the winter months with bobhouses, the ice-fishing huts beloved of New Hampshirites.

If one rose early before breakfast, it was usually possible to have filmed most of the major candidates by lunch: schmoozing a pot-bellied trucker, conducting a high-school band, gladhanding a postman, tobogganing down an icy hill, listening empathetically to a voter, or consuming a plate of bacon and eggs, sunny side up, then making sure to leave an over-generous tip.

Rather than the *New York Times* or the *Washington Post*, the *New Hampshire Union Leader* and the *Telegraph* of Nashua were the papers of record. The Wayfarer Inn in Bedford, nestled close to a covered wooden bridge and configured around a millpond, was the place to stay. Television producers especially loved its man-made waterfall, a perfect, if counterfeit, New England backdrop for live crosses to the studio in New York or Atlanta. Correspondents would stand before it, talking about how New Hampshirites liked authenticity in their candidates and how easily they could spot a fake.

The state's most famous water feature was overlooked by its most famous watering hole. Here, in the Wayfarer bar, reporters conducted much of their news-gathering, usually with a whisky or beer on the bar in front of them and, ideally, a loose-lipped campaign aide at their side. When finally he hung up his notepad, one legendary campaign reporter, the great Jack Germond of the *Baltimore Sun*, even had his bar stool officially retired.

Though Iowa could boast the first caucus of election season, it was New Hampshire, with the country's first fully fledged primary, which could make or break candidates – presidents, as well, as Harry Truman and Lyndon Johnson could both attest. Most of us had read the history, and virtually all of us were familiar with the reportage of Hunter S. Thompson, who had brought his gonzo journalism to New Hampshire in 1972 and found himself shooting the breeze with Richard M. Nixon and peeing in a urinal alongside George McGovern.

Lavatorial or otherwise, all of us craved the same intimacy, which only New Hampshire could deliver. And anomalous though it was to grant such an insignificant state such inordinate power – New Hampshire has a population the size of San Antonio, Texas, a demographic that is 97 per cent white and a cranky, contrarian streak summed up by its famed number-plate motto 'Live Free or Die' – none of us asked too many questions for we were all having too much fun. This was the Kentucky Derby of American politics, and everyone wanted to be in the paddock for an initial look at the runners.

The first election of the new millennium had promise. Not since the end of the Reagan era had the presidential nominations of both parties been up for grabs, and New Hampshire had attracted a compelling assortment of characters. On the Democratic side, Vice President Al Gore was several characters all in one, an angst-ridden candidate so unsure of himself that he even took advice on what shade of clothing he should wear. 'Earth colours' recommended his unofficial adviser, the author Naomi Wolf.

Up against Gore was the former New Jersey senator Bill Bradley, a basketball star with the charisma of a chartered accountant, whom reporters lent a more dramatic persona in order to enliven their own lives as much as his. For a time, it looked as if the movie star Warren Beatty might also enter the race, which was the cause of much merriment. No candidate had ever promised such skeletal riches – Cher, Mary Tyler Moore, Joan Collins, Julie Christie, Natalie Wood, Diane Keaton and even Madonna – though his journey to the White House never progressed much further than the driveway of his Beverly Hills home. At least the speculation allowed us to perform one of the great rituals of any presidential campaign: to talk up a frivolous celebrity candidate – a position filled more recently by Donald Trump.

On the Republican side, there were the usual publicity hounds and delusional no-hopers. Alan Keyes, a black radio talk-show host, right-wing ideologue and former diplomat, evidently thought it was possible to go from mid-ranking US ambassador to commander-in-chief in one Herculean leap.

Only marginally more plausible as a candidate was Steve Forbes, a nerdy businessman with Harry Potter glasses, vast riches, a celebrated name and the sense of entitlement that went with it. Given the strength of the Bible-belt right, Gary Bauer, a pocket-sized evangelical, hoped his candidacy would be blessed by providence, if not charisma. Yet his main contribution to the primary season was to produce its viral video sensation: the slapstick footage that showed him tumbling backwards off a stage and disappearing through the curtained backdrop, as he lost control of his frying pan in a candidates' pancake-flipping competition.

The press corps' favourite was the Arizona senator John McCain, a Vietnam veteran who came with a story of marvellous heroism and a campaign bus, the 'Straight Talk Express', that felt more like a frat-house on wheels. On board, McCain provided an endless supply of coffee and doughnuts, an even richer stream of pithy quotes, and something reporters valued even more, which was virtually round-the-clock access.

After the dissembling, obfuscation and perpetual spin of the Clinton years, here was the human rejoinder: an authentic candidate, comfortable in his own skin, seemingly untroubled by demons from his past and revelling in his insurgent candidacy against the Republican establishment and religious right.

Eight years later, after cosying up to his one-time foes in a second bid for Republican nomination that was both less unorthodox and more successful, McCain appeared before the American electorate in a dreadfully amputated form. Yet in 2000, he was so vital and unpredictable that virtually the entire press corps succumbed to a collective crush. When the Arizonian stood before town meetings in New Hampshire and exhorted his audience to become part of something much larger than themselves, one sensed that reporters were itching to shut their laptops, cast aside their notepads and sign up to his campaign as volunteers. Instead, they did something that was far more useful to McCain's hopes of pulling off an unexpected victory, which was to produce a narrative of the campaign that talked up his chances. There was no question, the Wayfarer bar was McCain country.

His great rival, George W. Bush, came with an absorbing storyline and an even more stellar bloodline: a grandfather, Prescott Bush, who was a senator and a father, George Herbert Walker, who had been president. Eyeing up a possible Bush restoration, reporters naturally seized upon the Oedipal over-tones of his candidacy. The works of Shakespeare were also mined for parallels, with George W. cast as Prince Hal, a son known for the discretions of his past, determined to redeem his father's reign.

As an aside, perhaps we should pause briefly to reflect on how campaign reportage relies on these kinds of tropes, and how Homer and the Bard are topped in the analogy league table only by American sport. Adopting the popular baseball argot, candidates invariably step up to the plate, swing for the fences, produce policies or strategies out of left field, get to first base if they survive beyond New Hampshire or Iowa, strike out if they do not, and demonstrate whether they are ready for the major leagues thereafter. They might even find themselves in the bottom of the ninth with the bases loaded. If successful, they would have gone the whole nine yards, produced various knockout punches, full-court presses and be on the verge of a slam dunk or home run. If not, they would be on the ropes and about to throw a 'Hail Mary' pass. My advice to anyone covering a US campaign would be to gain a rudimentary knowledge of Shakespeare, starting with the tragedies, and then invest in a glossary of American sporting terms. But I digress.

More than a decade on, and volumes of 'Bushisms' later, it is easy to forget that in the early days of his candidacy Bush appeared to have the superlative presidential résumé, and be capable of home runs, slam dunks and of maturing from Prince Hal to King Henry without even breaking a sweat. A Harvard MBA and a graduate of Yale, he was regarded as highly intelligent. His enormously profitable stewardship of the Texas Rangers baseball franchise gave him credibility as a corporate chief executive. As governor of Texas, he was regarded as an innovative policymaker, especially in the field of education. By becoming the first Texas governor to win two consecutive four-year terms, he had also demonstrated his vote-winning capabilities. His victories were thought to stem from a winning personality and his credo of compassionate conservatism, which allowed him to appeal to the centre while at the same time shoring up his base – twin attributes easily transferable to the national stage.

Helpfully for the profile writers, he could also identify a crucible moment in his life: the dehydrated haze of the morning after his 40th birthday, when he woke up with such a clawing hangover that he promised never to touch liquor again.

Admittedly, Bush did not seem to have much interest in

foreign affairs. Nor had he travelled widely. However, at a time when American hegemony appeared settled and unrivalled, it did not seem to matter. No candidate in the field had greater name recognition or fund-raising prowess, which in turn gave him another high-value political commodity, the air of inevitability.

As his key strategist, image-maker and intellectual blood bank, Bush could also call on one of the smartest political consultants in the land: Karl Rove, a modern-day Lee Atwater, whom he christened 'Turd Blossom'. In the early months of the campaign, it was Rove who came up with a reworking of William McKinley's front-porch campaign in 1896, whereby Bush rarely left the safety of the governor's mansion in Austin, and key supporters, donors and journalists paid visits to him.

Fearing closer scrutiny, Rove had come up with a candidate-protection programme, but at the start of the campaign it only enhanced the governor's aura of invincibility, to use another overworked expression from the campaign phrasebook. Here again, it is worth reflecting upon the respect that Bush once commanded. Even liberal-minded Europeans, who later dubbed him the Toxic Texan and worse, succumbed to his charm. Back in early 1999, I remember watching the swooning response of a London-based BBC producer at the sight of George W. greeting the then Conservative leader William Hague during a trip to the State Capitol Building in Austin. 'Wow, look at that charisma,' the producer gushed, when all Bush had done was walk into the room, thrust out his hand and said, 'Hi, how are you?' Though hard now to picture, it was typical of the flattering mood among journalists at the time.

George W. Bush's stumbling journey towards caricature only began later in 1999, when he started to venture further from his porch. First, he started confusing his Greeks with his 'Grecians', and his Kosovars with his 'Kosovarians'. Then, in December 1999, just a month before the New Hampshire primary, he flunked that infamous pop quiz in which he was asked to name the leaders of Chechnya (tough), Taiwan (less so), India (should have been straightforward) and Pakistan (Foreign Policy 101).

'Wait, wait, is this fifty questions?' the governor floundered.

'No, it's four questions of four leaders in four hotspots,' countered the schoolmarmish reporter, Andy Hiller, who worked for WHDH-TV in Boston but looked more like a plant from *Saturday Night Live*. Afterwards, Bush's press woman, Karen Hughes, tried to contain the fallout by arguing that the governor was running for the leadership of the free world rather than auditioning for a contestant's spot on *Jeopardy*, but the damage had been inflicted and has since been impossible to repair.

From reporters assigned to cover Bush on a daily basis came bizarre tales, not many of which ended up in print but that started to alter the conventional wisdom nonetheless. Frank Bruni of the *New York Times* told the story of the governor's attendance at a memorial service at Texas Christian University in September 1999 for the victims of a multiple shooting in Fort Worth in which seven were killed and a further seven injured. Throughout the service, as prayers, songs, bible readings and eulogies were offered up, Bush kept on sneaking glances at the press corps and pulling silly faces. 'Bush turned around from time to time to shoot us little smiles,' Bruni later reflected. 'He scrunched up his forehead, as if to ask us what we were up to back there. He wiggled his eyebrows, a wacky and wordless hello.' Given that Bush had signed a law allowing Texans to carry concealed weapons and enjoyed strong backing from the gun lobby, his presence in the outdoor stadium was bound to attract close scrutiny. Yet that did not stop him acting like a mischievous pageboy at a society wedding, a reprise of his role in his father's White House.

Certainly, the voters of New Hampshire thought they had spotted a joker, and, in any case, they had fallen for McCain. So, on election night, we all pitched up at the Arizonian's hotel, where we saw him celebrate a lopsided victory of 49 per cent to 30 per cent. Unable to raise his arms above his shoulders, because of the injuries he had sustained during his stay at the Hanoi Hilton, McCain did a victory jig with his shuddering hands stretched out in front, like some smiling zombie in a low-budget science-fiction flick looking for a victim to strangle. Weeks later, as the campaign circus moved to South Carolina, he almost had to be restrained from performing the same manoeuvre on George W. Bush.

The South Carolina primary was by far the grubbiest campaign I have ever covered, a view shared by veterans of the trail who had followed Richard Nixon in his squalid pomp. The Republican high command had set up South Carolina as an asbestos firewall to block dangerously liberal-minded candidates from progressing any further. McCain, whose views on campaign finance and immigration reform were considered heretical, was precisely the kind of subversive candidate they had in mind.

Rather than rely on the trusty firewall, however, the Bush campaign and its surrogates went nuclear and sought to eviscerate the Arizonian as soon as he headed south from New Hampshire. Push-pollers, for whom leading questions were near-lethal weapons, rang up voters to ask whether they would countenance a candidate who had fathered an illegitimate black love child ever becoming president (the McCains had adopted a young

Bangladeshi girl). Cindy McCain was accused of being a drug addict (she admitted to once having a dependency on painkillers). The senator was called a 'fag candidate', because of a meeting held with the gay campaign group the Log Cabin Republicans. During his five and a half years as a prisoner of war in Vietnam, he was accused of having become psychologically unhinged, brainwashed even, which explained both his hair-trigger temper and blasphemous views. To hammer home the point, George W. Bush appeared at the shoulder of a disgruntled POW, who accused McCain of returning home and forgetting those he left behind, which was the most wounding falsehood of all.

The Texas governor, meanwhile, conducted a textbook South Carolina campaign. Closely adhering to the famed 'Southern Strategy' pioneered by Nixon and perfected by Ronald Reagan, he came down on the side of the redneck traditionalists who demanded that the Confederate Flag still fly atop the State Capitol Building in Columbia. Tellingly, he also launched his campaign from the Great Hall of China-like stage of Bob Jones University, an establishment known for continuing to ban interracial dating on campus.

Meeting backstage ahead of a televised debate, McCain challenged Bush about the tawdriness of his campaign. 'John, it's just politics,' the governor blithely replied. Then, as the Bush campaign intended, McCain fell for the trap of fuming retaliation and cut a television spot comparing Bush's slander to Bill Clinton's lies. By his South Carolinian accusers, McCain had been called mentally deranged, a closet homosexual, a sexual degenerate and a betrayer of his fellow POWs. In likening George W. Bush to Bill Clinton, however, he was judged to have gone completely beyond the pale.

In another cruel injustice, the exit polls confirmed that South Carolinians thought it was McCain rather than Bush who had fought the most negative campaign. I was at the McCain hotel when that poll came through, and the NBC correspondent David Bloom immediately grasped its significance. 'Crushed,' he said as he walked into a deflated press room. It was the hinge point of the campaign, and one that paved the way for Bush's eventual victory. It also started a chain of events that ultimately led David Bloom into Iraq, where tragically he was among the journalists to lose his life.

South Carolina was the sorriest of spectacles, but I recall watching Bush on a day when the nobler instincts of his character came to the fore. Towards the end of a question-and-answer session before a crowd of a few hundred people, a teenage girl who clearly had seriously impaired vision asked what the Bush administration would do to help provide the specially designed glasses she needed to see better. Never a man for the small detail of policy, the governor could not give her an instant answer, but on hearing that she was having to make do with an inferior pair of glasses and was unable to afford new ones, he instantly came up with a solution.

With the irrepressibility of a charity auctioneer, he appealed to his wealthy donors seated in the room to stump up the cash. Sure enough, the girl left with the down payment on a new pair of spectacles. 'Compassionate conservatism', I always thought, was more than a bumper-sticker slogan for George W. Bush. Real conviction lay behind those words.

However, what South Carolina also demonstrated and foreshadowed was the extent to which he lacked the intellectual self-confidence, independence of mind or strategic smarts to counter more strongly conservative voices around him. During the campaign, it was Karl Rove. During the presidency, it was Dick Cheney and Donald Rumsfeld. A decent-minded man rarely prone to malevolence, Bush, I always suspected, would have preferred the higher road to the White House. Instead, he deferred to advisers when they demanded in South Carolina that it deviate through the gutter.

Three days after his defeat in the Palmetto state, McCain briefly mounted a mini-comeback by winning the Michigan primary. That night, I found myself pursuing Karl Rove around a packed hotel lobby in Detroit with a live microphone in my hand, trying to get some reaction. 'What are you telling the governor?' I kept on asking. 'What are you telling the governor?'

'I'm telling him there's a guy from the BBC who won't leave me alone,' came his deadpan reply.

What Rove probably told Bush was that Michigan would be McCain's last hurrah. As in New Hampshire, registered Democrats and independents were allowed to vote in the Michigan primary, and they had provided his margin in victory. Thereafter, the political calendar was packed with closed primaries in conservative states where only Republicans could vote, which heavily favoured Bush.

The McCain camp, by contrast, was confronted by a demoralising paradox: the senator was successfully assembling precisely the kind of broad-based coalition needed to win the presidency but not the Republican presidential nomination.

Michigan did indeed end up producing the last full-throttled roar of the 'Straight Talk Express', but even there McCain looked punch-drunk from South Carolina. Perhaps he never fully recovered, and when he ran for the presidency eight years later he still looked out on his feet. There was a lightness and freeness of spirit about John McCain in 2000 that was almost entirely absent in 2008, and the only time that I found myself recognising the old John McCain – which is to say the younger John McCain – was when he delivered one of the most gracious ever concession speeches on the night of Barack Obama's victory.

History, I suspect, will be generous to McCain and record that he played a vital role in the election of America's first African-American president, not so much by fighting a flawed campaign but because he conducted a clean campaign. Even when confronting near-certain defeat, he never sought to make race an issue. It would be tempting to call his rejection of negative tactics another collateral effect of South Carolina, but it can be more simply explained: McCain was being McCain, a politician who preferred straight-talk to trash-talk.

To his credit, Bush also played his part in the rise of Obama, by reminding the GOP that it was the party of Abraham Lincoln, the Great Emancipator, and by giving African-Americans a higher profile in his administration than any of his predecessors, Republican or Democrat. Without Colin Powell or Condoleezza Rice, and the familiarity that came with seeing blacks occupying the highest offices of state, Barack Obama might not have risen so fast.

With the McCain insurgency over, there was a lull in the campaign, and a chance for its reporters to draw breath. Perhaps there was even an opportunity to assess our own performance after spending so many months analysing the utterances, stumbles, earth tones and misjudged pancake flips of others. Come election time, the central complaints levelled against news organisations are that we fail to explore issues, that the horse race is our myopic focus, that we are preoccupied with style over substance, and that we always get distracted by eye-catching trivialities. On all of these counts, I fear we are guilty as charged. But just as a country often gets the democracy it deserves, I suspect the same is true of campaign journalism.

We cover the primary season as if it were a horse race because that is essentially what it is. We tend not to fully explore all the issues because the candidates themselves are usually so hesitant to do so. We spend more time on personalities rather than policies because the personalities are generally more intriguing and arguably more germane. Campaign promises are easily cast aside, after all.

However noble our intentions at the outset, we often allow style to trump substance, and assign far too much meaning to mindless trivialities, such as whether candidates wear boxers or briefs and who cracks the funniest gags on *Letterman* or *Leno*. Here, there is a tendency to judge candidates on their entertainment value rather than their ability to govern. All I would say is that if you, dear reader, had to listen to the same candidate stump-speech event after event, day after day – by the end of the first month, most reporters can perform the campaign party trick of mouthing along to a candidate's stump speech, silently reciting its every word, while some can even identify the lines at which the candidate's wife will nod approvingly – you might surrender to the temptations of trivialities as well.

Consider also the deadline factor, which is normally complicated by the logistics factor. Dashing from one flag-bedecked campaign event to another, from the next Best Western to the next Hampton Inn, from Denny's to the International House of Pancakes, with a sugar hit at Krispy Kreme doughnuts on the way, all one can hope to deliver by the end is the most rudimentary wrap of the day. A splash of colour, a sprinkling of soundbites and a piece to camera delivered at maximum volume over the strains of Fleetwood Mac.

To flick through my diary from that year is to revisit the madcap 'If it's Tuesday, it must be Peoria' whirl of the trail. Take the week leading up to Super Tuesday, when primaries were contested on the two great seaboards, in New York and California. It started with a pre-dawn, cross-country flight out of Washington that got us into Los Angeles in time for a lunchtime interview with the talkback-radio host Michael Reagan, Ronald's first, adopted son.

Then we drove up the freeway to Bakersfield, where McCain was about to address an open-air rally. Ideally, we would have made it back to Los Angeles in time for a speech by Bill Bradley on the campus of UCLA, but my producer could not for the life of her remember where she had parked our rental car, and we spent more than an hour trudging from one McMansion-lined cul-de-sac to the next trying to hunt it down. Too late, we headed back to the glass-sheafed rotundas of the Bonaventure Hotel in downtown LA, where I bumped into another journalist on the trail and indulged in a rare bout of hurried, unchivalrous passion known affectionately by its practitioners as 'campaign sex'.

Early the next morning, we filmed at Santa Monica beach, partly so that I could write the feeble script-line, 'This is California, where the road to the White House is lined with palm trees and rollerbladers.' (In South Carolina, it had been palmettos and barbecue joints.) Then we took in Beverly Hills to harvest some more footage, before descending upon a southern Californian mega-church to interview members of the Christian Coalition. That night, Gore and Bradley locked antlers in their umpteenth televised debate, and then we headed to LAX to catch the red-eye to New York.

Around noon, Gore did something at a high school in New York – I cannot remember quite what – while Bradley's image-makers arranged for him to flip some hot dogs in the famed Gray's Papaya in Manhattan, something of a Big Apple electoral ritual. That evening, there was time for a quick supper in Midtown with my old friend the 'complete pilchard' correspondent from Jerusalem, before Bush faced McCain in yet another debate.

The following morning, we interviewed former mayor of New York Ed Koch and former governor of New York Mario Cuomo, and then headed to what is billed in my diary as a 'Brooklyn black event', which shows the extent to which candidates and reporters slice and dice the electorate into neat little blocs, or, in this instance, a very large significant one.

To nod to Bradley's sporting past, we filmed courtside at Madison Square Garden, the home of the New York Knicks, his old basketball outfit, and then headed to an open-air rally in a park in Greenwich Village, where the former senator was introduced by the actor Harvey Keitel, who had far more to say about himself than the candidate.

You get the idea. The week was not yet a hundred hours old, and we had already racked up more than 6000 frequent-flyer miles, filmed in half a dozen or so iconic venues, covered two debates, been welcomed into the presence of Democratic and Republican royalty, drunk gallons of dodgy coffee, endured the interminable ramblings of a Reservoir Dog, lost and found a rental car and enjoyed a fairly lively nightlife. So disorientating was the campaign that it felt like that party game where a hapless victim is blindfolded, spun around at high velocity and then set loose:

not very grown up and occasionally vomit-inducing but hugely entertaining all the same.

This hints at another factor to bear in mind in assessing the performance of the press: that many journalists were either drunk or hung-over. Covering a campaign was like embarking on a great Kerouacian adventure, a land-based booze-cruise that moved from one great battleground state to another, and from one dingy bar to the next. A few nights after the New Hampshire primary, a colleague and I somehow found ourselves at a sorority house at Dartmouth College playing 'pong' with a group of sorority sisters – a drinking game where a ping-pong table was dotted with half-filled cups of beer and liquor that had to be chugged down in one mouthful if the ball landed inside. On the eve of the Democratic convention, a few of us were invited to the Playboy Mansion, where the Hef was hosting a fund-raiser. Citing tiredness from a week covering wildfires in Idaho, I decided to have a quiet dinner with friends, a lapse that demonstrates the extent to which chronic fatigue can impair one's judgement.

Here, of course, there is a glaring paradox, for it was this same group of travelling inebriates that passed judgement on the probity of the candidates under our professional gaze. Post-Clinton, virtue was especially important, and in 2000 the main candidates were keen to talk about character, values and their own personal narratives, if only to distance themselves from the incumbent.

For the closing riffs of his stump speeches, George W. Bush would pretend, rather presumptuously, to take the presidential oath of office. 'When I put my hand on the Bible,' he repeated ad nauseam, 'I will swear not only to uphold the law of our land, I will swear to uphold the honour and integrity of the office to which I have been elected.' Then, he would add with a vainglorious flourish, 'So help me God.'

Honour and integrity were also the leitmotifs of McCain's campaign. The irony here was that both were pushing character at a time when Bill Clinton's soaring approval ratings, and the lack of public outrage over his affair with Monica Lewinsky, suggested that American voters did not much care any more. Candidates who had been adulterous, smoked pot in their student years, sniffed cocaine, dodged the draft or gone through the express lane of their local supermarket with seven items in their baskets rather than the maximum six were now viable.

Here, scandal-hungry journalists were either slow to catch on or just could not help themselves. Consider the brief flap in New Hampshire that year over our hapless pancake-flipper Gary Bauer, who had to defend himself against the charge that he had been alone in the same room as a young blonde campaign aide. When reporters could not prove any impropriety, they latched on instead to a new category of misdemeanour, the fabulously Orwellian 'appearance of impropriety'.

On the Richter scale of political scandals, it should hardly have registered at all, but the US media tended to adopt a different criterion: where there was the faintest whiff of smoke, there surely must be fire.

Certainly, it was a quantum leap from campaigns of old, where reporters happily turned a blind eye. Why, in 1960 Ben Bradlee, the then *Newsweek* Washington bureau chief, and Jack Kennedy idled away a few hours as they awaited the results of the West Virginia primary by watching a porn flick a few blocks from the White House.

Perhaps the most serious failure of campaign reportage,

especially in the era of continuous news, is the extent to which everything gets magnified and exaggerated, so that the trivial becomes cardinal and the quotidian becomes epochal. Moments are rarely anything other than defining. Initiatives are at all times make or break. Candidates are forever delivering the most important speeches of their lives. Set-piece events, such as the party conventions, receive the kind of over-hyped coverage associated with the Superbowl.

The televised debates are a case in point. Beforehand, the talk always is of knockout punches, even though most debates live in the memory about as long as a one-day cricket international and are about as exciting as a scoreless draw in a football match. Ahead of the first presidential debate, we always perform the ritual of trawling through the archive to produce short preparatory television packages showing the highlights from debates past. Alas, there has never been much blood on the canvas. Ronald Reagan delivered a couple of hefty blows against Jimmy Carter and Walter Mondale, and Dan Quayle was decapitated by Lloyd Bentsen in 1988 when he made the mistake of likening himself to Jack Kennedy. But that was about it.

Because the first televised debate between Richard Nixon and Jack Kennedy had turned the 1960 presidential race on its head, the assumption was that every subsequent face-off would have the same transformative effect. However, even the Kennedy–Nixon debates were bereft of a knockdown punch. It was not Nixon's glass jaw that was the problem but rather the flop sweat on his forehead and upper lip.

If televised debates had a tendency of being instantly forgettable, then so, too, did those other great set-piece staples of US campaigns, the party conventions. Up until the late 1960s, after which primaries became decisive, conventions used to pick the presidential nominee in rooms that were choked with smoke and testosterone, and often splattered with blood. Now, their central function was merely to anoint the nominee, and they had essentially become week-long infomercials.

Just about my only recollections from the Republican convention in Philadelphia are of the visuals: the images that the political consultants who choreographed these events hoped would plant themselves in our minds. 'Stormin' Norman Schwarzkopf, the hero of Gulf War one, was beamed into the convention hall from the floodlit deck of the USS *New Jersey* docked nearby, probably with little inkling that Gulf War two was just around the corner. The wrestling champion The Rock made a triumphant entrance on stage, like the great prizefighter that he was.

In sharp contrast, Dick Cheney, George W.'s vice-presidential selector and eventual pick, shuffled self-consciously to the speaking podium with a leather folder tucked under his arm, as if he were a backroom aide delivering a file rather than about to deliver a speech. Visibly uncomfortable in the spotlight, his appearance perhaps presaged his role during the Bush presidency, where his influence was mammoth but largely in the shadows.

Like everyone, I recall being amazed by the number of African-Americans on display: black keynote speakers, such as Colin Powell, Condoleezza Rice and the former gridiron star and congressman J. C. Watts; black preachers, who delivered impassioned invocations that could easily have echoed from pulpits in Selma or Birmingham; and so many black entertainers that journalists scoffed the GOP convention looked more like a minstrel show.

A BBC colleague, who had opened most of his news reports

that week with pictures of soul and R&B bands performing before the delegates on stage, even thought it necessary to advise viewers not to adjust their sets. 'Yes, this is the Republican convention,' he bellowed, over yet more footage of a black ensemble swaying from side to side. Still more surprising was the sight of the GOP's only openly gay congressman, Jim Kolbe of Arizona, delivering a brief, three-minute speech in prime time. Throughout, the Texas delegation, which had been allotted seats directly in front of the speaking podium, sat with bowed heads in mumbling prayer, with cowboy hats covering their hearts. However, it was George W., their favourite son, who had insisted that Kolbe speak, and also that African-Americans be given a much more prominent role – more proof that his conservatism was also compassionate.

Tellingly, I can hardly remember the actual words that were spoken in Philadelphia. Bush's acceptance speech, the supposed highpoint of the week, was serviceable at best and produced little more than the usual bromides. 'This nation is daring and decent and ready for change,' he said, with Poppy Bush staring down proudly from the stands of the basketball arena. 'We will use these good times for great goals.'

It was hardly the Gettysburg Address, but Bush was smart enough to keep it simple. In any case, by now he thought he had the measure of Al Gore. An aide had pointed out to him a profile from the *New Yorker* in which Gore spoke admiringly about the work of the French philosopher Maurice Merleau-Ponty and his opus *Phenomenology of Perception*. 'Venus and Mars, man!' was Bush's reaction. 'I can't imagine anybody who's less like me. That makes it easy for me to run against him.'

Up against the perpetually angst-ridden Gore, Bush would portray himself as a man comfortable in his own skin, the reformed frat boy up against a class nerd who used to watch *Star Trek* at Harvard and wile away hours in his dorm punching out tunes on the keypad of his phone.

For all Bush's swagger and Texan braggadocio, his was a fairly thin skin. Sometime during convention week, George W. either watched, or was told about, a BBC report that described him as a 'hollow man', a description that clearly irked him. Up until that moment, we had enjoyed friendly relations with Team Bush. In fact, his media advisers appeared to think that the mere act of sitting for a BBC interview immediately boosted his foreign-policy credentials. The governor himself could usually be relied upon for a quick soundbite or grab. However, when a colleague tried to buttonhole him on a rope line as he boarded a plane out of Philly, the usual cry of 'BBC, Mr Governor, BBC' was met with an icy burst of uncongeniality. 'Hollow man, huh?' he harrumphed, and then brushed past.

He need not have worried. Hollow man or not, he was getting much better press than his opponent, Al Gore.

—

Had it been rehearsed? Had it been focus-grouped? Would it be seen as a blatantly political ploy? Had there been any tongue? While it was customary during the course of campaigns to report on sexual peccadillos and marital unfaithfulness, never before had so much attention been lavished by commentators on a presidential candidate kissing his own wife. Al Gore had done so with such lustre as he mounted the stage ahead of his acceptance speech at the Democratic convention at the Staples Center in Los Angeles that it looked for a moment as if he might mount poor Tipper.

Afterwards, the *New York Times* likened it to an amorous

groom being invited to kiss his bride, but to others it was more like the passion held back for the honeymoon suite afterwards. Rarely have I witnessed such a visceral reaction from the press gallery. 'Gross!' the American reporters cried in unison, as if they had walked into the living-room to find their parents in flagrante. 'Yuck!' scoffed the Brits.

Naturally, the kiss revealed much more about Al Gore's relationship with Bill Clinton than about his rapport with his wife. Angered by the Lewinsky scandal and also repulsed by it – his own daughters were roughly the same age as Monica – the vice president was determined to demonstrate he was the anti-Clinton: a good husband; a loving father; a moral man. To offer more proof, his wife's lips provided the perfect prop, even if the subliminal message came dripping in saliva. Appearing later on CNN's *Larry King Live*, Gore stressed that the kiss was real passion rather than realpolitik. 'One of the political analysts said, "Were you trying to send a message?",' Gore commented, before adding, as if butter would not melt in his mouth, 'I was trying to send a message to Tipper.'

'Message received,' whispered his normally demure spouse, who was sat at his side.

In a normal political season obeying normal political rules, Al Gore's election should have been something of a formality. Peace and prosperity was not just a bumper-sticker slogan but also a reality for everyday Americans. Household incomes had never been higher. The economy was close to full employment. The budget was in surplus. Politically, as well, Gore was well positioned to reap a harvest. The Democratic Party was united, which was historically unusual. Bill Clinton was enjoying enviably high approval ratings. Senior Republicans had been the main victims of the impeachment crisis. Moreover, the view among delegates at the convention in Los Angeles was that, in George W. Bush, they were up against a complete knuckle-brain. The problem for the Democrats was that Al Gore was up against himself.

If ever there was a case of a candidate getting lost in his own campaign, it was Al Gore in 2000. Though he wanted to champion his signature issue, global warming, his advisers talked him out of it. Though he was one of the most prescient and innovative policymakers of the post-war era, and particularly well credentialed to fight a new-millennial campaign, he and his advisers opted for crude populism, a 'poor against the powerful' tirade that hailed from the mid-1930s.

Though he should have credited the American people with the guile to differentiate what was good about the Clinton years – the economy – from what was bad – its sordidness – he decided virtually to ignore the administration's record altogether. He therefore ran as an insurgent rather than an incumbent, even though most Americans had never had it so good.

From start to finish, Gore allowed himself to be defined by the focus groups and the polls, and disgruntled aides sighed that they had rarely seen a candidate so thoroughly dependent on the numbers. Watching from the sidelines, where Gore was determined he should remain, Bill Clinton could hardly believe his deputy's haplessness. Paradoxically, Gore should have paid much closer heed to the advice from Naomi Wolf. Her main recommendation had nothing to do with his wardrobe. Instead, she argued that the real Al Gore should be allowed out of the closet.

It was a measure of his insecurity that in the three presidential debates we saw three different Al Gores. During their first encounter in Boston, having tutted and sighed his way through

George W. Bush's answers, he came across as petulant and antsy. He was also daubed with so much make-up that he looked like the lead baritone in a light operatic society just about to perform *The Mikado*. In the second debate, after being stung by an acid shower of criticism in the aftermath of the first, Gore overcompensated by being unusually nice. Then, in the third debate, he alternated between the two. Gore had flunked the great 'who would you rather have a beer with?' test, even though, as has oft been pointed out, the free world might have been better served by a nerdy designated driver.

For me, the event that most neatly encapsulated Gore's problems was staged in Nashville, when he appeared at a late-night fund-raiser at the famed Wildhorse Saloon. With little more than a week to go before election day, it came to be known as the hoedown before the showdown. Tennessee, which he had represented as a congressman and senator for 16 years, was the last place Gore wanted to be at this late stage, but now he faced the hurtful prospect of becoming the first presidential candidate since George McGovern in 1972 to lose his home state.

Dispensing with the earth tones, he appeared in denim, the fabric of the south, for a concert that featured Patty Loveless, Billy Ray Cyrus and Tony Bennett. In the home of country and western, the New York crooner should have looked the most out of place, especially since he had come dressed in a shiny silk suit with a scarlet handkerchief flopping insouciantly from his breast pocket. Inevitably, however, it was the vice president who looked the more awkward of the two. Gore was so out of tune with the heartland, as the headlines would later put it, that he could not even clap in time to the music.

That night, perhaps the most telling moment came when

the master of ceremonies, Eddie George, the running back of the local NFL team, the Tennessee Titans, asked Gore where his footballing allegiances truly lay. With synthetic home-town pride and without any hint of irony, Gore proudly announced that the Tennessee Titans was his team, even though virtually everyone in the Wildhorse Saloon knew him to be a devotee, man and boy, of the Washington Redskins.

An elderly southern matriarch, with a turn of phrase dripping in sorghum and molasses, had told the BBC that Gore would rather 'climb a tree to tell a lie than stay on the ground to tell the truth'. Here was yet more proof. More than that, the Titans white lie revealed one of his recurring problems: his lack of an anchor, both personal and political.

Confidently expecting his son would one day take the oath of office as president, Al Gore Snr, a former Tennessee senator himself, had raised him in Washington. He was sent to an elite academy, schooled in the workings of the capital and dispatched to the finishing school of Harvard. However, Washington had turned him into a political being. So much so that when the politics changed, so too did his personality. The Gore paradox was that his rearing in Washington, combined with his experience as a congressman, senator and vice president, made him super-qualified to fulfil his parents' great master plan. Yet a life spent in Washington had stunted his development. He had spent too much time in the American capital to take its top job.

Throughout the campaign, Gore was also victimised by a hostile and unforgiving press. Tellingly, it was not the right-wing ideologues on Fox News that became his most troublesome critics. Far more hurtful was the friendly fire he came under from liberal-minded reporters. They were so determined to demonstrate their impartiality that they tended to overcompensate and ended up handicapping the race in Bush's favour.

In the first presidential debate, Gore demonstrated a much greater mastery of the issues and was clearly the more eloquent and intelligent of the candidates. However, the post-debate coverage was dominated instead by his huffing, sighing and heavy make-up. In a similar vein, Gore's habit of making small exaggerations became a much bigger story than Bush's gaffes and the gaps in his knowledge.

Nothing illustrated this more than the reporting of his supposed boast during an interview with Wolf Blitzer on CNN that he had invented the worldwide web. Gore actually said that during his years as a congressman he had taken 'the initiative in creating the internet', which was an overstatement for sure, but one with a grounding in truth. No lawmaker on Capitol Hill had made a greater contribution to nurturing the worldwide web, as some of its original designers happily put on the record.

Another of Gore's presumed lies, which in its later reporting seemed even more outlandish, was his boast that he had inspired the character Oliver Barrett in Erich Segal's campus romance *Love Story*. Again, however, it was not a barefaced fib. As Segal himself later explained, Barrett had been a composite character, which drew on Gore and his Harvard roommate, the actor Tommy Lee Jones.

From his robotic speeches to his habit on even mildly temperate days of sweating through his shirts, there was a snideness about the reporting of Al Gore that would have been considered a breach of impartiality had it been targeted at Bush. It was a cannibalistic meanness, for a liberal-minded press was devouring one of its own. Another motive was also at work. Journalists often write out of self-interest, and many had simply decided that a Bush victory

W

was better for business. The first father–son presidential combo since John and John Quincy Adams – 'Bush 41' and 'Bush 43', as they took to calling themselves – offered a much better story than a continuation of the Clinton years without its central protagonist.

What had so far been a fairly uneventful general-election campaign finished with another trope: an October surprise, even though it came 48 hours late, on 2 November. Ever since Henry Kissinger stepped before the cameras in October at the fag end of the 1972 campaign to announce that peace was at hand in Vietnam, journalists awaited an unexpected event or revelation with the potential to transform the race completely.

Bona-fide October surprises were actually extremely rare, but just four days before election day it was reported that in 1976 George W. Bush had been pulled over by the police in Kennebunkport, Maine, at the end of a night of drinking with the Australian tennis ace John Newcombe, for driving too slowly. After being breathalysed, he tested positive to driving under the influence and was given a $150 on-the-spot fine. Now, it threatened to cost him the election.

Not to have pre-empted the story with a timely public confessional was considered by Karl Rove to be the single biggest tactical error of the entire campaign, and later he estimated it had cost Bush the states of New Mexico, Wisconsin, Iowa, Oregon and Maine – victory in which would have made Florida entirely superfluous. Looking back, however, perhaps what was most intriguing about the DUI October surprise was the source of the story.

It was first put to air by a Fox affiliate in Maine, whose scoop was picked up immediately by Fox News, which broke it nationally. In Britain, the *Sun* had long claimed to have been chiefly responsible for a string of Conservative victories. 'It's *The Sun* Wot Won It', the paper claimed on its front page after John Major's come-from-behind victory at the 1992 general election. In America, its Murdoch-owned corporate stablemate had come close to producing a very different headline: 'It Was Fox News Wot Lost It'.

—

Perhaps sensing that his days as the face of CBS News might be numbered, Dan Rather arrived for duty on election night bristling with Ratherisms. The Texan newsman unleashed this arsenal with the fervour and profligacy of a buckskin-clad cowboy engaged in his very own private Alamo, determined to fire every bullet and empty every shotgun before his anchor desk was finally overrun by network executives brandishing a slew of falling ratings.

For Rather, the election was not merely close, it was 'tight as the rusted lug nuts on a '55 Ford', it was 'a too-small bathing suit on a too-long ride home from the beach', it was 'spandex tight'. As for the key battleground state of Florida, it was 'hot enough to peel house paint'. With its outcome increasingly uncertain, Dan went ape: 'Turn down the lights, the party got wilder.'

The mad tumble of events had started just before eight o'clock, when the networks first put Florida in the Democratic column, which appeared to foreshadow a Gore victory nationwide. Then, two hours and four minutes later, they retracted Florida from Gore and declared it too close to call. Over the next four hours, I have never known a newsroom to be at once so suspenseful and so feverish. At times, it felt akin to maintaining an all-night vigil in a hospital waiting room when the patient stood only a 50/50 chance of survival. At others, it had the revelry of the countdown to midnight on New Year's Eve.

Finally, at 2.16 am, after freshly counted votes started streaming in from the Florida panhandle, which was an hour behind the rest of the state, the networks made their long-awaited call. The Sunshine State had gone . . . Bush. With Florida came victory, and Fox News was the first out of the traps with a full-screen graphic of emphatic certainty announcing that George W. Bush would now become the next president.

Minutes later, with the same definitiveness, the other networks followed suit. 'Sip it, savour it, cup it, photostat it, underline it in red, press it in a book, put it in an album, hang it on the wall,' suggested Dan Rather, mistakenly thinking it would be his final broadside of the night. 'George W. Bush is the next president of the United States.' Gore thought so too, and telephoned the Texan governor to congratulate him on his victory.

As Gore set off in his vice-presidential motorcade to deliver his concession speech at the War Memorial Plaza in Nashville, his number-crunchers at base were still keeping track of Florida's late-reporting precincts and noticed he was fast gaining ground. With votes left still to count, Gore was only 5000 behind. So, like lawyers who have uncovered a vital piece of evidence that exonerates their client just as he is about to mount the gallows, they put frantic calls through to the motorcade and managed to halt it just in time.

An awkward phone call followed, in which Gore withdrew his earlier concession. 'There's no need to get snippy about it,' said Gore when Bush expressed incredulity. And then the networks went into breakneck reverse. Now, Florida was too close to call. 'We don't just have egg on our face,' observed Tom Brokaw, the NBC anchor, 'we have an omelette.'

Dan Rather also admitted the networks had erred: 'We lived by the crystal ball. We're eating so much broken glass.' As for his take on the main protagonists, Mssrs Bush and Gore: 'They both have champagne on ice, but after the night is over they might need a pickaxe to open them.'

I spent much of that night racing between our on-air set in Washington, trying to provide a commentary, and the video-editing suite, where my picture editor played his edit deck like a pinball machine. In television news editing, the general rule of thumb is that it takes an hour to cut a minute. The storyline careered all over the place at such a pace, however, that often we had less than fifteen minutes to cut three.

Time pressures made the mechanics of laying pictures and voice difficult enough. (Never, before or since, have I seen an editor lay both at the same time, as we did that night.) A harder challenge was making sense out of chaos. Looking back from this distance, the night had a neat timeline: Gore edges ahead, falls back, realises he has lost, concedes defeat, then retracts. On the night, however, with the momentum shifting constantly, and with spin and counter-spin coming from both camps, I fear that we, like the US networks, only added to the mayhem. Wrapping up our coverage shortly after breakfast time, I offered an exhausted final thought from that well-thumbed compendium of statements of the complete obvious: 'The election will not be over until Al Gore concedes.' But none of us suspected that it would be a further 35 days before he did so.

Even as I spoke, teams of lawyers were already boarding the first planes out of National Airport heading south to Miami, Palm Beach and Tallahassee. The marrying of the American political and legal systems, a process that had started with Watergate and continued through the Clinton impeachment, was about to reach its zenith. In truth, I was not quite sure whether we as journalists were sufficiently well credentialed to cope. In a trade traditionally populated by history and English literature graduates, linguists and the occasional classicist, the Florida recount merely confirmed what I had thought throughout impeachment: that by far the best grounding for any Washington-based reporter was to have spent two years studying jurisprudence at law school.

Aside from the angry partisanship, perhaps the most discouraging trend in Washington politics over the past 30 years has been the extent to which law has overtaken history as its academic touchstone, and how the juridical letter of the Constitution has come to crush its spirit. As Louis Menand observed in the *New Yorker*, a magazine where the in-house legal-affairs writer was about to make a big name for himself, we were about to embark on a 'civics lesson from hell'.

A few hours after finally retiring to bed after our election-night marathon, we awoke to a politics transformed. Footage had already come through from Florida showing polling stations looking more like crime scenes, cordoned off with yellow police tape, with blinking squad cars parked outside. This unfolding national melodrama had a new nomenclature – dimpled chads, pregnant chads, hanging chads – and a new complement of characters. The first, unlikely cast members became the befuddled pensioners of Palm Beach County, many of them Jewish, who had been so bamboozled by a complicated ballot paper, the notorious butterfly ballot, that many had speared the hole earmarked for Pat Buchanan, a fringe candidate regularly accused of anti-Semitism.

Then the focus shifted to the supervisor of elections in Palm Beach County, the exotically named Theresa LePore, the registered Democrat who had designed the ballot's perplexing layout. Rather usefully for his brother, the Florida governor Jeb Bush now became a central figure. So, too, did his secretary of state, Katherine Harris, who wore such heavy and glossy make-up that she was billed as the Cruella de Vil of the Florida recount.

Now that the cinematic character of the election had shifted from campaign road movie to courtroom drama, with the occasional nod towards Disney, the legal hired guns and trial lawyers became inadvertent stars. As the court-ordered recounts started, so, too, did the boggled-eyed voting officials who peered through thick magnifying glasses examining ballot papers as if they were rare stamps. The candidates, meanwhile, largely disappeared from view, having become almost superfluous to the story. Not much they could say publicly could materially affect the outcome. Now, it was down to their lawyers and the judges.

Once writs had gone airborne, it was only a matter of time before the US Supreme Court intervened. On 9 December 2000, more than a month on from election day and just 24 hours after the Florida Supreme Court had ordered all the votes to be counted again by hand, the Supreme Court's nine justices, in a 5–4 decision, stayed the recount. Two days later, it heard oral arguments in *Bush vs. Gore*. That morning, boisterous cheer squads from both sides besieged the court, with a donkey deposited at the foot of its marble steps by the supporters of Al Gore that served as a mascot for the Democrats and a four-legged reminder, presumably, of the deficiencies of the law.

In this normally subdued corner of Capitol Hill, there was more pandemonium on the night the justices delivered their decision. Handed the ruling in the bowels of the Supreme Court, a posse of journalists and legal analysts came sprinting out of a side door, like lunatics escaping an ornate and pillared asylum, with mobile phones in one hand and the freshly printed judgment in the other. Then they stood before the cameras in the chill late-night air, illuminated by giant Klieg lights and flanked by rivals from other networks, ferociously racing to become first to break the news.

Deciphering the ruling was like trying to crack a code, and the correspondents were experiencing an exquisite form of torture: rarely in their professional lives would they have broadcast live before such massive audiences, and rarely would they have appeared on screen with so little idea of what they were talking about. On ABC News, the anchor Peter Jennings was as unflappable as ever. 'Nobody should be embarrassed about trying to work out a Supreme Court ruling on the fly,' he said, before crossing over to its correspondent, Jackie Judd, of blue-dress fame, and Jeffrey Toobin, the *New Yorker*'s legal eagle. 'Jackie, why don't you start?' Jennings said coolly.

'I'm going to turn it over to Jeffrey Toobin,' she said.

'I was hoping to turn it to Jackie,' replied Toobin.

Both had trampled all over the correspondent's second commandment, that one should never voluntarily cede airtime to a rival. But both had upheld rule number one, which is never to look stupid on air.

Further down the row, CNN's legal analyst was less judicious. He got the ruling badly wrong, suggesting in the haste of the moment that the recount would be allowed to continue. He did not survive at the network much longer.

As this absurd slapstick unfolded, I was in the warmth of our television studio in Washington but felt much the same discomfort. Naturally, London was desperate to know the outcome, but as luck would have it a fellow correspondent happened to be on anchoring duties that night, and he kindly allowed me a few minutes to read the ruling off-camera rather than attempt to decode it live on air.

I was unable to make sense of the majority ruling, which was a jumble of legalese, but the dissenting opinions were easy to divine. So angry was the tone from the Democrat-appointed justices that it became instantly clear that the court's 5–4 ruling favoured George W. Bush.

As soon as it intervened in the disputed election, most assumed SCOTUS would rule along partisan lines, and so it proved. Put simply, it had decided that a state-wide recount was the ideal way to settle the disputed election but that there was not enough time to complete it. A heavily politicised legal system had delivered an overtly political decision, and one that the pro-Bush justices admitted guiltily should not be relied upon as a precedent.

'Whew, it may not be everything we want,' opined Dan Rather, 'but at least we're still breathing.'

Al Gore conceded the following evening, and George W. and Laura, his first-lady-in-waiting, could now finally RSVP to the organisers of the 'Black Tie and Boots Ball', a Lone Star extravaganza held on the eve of inauguration day. Seemingly dreamt up to prove once and for all that Texas did things bigger and better, the ballrooms were decorated with 20,000 yellow roses, a live steer, various dead armadillos, a mechanical bucking bronco and cowboys that dangled from the ceilings. A menu weighted more heavily towards turf than surf included 2.5 tonnes of brisket and 20,000 shrimp, and more than 5000 Texan wives came dressed in so many sequins that Bill Clinton's Arkansas ball quite literally paled in comparison.

The country artist Lee Greenwood sang that rousing anthem

of the Reagan years, 'I'm Proud to Be an American', and a group of high-kicking Texan Rangerettes dressed in scarlet tunics, knee-high white cowboy boots and sky-blue miniskirts also performed their patriotic duty. But the legs that hogged the headlines belonged to George W. Bush, who pulled up his tuxedo to display custom-made cowboy boots embossed with the presidential seal, like a cancan girl lifting up her skirt to reveal the top of her stockings.

The following day, having rehearsed it so many times on the campaign trail, W finally got to recite the oath of office for real. All Al Gore got to deliver, meanwhile, was a rueful one-liner: 'You win some, you lose some, and then there's that little-known third category.'

Chapter 4

9/11

August could hardly have done more that year to cement its reputation as the red-letter month of the journalistic silly season. Washington was engrossed by a B-grade sex scandal involving a C-grade congressman, a Californian non-entity called Gary Condit who came with that Beltway blend of an over-sized ego, over-active libido and blow-dried hair.

He was alleged to have had an affair with a young staffer, Chandra Levy, an intern, no less, which gave the story a Lewinsky-lite allure. What turned it into round-the-clock news, however, was the more sobering fact that she had not been seen for weeks and might even have been pregnant at the time of her disappearance. With little else vying for airtime, the cable news channels performed their usual alchemy of turning a mini-imbroglio into a mega-scandal. There were the banner logos, 'The Search for Chandra', and the mandatory chorus of bloviators and talking heads – perma-tanned LA trial attorneys, ranting ideologues, under-employed political consultants, the latest right-wing pin-up, and sanctimonious virtue tsars all shouting over themselves.

Congressman Condit also performed his duty by agreeing to sit for a prime-time confessional. 'Did you murder Chandra Levy?' asked the interviewer Connie Chung. Throughout the summer of

2001, it was Washington's most burning question and guiltiest pleasure.

President Bush was out of town, having decided to spend August on his ranch in Crawford, Texas, or the Western White House, as his aides preferred to call it in the hope – forlorn as it turned out – that people would not think him a slacker. There, he cleared brush, challenged his Secret Service detail to race him in the hundred-degree heat, went mountain-bike riding and pondered whether America should allow scientists to perform research using stem cells. Unbeknown to us at the time, on 6 August 2001 Mr Bush was also presented with a presidential briefing item entitled 'Bin Laden Determined to Strike in US'. It did not appear to trouble him unduly. 'All right,' he reportedly told his CIA briefer, 'you've covered your ass now.'

Oblivious to the heightened terrorist alerts, most of us thought the president had picked a perfect time to be out of the capital. That year, August brought not only its customary humidity but also the worst floods since the Second World War. An eruption of exploding manhole covers also terrorised shoppers in the streets of Georgetown. In a frivolous dispatch, penned during lulls in the Condit scandal, I described my heroic efforts in holding back the invading waters from my basement apartment by forming a flood barrier with back issues of the *New York Times*, and reported how visits to Barnes & Noble on M Street had never been more treacherous. 'Twin disasters struck Washington DC last weekend,' I wrote at the time, offering further proof that in the absence of any real great drama that summer we had to invent our own.

Devoid of much of its normal thrusting energy, America muddled along – revisiting its heroic past as much as dwelling too often on its tawdry and unadventurous present. At the movies, the summer blockbuster was *Pearl Harbor*. On television, it was HBO's *Band of Brothers*. Both were part of the Second World War revivalism, now bordering on idolatry, that followed the publication of Tom Brokaw's surprise bestseller *The Greatest Generation* and Steven Spielberg's wartime epic *Saving Private Ryan*. As if to prove the point, *The Wild Blue*, a book by the Second World War historian Stephen Ambrose about the young Americans who flew B-24s over Europe, topped the *New York Times* bestseller list. On Broadway, it was 'Springtime for Hitler', and the most pressing matter on the minds of many New Yorkers was how to get a ticket for the smash-hit musical *The Producers*.

On Condit duty throughout August, I planned to go on vacation in early September. Before heading off, I filed a story out of New York relevant now only for its utter triviality. Scandal had rocked the world of Little League baseball. It centred on a phenomenal 11-year-old pitcher from the Bronx who had been the standout star of the recent World Championships. At five foot eight inches tall, he towered over not only his fellow Little Leaguers but some of his adult coaches as well, which raised inevitable doubts about his eligibility. Predictably enough, when reporters examined his birth records, they discovered he was actually two years older than he should have been – another story that was turned into a modern-day morality tale to fill a few column inches in New York. Did I mention that the silly season had rarely been sillier?

September is such a perfect time to holiday in North America – or so I used to think. I headed off to visit friends in Calgary, Canada's take on Dallas, and then drove through the Rockies, where the turning trees were a blaze of bronze and tangerine, and on to Vancouver, that haven of liveability. Then I followed the Pacific coast down to Seattle.

On 10 September 2001, I remember enjoying the most blissful of days. I wandered through the Pike Place Fish Market, overlooking the harbour. I had a latte at the original branch of Starbucks, a heritage site for some, a pilgrimage site for others. I enjoyed the architecture of Frank Gehry's Experience Music Project, a futuristic building whose curvaceous, shining metal skin looked like an early prototype for his opus in Bilbao. In a second-hand bookstore, I even came across a book I had been hunting down for years, *Mr Kennedy and the Negroes*.

Work seemed a million miles away. I did not know yet, but the distance the next morning would feel greater. Pondering the giant strides being made in American brewing, I drank a few Sierra Nevada pale ales and spent the evening in the company of *Mr Kennedy and the Negroes*. Before turning in, I flicked through the news channels, as holidaying correspondents are prone to do, to reassure myself that nothing of any great significance was happening in my absence. Then I fell asleep.

Needless to say, the biggest story of my working life, the most consequential event a Washington correspondent could ever cover, the moment that the world changed forever, the instant my career was severed in two, struck while I was still comatose. Asleep in Seattle!

Switching on the television in the morning, still oblivious, my first glimpse of Lower Manhattan on 11 September was a tight close-up – an almost microscopically tight close-up – of the gash in a small section of one of the towers. In the slow motion of initial recognition, I recall thinking that a Cessna or other light plane must have ploughed into the tower. Big, but not that big, I remember thinking, inclined as journalists are to immediately assign a ranking to every event. Then the picture switched from a close-up to a panoramic view of Lower Manhattan. With manic suddenness, the usual currencies of news were completely worthless. What confronted us on our screens stretched the bounds of understanding.

I grabbed my mobile to check it for messages, but its crystal display registered my irrelevance. Just one missed call. From my mother. After trying repeatedly, I eventually managed to get through to the bureau in Washington, knowing that I was surplus to requirements and feeling almost apologetic for calling. My harried bureau chief was considerate enough at least to pretend that I could make some useful contribution. With dozens of planes still in the air, and some of them thought to be under the control of hijackers, he suggested I head for Los Angeles, where the next wave of attacks was expected to come. With airplanes already grounded, LA was a three-day drive away, and he knew as well as I did – although, again, he was generous enough to leave it unsaid – that I had completely missed the story.

I recount all of this with abject apologies, hoping that my passport from Correspondentland grants me a degree of diplomatic immunity. I know now, and knew then, that missing a story – even a story on the scale of 9/11 – did not merit even the tiniest of quivers on the gauge of human suffering. On that awful morning, I promise you that my first thoughts and tears were for the poor people in those towers. But I hope you will forgive me when I admit to feelings of self-pity as well: a combination of professional helplessness tinged with professional jealousy, since I knew that my friends and colleagues in Washington were busy covering the defining story of our careers.

Still more shamefacedly, the only time that day when my spirits were briefly lifted was when I learnt that many of my colleagues were even further from Washington than I. One, the human megaphone from Rabin's funeral, was in Nicaragua, where even his voice was out of range. I also discovered that Christopher Hitchens had been marooned in Washington state, which again raised my spirits. Yet the scar tissue from being absent from my post on 9/11 is still in the process of forming more than a decade later.

Over the years, I have concocted various consoling *ex post facto* rationalisations. I would have botched the story. I would not have immediately grasped its immensity. There were correspondents that day, after all, who did not acquit themselves brilliantly – though there were countless others whose coverage was riveting and heroic. Stephen Evans, our New York business correspondent, was even in the lobby of the World Trade Center when the first plane hit.

Perhaps I saved myself the hassle of becoming embroiled in some of the far-fetched conspiracy theories soon appearing on the web that claimed that the BBC and its correspondents were complicit because we apparently reported that one of the nearby towers, Tower 7, collapsed 20 minutes before it actually did. (Not that I suspect it will make much difference to our accusers, but I promise you that the BBC is far too bureaucratic, unwieldy, gossipy and downright honest to do conspiracies.) For a time, I tried to convince myself that it was actually a positive that I had missed 9/11, because it gave me a measure of detachment in covering the aftermath.

Instead of playing a central role on 9/11, I went through the motions of professionalism on the periphery. I set off for Los Angeles, but I made it only as far as Portland, Oregon, where I hired a local cameraman and started to gather material. Main

Street reaction sort of stuff. Already, the city was bedecked in flags. Hand-painted patriotic signs of support hung from overpasses on the freeway. Long lines had already started to form outside blood-transfusion centres. Evening church services were packed.

Then, rather like a castaway stranded on a desert island who suddenly spots footprints in the sand, I also discovered that other Washington-based colleagues were also on the west coast. Immediately, we hatched plans for our speedy return and even had a Lear jet on standby in Los Angeles, ready to take off the minute that American airspace reopened. Just outside London, another chartered plane was also on standby, at Stansted Airport, ready to fly all the big-name correspondents and presenters from the BBC and its rivals over to New York. The passenger manifest included some of the most illustrious names in broadcast journalism, the most irrepressibly vain as well, so inevitably the plane soon came to be dubbed 'Ego One'.

Eventually, after three interminably long days, hundreds of phone calls to my travel agent, dozens of bookings on planes that never left the runway and four cross-country flights that did eventually take off, I made it back to Washington. Leaving Portland, I can still recall rushing to the departure gate past a row of newspaper-vending machines and noticing that none of the front pages carried pictures of the towers aflame, the smouldering Pentagon or the grainy black-and-white CCTV footage of the hijackers about to board the planes. There was no sign of any flags at half-mast, candles, flowers, photocopied flyers with the faces of relatives under the word 'MISSING'. The lightning – and lightening – sensation that the attacks had not happened lasted for all but a millisecond: the tiny slice of time that it took to realise the front pages were from the morning of 11 September. Yesterday's newsprint had never been so out of date.

By the time I returned to Washington, shiny enamel flag-pins were affixed already to reporters' lapels. Graphic renderings of the Stars and Stripes fluttered in the corners of the screens. NBC's famed peacock logo even took on the colours of Old Glory. In the mood of ultra-patriotism that instantly prevailed, some US reporters seemed to think they should be flag-wavers first and journalists second – although, for many, the feeling of being participants in this great drama rather than spectators was not entirely unforgivable.

On the morning of the attacks, members of the White House press corps had sprinted from the West Wing, fearing it was about to come under aerial attack. The tight pool of reporters accompanying George W. Bush on a trip to Florida found themselves being flown aboard Air Force One from one military installation to the next, as the Secret Service weighed whether it was safe to return to Washington.

One sensed from the outset that much of the American media, and especially the White House press corps, were clamorous for the president to rise to the occasion. To begin with, however, he fell embarrassingly short. In Sarasota that Tuesday morning, before a class of second-graders, he finished listening to *The Pet Goat* – all seven minutes of it – even after Andrew Card, his chief of staff, reported that a second plane had flown into the South Tower and that 'America is under attack'.

Twenty minutes later came his first presidential statement, when he spoke with a lazy informality about 'those folks who carried out this attack'. Even when addressing the nation from the Oval Office that night, the president struggled to find the apposite words, even though he could now call on his team of speech-writers. 'These acts shattered steel, but they cannot dent the steel of America' sounded like a line from a first draft, perhaps even a second, that should have been culled before it reached the third.

It was days before he grew into the role assigned to him by the press, of the strong national leader. This transformation started in the wreckage of Ground Zero, bullhorn in hand, with an ad-libbed speech that came to be likened to the eloquence of King Henry on St Crispin's Day. Then it continued with an address before a joint session of Congress nine days after the attack in which he claimed, with still more self- and national certainty, that America had found 'our mission and our moment'.

The then dean of the Washington press corps, David Broder, compared the president's speech to Lincoln's – the highest of oratorical accolades. It sounded rather like a courtier shouting 'The king is dead. Long live the king!' and offered more proof of the deferential mood among journalists at the time. A year afterwards, the former CNN correspondent Christiane Amanpour spoke of reporters self-muzzling, but that implied they wanted still to play the role of attack dogs. Alas, they were far more supine.

I fear, too, that some of this jingoism and fealty crept into our own coverage. The spirit of Le Monde's famous headline on 12 September, 'Nous Sommes Tous Américains', certainly found an echo among the foreign press corps. No doubt, we were more dispassionate than our US colleagues, but neither were we without passion. As I said at the outset, most of us were lovers of America and completely enamoured of New York.

In the week after 9/11, I remember being irritated by an editor in London who suggested, sarcastically, that there were other ways to start a television piece than with the slushy sentimentalism of baseball fans joining in the singing of the national anthem, a flag being hoisted, or any other patriotic ritual, such as the singing of 'America the Beautiful'. Looking back, however, I suspect she was doing her job rather better than I.

Aware that the press was in such close alignment, the Bush administration even felt confident enough to start singling out miscreant broadcasters from the podium of the White House briefing room. Most notoriously, the comedian Bill Maher, the host of *Politically Incorrect*, came under fire for suggesting it was 'cowardly' to fire cruise missiles from 2000 miles away and, more controversially, that the suicidal hijackers could not be described as cowards. Rounding on Maher from his lectern in the White House briefing room, the president's press spokesman, Ari Fleischer, reminded Americans that they needed to 'watch what they say, watch what they do', which appeared to turn the First Amendment on its head.

Rather than defend Maher, ABC, the network that broadcast his late-night show, took heed and decided against renewing his contract. After that, there was not much need for further censorship, because the mainstream media censored itself by banishing such subversive thoughts. On at least one occasion, the White House even targeted a dissident reporter, Dana Milbank of the *Washington Post*, having taken an intense dislike to his wounding wit and disrespectful tone, along with an article he went on to write in October 2002 under the headline 'For Bush, facts are malleable'. It was suggested to the *Post*'s management that another reporter might do a better job of covering the presidency – a recommendation they thankfully ignored.

Few things better illustrated the absence of reproach in the media coverage post-9/11 than the blithe acceptance of the Bush administration's standard line that nobody could have foreseen such a calamity. Condoleezza Rice, the then national security adviser, stated it most boldly in May 2002: 'I don't think anybody could have predicted that these people would take an airplane and slam it into the World Trade Center, take another and slam it into the Pentagon; that they would use a plane as a missile.'

Alas, it required no great leap of imagination. A cursory glance at Tom Clancy's *Executive Orders* would have sufficed – an airport novel that came up with precisely that kind of scenario, with a plane obliterating Capitol Hill just as the president is delivering a speech. The White House had also come under a kamikaze-style attack during the Clinton administration, when a suicidal aircraft mechanic crashed a Cessna 150 into the South Lawn. By strange coincidence, he stole the plane on the night of 11 September 1994.

Then there were the warnings. In January 2001, just days after George W. Bush took office, the former senators Warren Rudman and Gary Hart, of *Monkey Business* fame, published the report of the US Commission on National Security/21st Century. Its key finding was that a combination of 'unconventional weapons proliferation with the persistence of international terrorism will end the relative invulnerability of the US homeland to catastrophic attack.'

There was also that security briefing at his ranch in Crawford on 6 August talking up the possibility of an attack orchestrated by Osama bin Laden, the existence of which was suppressed until April 2004. Among various other alerts, there was the famed Phoenix memo from an FBI agent in Arizona warning that bin Laden had sent students to attend civil aviation schools. Despite these lapses, no high-ranking administration figure lost his or her job in the aftermath. Nor did the American press demand any scalps.

Rather, leading lights in the administration became overnight sensations. Such was the star power of Defence Secretary Donald Rumsfeld, the one-time college wrestler who helped pull bodies from the rubble of the Pentagon, that fans wanted to know the brand of his rimless glasses and what grooming oil he used to slick back his silver hair. The president took to calling him 'Rumstud'. Spouting his 'known knowns', 'known unknowns' and 'unknown unknowns', his press conferences became command performances, and were by far the best theatre that post-9/11 Washington could muster. Unfortunately, the Pentagon press pack often served as his stooges and seemed almost hypnotised by his epistemological wordplay. In the view of a BBC colleague, Justin Webb, the press conferences looked like 'spanking sessions for a generation of defence nerds'.

Typical of the fawning coverage was Bob Woodward's fly-on-the-wall book *Bush at War*. Consider his description of the president's reaction at being told that a second plane had ploughed into the World Trade Center. 'Bush remembers exactly what he was thinking,' Woodward recounts, before delivering a self-serving quote from the president. '"They had declared war on us, and I made up my mind at that moment that we were going to war."' Then Woodward takes up the story, in a manner that reinforces the impression that the president was fully in command. 'Bush decided that he needed to say something to the public.'

And that is it. Inexplicably, Woodward failed to describe *The Pet Goat* episode in that Sarasota classroom, used to merciless effect by the film-maker Michael Moore in *Fahrenheit 9/11*, and which still makes for excruciating viewing. Even after

Card had whispered in his ear, Bush continued to listen to the children reading the book. A minute later, he actually picked up the book himself from the shelf, started to look at it in complete puzzlement, and then cracked a lame gag, like the jester of old. When the children had finished, he thanked them for showing him their reading skills and congratulated them on spending more time reading than watching television. Then he expressed gratitude for making him feel so welcome.

At this point, he could easily have left the classroom to get an update from his aides, but instead he allowed the school principal to step in and thank him for coming. Though Woodward did not touch on any of this, Bush's performance in Sarasota suggested that he was not even in charge of the classroom, still less the country. The contrast with Woodward's work, alongside Carl Bernstein, on Watergate almost 30 years earlier could not have been starker. Then, he had helped demolish a Republican president. Now, like so many other Washington-based reporters, he provided buttressing when Bush wobbled badly.

In those months after 9/11, Washington became a far more dismal city in which to live and work. Inelegant concrete barriers soon encircled every single major government building and landmark, giving some of L'Enfant's boulevards the look of freeway entrance ramps. Even at the Lincoln Memorial, a monument as solid as a fortress, ugly security barriers fell within the Great Emancipator's brooding stare. Batteries of surface-to-air missiles were even positioned within sight of the Capitol's dome.

For weeks afterwards, it was impossible to watch a plane land at National Airport on the banks of the Potomac, a few seconds' flying time from the White House, without wondering if it might suddenly change direction at the very last moment and spear into a building. Years on, I still caught myself peering into the sky to check if incoming aircraft had lowered their landing gear.

Flying into Washington, passengers made sure they had visited the toilet well before coming in to land. To do so during the final approach was to risk having your arm or jaw broken by an air marshal. Washington now had even less of the feel of *The West Wing*. Instead, it mirrored *24*, the new Fox show that premiered in November 2001, where an anti-terrorism agent played by Kiefer Sutherland tried each week to save America from prime-time Armageddon.

Still more depressing was New York. Usually, I travelled there by train from Washington, partly to enjoy the invigorating sight of the spires of Manhattan's skyline as you rumbled through the industrial swampland of northern New Jersey. The first time I made the journey after 9/11, however, Lower Manhattan was unrecognisable. Peering through the smokestacks, freeway overpasses and rusting pylons, I mistook it for an outlying suburb of Newark.

With no shortage of heart-rending stories to tell, or images to shoot – jagged and cindery, the remains at Ground Zero smouldered for months afterwards – the main challenge for journalists was literary. Words seemed not only inadequate in describing the attacks but also superfluous up against the instant iconography of the planes darting into the Twin Towers. Anyone with access to a television or the internet had such a visual association with 9/11 that it was hard to come up with any commentary, other than the repetition of simple facts, that added much to their experience.

What could one say, for instance, about the crackly tape recordings of victims making 9/11 emergency calls or telephoning their relatives while the towers were aflame, in the certain knowledge that they were saying their last goodbyes? All that was needed were short biographies of the office workers making the calls. That is perhaps why 'The Portraits of Grief', the *New York Times*'s brief pen portraits of the victims, were so compelling. We knew what had happened. What we wanted to find out was to whom it had happened.

'The Portraits of Grief', which fleshed out a victim's personality from small illustrative details, provided this human mosaic. We heard of Leon Smith Jnr, the big-hearted fire-truck driver; Dianne Bullis Snyder, a wife, a mother, a doer; John F. Ginley, a quiet family man; Mohammad Salman Hamdani, the all-American Jedi; and Todd Isaac, a jolly snowboarder.

Even when the *New Yorker* drew upon its vast literary resources to provide short prose poems, they felt meagre. John Updike, who had been 'summoned' to the roof of his Brooklyn apartment building to 'witness something great and horrendous', spoke of how 'the south tower dropped from the screen of our viewing; it fell straight down like an elevator, with a tinkling shiver and a groan of concussion distinct across the mile of air.' More convincing was his description of 'the mundane duties of survivors – to pick up the pieces, to bury the dead, to take more precautions, to go on living'.

In the same pages, the novelist Jonathan Franzen tried to capture the convolutions of the New York mind. 'Besides the horror and sadness of what you were watching,' he wrote, 'you might also have felt a childish disappointment over the disruption of your day; or a selfish worry about the impact on your finances, or admiration for an attack so brilliantly conceived and so flawlessly executed, or, worst of all, an awed appreciation of the visual spectacle it produced.'

Updike had spoken of the 'false intimacy of television', but, whether false or not, it made much of what was written in the aftermath of 9/11 redundant. The familiarity with these terrible events was visual, visceral and unspoken. However erudite, literary renderings tended only to provide fresh perspectives rather than adding more emotional depth. Strangely, perhaps the most apposite words came from a dead poet, W. H. Auden, and his poem 'September 1, 1939':

> The unmentionable odour of death
> Offends the September night.

Likewise, there were surprisingly few champions in the literary sport of encapsulating 9/11 in novels. In *Underworld*, a stupendous tour de force that seemed almost to foreshadow the 9/11 attacks by featuring the Twin Towers shrouded in cloud on its fly-jacket, Don DeLillo captured America's Cold War paranoia better than any other novelist. Yet *Falling Man*, which filtered the aftermath of 9/11 through a lawyer working that day in the World Trade Center who sought solace by screwing a fellow survivor and disappearing into the windowless poker rooms of Las Vegas, was a disappointment.

Similarly, John Updike's *Terrorist*, which offered a twist to the canon by approaching 9/11 from the perspective of a radicalised young American Muslim rather than a victim of the attacks, was far from his best work.

In Philip Roth's *Everyman*, the main protagonist had moved away from Manhattan in the aftermath of 9/11, a metaphor perhaps for the author's apparent squeamishness at tackling the subject himself.

Just as the authors of the great American novels have not yet produced the great 9/11 novel, nor has anyone else. Jonathan Safran Foer's *Extremely Loud and Incredibly Close*, which told the story of a nine-year-old boy who lost his father in the Twin Towers, was heart-rending and fantastical, and it captured not only the depthless anguish of September's bereavement but its randomness as well. Joseph O'Neill's *Netherland* encased the melancholy and desolation that hung in the still-putrid air of Manhattan. But I have not yet completed a post-9/11 novel with complete contentment. It was not so much a failure of imagination. Instead, the problem for novelists is that no new stories were needed when there were more than enough from the day itself.

Again, this explains the success of that other surprise bestseller, *The Report of the 9/11 Commission*. Try as they might, novelists and film-makers have not yet managed to turn 9/11 into a major cultural event. Rather like the Second World War, which has never been commemorated with appropriately epic works of fiction, simple, real-life narratives have had more than enough drama, pathos and sentimentality.

The fact that *The Report of the 9/11 Commission* made it so effortlessly to the top of the national bestseller lists was all part of what came to be described as the new normalcy. An anxious America of colour-coded security warnings, the rote removal of shoes at airports, National Guardsmen in musty combat fatigues at railway stations, worries about owning property in Washington or Manhattan because of the possible detonation of dirty bombs and runs on hardware shops to buy up plastic sheeting and duct tape.

I remember telling London that the duct-tape panic was a complete media beat-up, a confected alert from our friends at cable news. Americans simply were not that paranoid. Then I went to an old-fashioned hardware store near the bureau, in an area populated by urban professionals – lawyers, college lecturers, accountants, journalists – and discovered that Americans were that paranoid now. The shelves were completely empty.

More so than the run on duct tape, the low point for me came when I watched a wheelchair-bound woman in her 80s being told to remove her white slippers, presumably to ensure they were not packed with explosives. Paranoiac madness or what the writer George Packer called a 'mental state of emergency'.

However much one wanted to return to 10 September, there *was* reason to be afraid. Ominous warnings about chemical and biological weapons were borne out in early October 2001 when anthrax-laced letters turned up in the post of news organisations and the offices of two senators, including the Democratic senate majority leader Tom Daschle.

Cordoned off with yellow tape, and patrolled now by police officers wearing chemical-warfare HAZMAT suits, Capitol Hill resembled the set of a big-budget science-fiction movie with extremely high production values. With ABC News, CBS News, NBC News and the *New York Post* all coming under anthrax attack, it was not long before all of the mail sent to our bureau in M Street was also being screened for deadly spores. Danger normally comes in combat zones and war-torn countries, but now it came through the mail. I distinctly remember the moment I heard that NBC News had been targeted, for I felt physically sick.

Strangest of all was the sight of policemen dressed in HAZMAT suits at the headquarters of the *National Enquirer* in Boca Raton, Florida, the first media organisation to be targeted. 'The *Enquirer* Hit By Anthrax Attack'. Not even the tabloid's inventive sub-editors could have produced a headline as outlandish as that.

Usually so optimistic, America had become a place of fear, anxiety and paranoia. Crucially, however, there was curiosity too. Part of the public response to 9/11 was a quest for understanding, with many Americans now considering it part of their civic duty to find out 'why they hate us'. Search engines spewed out information on al-Qaeda, Osama bin Laden, the Northern Alliance and General Pervez Musharraf of Pakistan.

Ahmed Rashid's *Taliban*, a once-obscure history of a once-obscure band of Islamic zealots, became an unexpected bestseller. So, too, did *Islam: A Short History* by the religious scholar Karen Armstrong, and *Holy War, Inc.* by a British journalist, Peter Bergen, who had once interviewed bin Laden.

With more weighty matters to discuss, the green rooms of the cable news channels now played host to more serious-minded pundits. Retired colonels edged out political hacks. Former intelligence officers, especially those with expertise in Afghanistan and Pakistan, took precedence over Hollywood divorce attorneys. The BBC also benefited from this thirst for knowledge, not least because so many of the US networks and newspapers had defenestrated their networks of foreign bureaux. Our ratings in America soared.

Naturally, the fun went out of American reporting, for gone in an instant was the frivolity of the Clinton era and the relatively relaxed pace of the start of the Bush years. With the aftermath of 9/11 now the single preoccupation, trips beyond the Beltway to cover a lighter menu of stories also came to an immediate halt. Keen to explore as much of America as I could – my running tally of 'states visited' was closing in fast on that magic number 50 – my editors had been surprisingly indulgent when it came to recreational reportage. They had let me file from 'The Big Easy' on how the jazz clubs of Bourbon Street were being elbowed out by strip joints; from Las Vegas on the Y2K fear, hilarious in retrospect, that on the stroke of midnight at the start of the new millennium electronic gambling machines would turn into silver waterfalls; and even from Tinseltown, where I had donned a black tuxedo for red-carpet duties at the Oscars. Instead, the American 9/11 beat was limited pretty much to Washington, New York and the occasional nearby military base.

An exception was to fly, via Puerto Rico, to America's Caribbean redoubt: the most controversial new landmark in the Bush administration's war on terror.

Chapter 5

Happy Meals at Guantanamo

Much of Guantanamo Bay felt more like a resort than an encampment, a heavily militarised holiday camp on the craggy shores of the Caribbean. On every night of the week, the Downtown Lyceum, an open-air cinema with terraced bleachers, offered the latest in Hollywood escapism. Tuesday and Sunday were bingo nights at the Windjammer Cafe. The Cuban Club promised 'the genuine taste of the Caribbean'. If that did not suit, there was Rick's Lounge for the officer ranks, the Tiki Bar, a late-night hotspot with views across the moonlit-dappled water, a Reef Raiders dive club, an 18-hole golf course, 11 beaches and, inexorably, an O'Reilly's Irish pub.

Were it not for its battleship-grey paint job, the roll-on-roll-off ferry connecting the two halves of the base, on the windward and leeward sides of the bay, would not have looked out of place steaming into Martha's Vineyard. The bayside clapboard homes of the naval commanders again recalled New England and could have provided the backdrop for a Ralph Lauren fashion shoot.

The weather was perfect. Unblemished blue skies, with a soothing breeze blowing off the sea. Needless to say, there was a Pizza Hut, a Subway and a McDonald's, the only branch on the island of Cuba. It came complete with golden arches and the normal architectural blandishments of dull-brown brick walls, plate-glass façades and mansard roofs. The only thing missing was a Toyota dealership next door.

Other parts of Gitmo looked like a museum of the Cold War – albeit a working museum, since this was one of the few corners of the world where it had not yet ended. A 17-mile fence-line hyphenated with tall watchtowers separated Cuban Cuba from America's century-old outpost, the first beyond its shores. US Marines looked out over a no-man's-land known still as the Cactus Curtain. Cuba's Frontier Brigade stood guard on the other side.

Even though many of the 55,000 landmines had been cleared on the orders of Bill Clinton, it was still thought to be the biggest minefield anywhere in the western hemisphere and the second most dangerous in the world. US forces patrolling the fence-line even kept up the Soviet-era precaution of covering their mouths whenever they spoke, lest Cuban lip-readers picked up what they were saying by peering at them through binoculars.

Just two years on from 9/11, Gitmo already housed a relic of the Bush administration's war on terror: Camp X-Ray, the temporary detention centre where 'enemy combatants' had been brought from Afghanistan wearing orange boiler suits, goggles, restraints, earmuffs and face masks. Its makeshift wooden watchtowers had not yet been dismantled, nor had its open-sided wire cells with mesh walls and corrugated tin roofs that made them look more like dog kennels.

We had been invited to Guantanamo by the Pentagon to look at its replacement, a purpose-built prison constructed in a remote corner of scrubland once populated by iguanas and banana rats. On arrival at Gitmo's airstrip, we were loaded onto a white-painted school bus, ferried across the bay and introduced to our Pentagon guide. She was an attractive African-American lieutenant colonel with a winsome smile, a velvet voice and more than a passing resemblance to Halle Berry. In their battle for journalistic hearts and minds, the US military had unleashed a devastating new weapon: a smart bombshell.

She had put together a busy itinerary. There were interviews with camp cooks, who showed us, with the aplomb of television chefs, their new Muslim-friendly dishes – though 'culturally appropriate' was the phrase *de jour*. The menu included halal meat, baklava pastries and even special dough that they proudly called Taliban bread. During the fasting month of Ramadan, especially large breakfasts were prepared to help the inmates last until sundown.

After a tour of the kitchens, we were shown the state-of-the-art medical facilities, which offered detainees at least as high a standard of healthcare as American veterans returning from Afghanistan. A library for the detainees included Arabic editions of Harry Potter. Newly built cells had arrows stencilled into the floor facing towards Mecca and were all equipped with a copy of the Koran. Surgical masks had also been handed out, which the detainees hung from the ceiling to protect their holy books from ever coming into contact with the ground. In a further demonstration of tolerance towards Islam, loudspeakers were dotted around the detention centre from which the call to prayer was broadcast five times a day.

At the end of the briefings, we were finally allowed behind the wire, where virtually all the 700 inmates were bearded and wore crocheted prayer caps and flip-flops. White overalls indicated compliant prisoners who did not pose much of a threat to the guards – the majority – and orange clothing marked out supposed troublemakers. At the time of our visit, in late 2003, none of the inmates had been granted access to a lawyer or even told where they were being held. No one had been charged with any crimes, and some faced the prospect of spending the rest of their lives at Guantanamo without ever getting their day in court.

Ahead of time, we were warned that our visit would come to an immediate end if any of us tried to speak or communicate in any way with the detainees. Today, however, it was a squawking warning siren and the panicked shouts of the prison warden that brought it to a premature conclusion. Rushed from the facility, we were told that there had been some kind of security breach, and it was no longer safe for us to continue our tour. Later, however, we learnt that the siren normally sounded when an inmate attempted to commit suicide – or made a 'gesture towards suicide', in the terminology favoured by the Pentagon.

In the face of criticism from international human-rights groups, our Pentagon handlers aimed to demonstrate that compassion was being shown towards their captives. But they also left us in no doubt that the enemy combatants were the 'worst of the worst', as Donald Rumsfeld had described them. A reservist drafted in from the mainland, where he ran a prison in the Midwest, put it succinctly: 'I have no doubt in my mind that if they had the chance they would kill us all. They'd kill you in a heartbeat. They'd kill women and children. They'd burn down our houses and destroy our way of life. That's their intent.'

More sympathetic was the camp's new Muslim chaplain, a Chinese-American called Captain James Yee, who wore the Stars and Stripes on his sleeve, an Islamic crescent on his military cap and carried around a copy of the Koran wherever he went.

A former Lutheran who converted to Islam during the first Gulf War, Captain Yee now provided pastoral care for the inmates and probably spent more time in conversation with them than any other American on the base.

'As a Muslim, do you think it is moral that people are being held without charge?' I asked him.

'I try not to think about the idea of being charged or not charged,' he replied, rather vaguely. 'Whether they are charged or not, I can't control that. But what I can control is . . . helping them get through every day.'

Next up was a meeting with the head of the detention facilities, Geoffrey D. Miller, a two-star general who spoke fluent war on terrorism and had a penchant for quoting Thomas Jefferson: 'the price of freedom is eternal vigilance'. Straight out of central casting, he made me think that the first question I should ask was 'Did you order the Code Red?'. To which he presumably would have replied, 'You're goddamn right I did!'

But, rather than ventriloquise Jack Nicholson, Miller presented himself as a benevolent reformer, mindful of both the sensibilities of his Muslim inmates and the criticisms of human-rights groups. 'Did you see those kitchens?' he asked. 'Has the lieutenant colonel been taking good care of you?'

He was also obliging enough to offer up a global scoop. Guantanamo Bay housed three juvenile enemy combatants, aged between 13 and 15, who were kept in a prison annex called Camp Iguana. It had the feel of a kind of terroristic crèche, with a small play area and a panoramic ocean view – something of an oddity for children who had grown up in landlocked Afghanistan. Miller announced that these legal castaways were about to be set free. Nothing numbs the inquisitive impulses of a journalist quite as instantly as a spoon-fed exclusive, so we dutifully went off to break the news to our editors at home.

Throughout the trip, we were fed other titbits of information, all of which were designed to show that the conditions at Gitmo were nowhere near as bad as was widely thought at the time. The message throughout this Pentagon PR offensive was that 'America's Caribbean gulag' was getting an unfair rap. My favourite nugget was delivered by our Halle Berry lookalike. One morning, as we drove in our school bus past the golden arches of McDonald's, she chirpily pointed out that detainees who provided interrogators with actionable intelligence got a fast-food reward: a Happy Meal from Guantanamo. This was presented as a key interrogation tool, although she was unable to say whether the meal came with a small moulded toy.

None of us swallowed this, of course, and I suspect it actually added to our increasingly mutinous mood. Already, we were aggrieved that the Pentagon trip came with such prohibitive restrictions. We were not allowed to speak to inmates – which was understandable – or to film anything behind the wire. Instead, we were given Pentagon 'B-roll', as it is called: stock generic shots that showed the stainless-steel operating theatres, and the arrows on the floors of the cells and the copies of the Koran. Everything that the Pentagon wanted us to see and broadcast to the rest of the world.

The only shot of the detention centre we were allowed to take for ourselves was from outside the wire – and one that featured in virtually every television report filed from Guantanamo – showing me entering through the gate. Under the conditions that news organisations signed up to ahead of time, and had long been fighting, the Pentagon could review our footage and delete sections that it deemed infringed the guidelines. Our prime reason for travelling to Guantanamo Bay had been to see the newly refurbished building on the base where the first military tribunals were about to start, but again we were not even allowed inside. Moreover, the windows had been fitted with mirror glass. The secrecy was all the more disconcerting given that the Pentagon had trumpeted the supposed transparency of the military-tribunal process.

Within days of leaving Guantanamo, our interview with the Muslim chaplain suddenly became part of a larger news story. Captain Yee, the quiet chaplain who had been put forward as a poster boy of the Pentagon's goodwill, was arrested and imprisoned on charges of mutiny, aiding the enemy and espionage. He had been recorded making regular phone calls to Damascus. He kept a personal journal that included a log of alleged atrocities against inmates, whom he apparently referred to as his brethren. Information was leaked to the press that he kept hand-drawn sketches of prison quarters along with notes of what was said during interrogations.

As further evidence of his disloyalty, Yee was reluctant to eat in the company of his fellow West Point-trained officers. Added together, the evidence was enough to persuade his one-time cheerleaders to manacle him in a so-called 'three-piece suit' – a primitive set of wrist and ankle shackles, connected to a heavy leather belt. Then he was thrown into the navy brig in Charleston, South Carolina, where he was held in solitary confinement for 76 days.

Not for the first time in post-9/11 America, the evidence did not survive close scrutiny. The calls to Damascus were easily explained. His wife was Palestinian-born and had decided to await his return from Cuba with her Syria-based family. Yee did not eat with his fellow officers because the mess hall did not serve halal meat. As for the journal, Yee simply chronicled what he saw. Rather, the case against Yee seemed to be based on groundless suspicions raised by colleagues who thought he spent too much time with inmates and seemed overly sympathetic towards their plight. Eventually, the case against him collapsed, and he was granted an honourable discharge. To this day, he is awaiting an apology from the Pentagon.

Neither was Major General Geoffrey D. Miller quite the forward-thinking reformer that the Pentagon would have us believe. Hand-picked by Donald Rumsfeld to generate more actionable intelligence from the Guantanamo inmates, he brought in expansive new guidelines granting interrogators much more latitude. Dogs were allowed to frighten detainees. They were stripped naked. The new guidelines also allowed for the use of stress positions.

Miller had also been the driving force behind the prosecution of Captain Yee, one of the few officers to voice concerns about the tough new regime. Then still fairly obscure, Miller achieved much wider fame when he became a central figure in the Abu Ghraib scandal in Iraq. He had first visited the prison in 2003 with the apparent aim of 'Gitmo-ising' the facility and later went on to oversee it. Whether by coincidence or design, the first of the infamous pictures showing military policemen desecrating Iraqi prisoners were taken shortly after Miller's first visit.

As for the Happy Meals at Guantanamo, it soon emerged that interrogators preferred a very different menu of techniques to extract information. Allegations surfaced of inmates being taunted by female interrogators and prostitutes, who flashed G-strings, wore miniskirts and smeared fake menstrual blood on the cheeks of prisoners. Waterboarding, a form of torture that simulates drowning by pouring water into the breathing passages, was also used, a technique once favoured by the Khmer Rouge in Cambodia.

Back in Washington a few months later, I ended up having dinner with the military spokeswoman who had been our guide. She was the most charming company, and she revealed that after leaving the military she ideally wanted to become a novelist: not quite the radical career change that once it might have seemed.

—

After 9/11, and especially in the run-up to the Iraq war, the character of Correspondentland changed completely. A BBC colleague who accompanied me on that trip to Guantanamo was part of a new breed of journalists who had suddenly come into their own. Not only was he fluent in American politics but he was also an expert in nuclear proliferation, working in his spare time on an exposé of A. Q. Khan, the founding father of Pakistan's nuclear capability – the 'Islamic bomb', as it was often called – who was believed to be trading secrets to rogue states such as North Korea and Libya.

Though we all tried to catch up by replenishing our Rolodexes with the names of spooks, academics who specialised in proliferation issues and chemical, biological and nuclear weapons experts, these kinds of journalists were way out in front, since they had courted them for years. Security specialists with good contacts in the intelligence community were at a premium. So, too, were South Asian hands who knew their way around Afghanistan and Pakistan. Former Kabul correspondents, who had been neglected for more than a decade after the withdrawal of the Soviet Union, found themselves instantly rehabilitated and heading back to the Hindu Kush.

In this reordered hierarchy, Arabists vaulted to the top: correspondents who could pronounce, remember and link the names of terrorist suspects, and read for themselves the jihadist websites that fired their imaginations. Journalism had a new caste system, and previously obscure reporters rapidly found themselves in high demand. Washington had always tended to favour show ponies. Now, workhorses, with a methodical approach and unflashy prose, proved their worth.

This helps explain why, as the Bush administration prosecuted its case for regime change in Baghdad, so many journalists who lacked this kind of expertise came to rely so heavily on those who didn't. Of these, Judith Miller of the *New York Times* was the Brahmin among Brahmins – an obsessive reporter with razor-sharp elbows and a highly developed diva complex, who for years had been preoccupied with the destructive power of weapons of mass destruction. Now folkloric is the story of how she once invited her boyfriend to watch her swim laps at the pool of the Washington Hilton, and then pondered, as she stretched in the afternoon sun, which was the more destructive, chemical or nuclear weapons.

With attention shifting to Iraq, every news organisation craved its own Judith Miller. The Pulitzer Prize-winning article she had published eight months before the attacks, on the determination of al-Qaeda to equip itself with weapons of mass destruction, now seemed brilliantly prescient. So, too, did her book published that summer entitled *Germs: Biological Weapons and America's Secret War*, which by Christmas topped her paper's own bestseller list.

Thus, when a series of eye-catching reports on Saddam

Hussein's weapons of mass destruction programme appeared in late 2001 and throughout 2002 with Miller's byline attached, everyone took notice. Based on raw intelligence from the vice president's office, key Pentagon officials and their favourite Iraqi defector, Ahmed Chalabi, her stories warned that the Baghdad regime had taken delivery of a particularly virulent strain of smallpox, and that Saddam Hussein had started renovating his storage facilities for biological and chemical weapons.

More alarming still was the revelation that he sought to import the type of aluminium tubes that were essential components in the development of nuclear weapons. With the stories given pride of place in the top right-hand corner of the front page of the *New York Times*, the same fearful tone found an echo in everyone's follow-up stories. If the information had come from Miller and had the imprimatur of the *Times*, it must have the stamp of truth.

To this day, I think that one of the main reasons why journalists proved so malleable in the run-up to the war on Iraq was not because of the persuasive powers of the Bush administration but more down to the authority of the *New York Times*. When the two worked in tandem, they were an unstoppable combination.

To offer a word in our defence, it was not as if we had taken complete leave of our senses or were entirely unthinking or uninquiring. After all, our own sources validated much of Miller's reportage. Washington was heavily populated with former United Nations weapons inspectors proffering dire warnings of their own. Even French diplomats would quietly tell you, off the record and not for attribution, that they believed Saddam Hussein had built up a formidable stockpile of chemical weapons. Their disagreement with the Bush administration was not over the existence of weapons but in how to prevent their use. As for the Bush administration's most vocal critic, the former weapons inspector Scott Ritter, he appeared on the cable networks so frequently and at such a high volume that he tended to drown out his own message.

Among the ironies of American journalism in the run-up to Iraq was that this phase of suspended scepticism only began drawing to an end after the Bush administration delivered its most detailed presentation of the case against Saddam. When the US secretary of state Colin Powell went before the UN Security Council in February 2003, with the CIA director George Tenet sitting meaningfully behind, all of us expected an Adlai Stevenson moment: the dramatic, incontrovertible evidence that would register just as powerfully as the black-and-white aerial-reconnaissance pictures revealing the Soviet missile launchers on Cuba that the Americans had produced at the height of the missile crisis in October 1962.

Instead, the best that Powell could produce were a few PowerPoint graphics, some inconclusive satellite imagery and a mocked-up vial of anthrax that he dangled suggestively between his fingers. You could almost hear the collective cry of 'Is that it?' echo across the newsrooms of the capital.

However, even if the Powell speech helped restore a greater sense of journalistic balance, there was still widespread press support for the war. For many, the Bush administration's 'mushroom cloud' argument remained persuasive: why take the chance that Saddam might one day have a nuclear capability when his regime could be decapitated in a short sharp war?

With or without the press, with or without cast-iron evidence, and with or without an international 'coalition of the willing', the Bush administration was about to wage war against Saddam

Hussein, and blood was about to be spilt. That much had become clear during George W. Bush's State of the Union address in January 2002, when he declared that Iraq was part of an 'axis of evil' alongside North Korea and Iran. As part of our live coverage, I watched it from a radio studio alongside a former member of Bill Clinton's national security team, who physically recoiled when Bush delivered his 'axis of evil' line. This dovish foreign-policy expert was so startled and agitated it was almost as if he was watching the second plane hit the South Tower. He thought it the most belligerent speech he had ever heard a president deliver and feared it ran the risk of squandering all the international goodwill that had followed 9/11.

The prescience of these fears became immediately apparent when the press corps and I travelled with Bush in the months after the 'axis of evil' speech. Arriving in Seoul a few weeks later, we saw protesters gathered outside the military base where Air Force One touched down brandishing 'No Bush, No War' placards. In the capital itself, South Korean Government officials were privately seething that Bush had so publicly trashed the 'sunshine policy' of the then president Kim Dae-jung, which sought détente with Pyongyang.

Out of politeness to his hosts, Bush consciously decided not to repeat the phrase 'axis of evil' while on Korean soil – in the filing centre, we dubbed it the 'Don't Mention the Axis of Evil' tour. But we suspected he might not be able to bite his lip for the duration of the trip. Sure enough, early one morning we were all choppered in great hulking Chinooks to one of the American outposts in the demilitarised zone, the famed DMZ. There, the White House staged a photo opportunity, where Bush peered, Patton-like, through binoculars at the North Korean watchtowers in the hostile distance. As he stood on the ramparts, one of his US military guides recounted the story of a deadly attack on American GIs in the 1970s, and how the axes used in the killings now had pride of place in a 'peace museum' on the North Korean side of the DMZ. Bush relayed the harrowing story to reporters watching from below and then added, 'No wonder I think they're evil.'

With 37,000 US troops still stationed in South Korea, guaranteeing its security, US presidents could normally expect a grateful welcome in Seoul. Not Bush after his 'axis of evil' speech.

The same was true of a visit a few months later to Berlin, another bastion of the Cold War where successive US presidents suffering slumps in support at home had gone to boost their flagging morale. Here, the surname Bush also carried some weight, since after the fall of the Berlin Wall George Snr, the then president, had been welcomed like a liberator. Bush Jnr, however, was unable to tap into this reservoir of goodwill and was greeted instead by the now-familiar scene: thousands of protesters carrying placards such as 'We Don't Want Your War', 'Stop Bush's Global War' and 'Axis of Peace', and those life-size papier-mâché puppets of Bush, bobbing manically from side to side. Europeans may have temporarily become Americans in the immediate aftermath of 9/11, but not in the lead-up to Iraq.

Rather than prompting any great introspection, I suspect these visits merely reinforced the 'for us or against us' bunker mentality that had now taken grip in the Bush administration. They also confirmed the existence, as Donald Rumsfeld described it, of an Old Europe, which was instinctively antagonistic towards Washington, and a New Europe to the east of Berlin, which was much more closely aligned.

Lending grist to the Pentagon's mill, just about the only place where George W. Bush was guaranteed an enthusiastic welcome was in the former satellite states of the Soviet Union. Whereas in cities such as Berlin and Paris the president's image-makers rarely allowed him to step outside, in places such as Vilnius and Bucharest they encouraged him to take part in massive outdoor rallies.

His speech in the Romanian capital, opposite the communist headquarters where in 1989 Nicolae Ceaușescu had to be lifted off the roof by helicopter, lingers in the mind because I had never seen Bush greeted with such delirium, even before a crowd of Texan Republicans. Under driving rain, in the most horrid of conditions, tens of thousands had gathered in Revolution Square, waving postcard-sized Romanian and American flags and bobbing their umbrellas up and down in time to the music. Loudspeakers belted out Elvis Presley's 'A Little Less Conversation' – a rather neat musical summation, it could be argued, of the Bush doctrine.

Yet it was the president rather than the king that the crowd wanted to hear. 'Salut!' shouted Bush, after bouncing onto stage wearing a hefty bullet-proof jacket under his overcoat that seemed for once an unnecessary precaution. Addressing freedom-loving new friends, Bush had rarely been more fluent at the podium. To wild cheers, he noted that 'the people of Romania know that dictators must never be appeased or ignored. They must be opposed.' For a brief moment, rays of sunlight breached the charcoal skies and a rainbow started to form. Noticing the change in the weather, Bush interpreted it as a sign from the heavens: 'God is smiling on us today.' Rarely in any doubt about the righteousness of his cause, he firmly believed it to be true. New Europe got it, I dare say he left thinking. Old Europe most definitely did not.

The Old European exception, of course, was Tony Blair.

From the moment at the Crawford ranch in April 2002 when he first signed up for the Iraq war, Blair became the American president's most useful ally. With an eloquence and coherence that eluded Bush, Blair built the case against Saddam Hussein with far greater intellectual and moral force. It helped shore up not only international support at the United Nations but also Democratic support in Congress. Blair helped provide Bush with diplomatic and political cover, even if it earned him the scorn of much of the British public, along with the sobriquet 'Bush's poodle'.

Another eloquent English progressive, accused by his friends and former comrades of lurching precipitously to the right, lent his voice as well. As he laid out the case against Saddam Hussein, Christopher Hitchens became a frequent visitor to our bureau, as he had been during the impeachment saga – although this time he appeared significantly more sober. With a bronze bust of Sir Winston Churchill sitting, shrine-like, in the Oval Office and Tony Blair regularly flying in from London, Englishmen had never received a warmer welcome in Washington.

This was more than could be said for the French – or the 'cheese-eating surrender-monkeys', as the New York tabloids took to calling them, or the founding member of the 'axis of weasels'. I, like everyone else who used the government cafeteria on Capitol Hill, found myself eating newly renamed Freedom Fries. So, too, did the reporters aboard Air Force One, where French toast was banished as well. French wine was poured down drains, while a newspaper suggested that couples refrain from French kissing and opt for a 'liberty lip lock' instead. Even the wonderful little Parisian-style street café opposite where I lived in Georgetown came under fire for insisting still on flying the red, white and blue of the *drapeau tricolore*. The butcher up the road hit back with the war-on-terror trifecta of Old Glory, the Union Flag and the Australian colours, in appreciation of Australian Prime Minister John Howard's rock-steady support.

If the sight of French red wine being poured down drains provided the pictures for our most frivolous 'waiting for war' stories, then a trip to Dover Air Base in Delaware was by far the most grave. It was the home of the US military's largest mortuary and a base that had forced its way into the American consciousness during Vietnam because of the sight on the evening news night after night of so many flag-draped coffins being flown back from South East Asia. The 'Dover test' remained something of a yardstick, a gauge of how many American casualties the public would countenance, and thus of a given conflict's political acceptability.

In the early 1990s, the filming of the return of caskets had been banned precisely for that reason, the thinking presumably being that the American public had become a lot more squeamish. Even though that ban remained in place, the Pentagon agreed to show us the base's upgraded facilities. A determinedly on-message officer from the base's press team took us to the medical facilities available to casualties returning from the front and to the military-tailor shop. Its only task was to fashion ceremonial uniforms for the returning dead, and it boasted a complete collection of ribbonry, braiding, enamel badges and insignia from every US regiment and branch of the military.

Morbid though it sounds, what we really wanted to see was the mortuary, the section of the base where cameras were prohibited and which thus had the most news value. While his boss briefly stepped away, a determinedly off-message Pentagon PR flack sneaked us into the mortuary, where the gurneys were already lined up in readiness for the first fatalities from Iraq. In those days, subversive military press officers were thin on the ground, but we were fortunate to be in the hands of one in the ten minutes or so that we had to film. In short time, he had handed us a rather macabre scoop.

War eventually came with the much previewed 'shock and awe' of the first night-time assault on Baghdad. Like virtually everyone else in Washington, including the president himself, we watched it unfold on cable television. From the safety of the bureau, we admired the courage of our team that had chosen to remain at the Palestine Hotel in the Iraqi capital – most US networks had by this time evacuated – and envied the reporters embedded with the US and British troops, who we suspected would be joining them in a liberated Baghdad within the month.

With the diplomatic manoeuvrings over, and the action unfolding on the ground, suits correspondents plummeted down the running order again, leaving boots correspondents with the lead. From 9.34 pm on 20 March 2003, when the war started, to when the statue of Saddam Hussein was hauled down in Firdos Square by a US Marines recovery vehicle – footage shown every 7.5 minutes on CNN and every 4.4 minutes on Fox, which suggested that American forces now controlled central Baghdad but were still a long way from winning the war – we felt like spectators.

During this time, I can recall leaving Washington only once. I was dispatched to Palestine, West Virginia, a hamlet nestled in the Appalachians that was the home of Private Jessica Lynch, the war's most unlikely star. Awoken before dawn by London and told to get to West Virginia to file in time for the evening news – lunchtime US time – I thought the details of the story seemed just too good to be true.

Private Lynch, the 19-year-old member of a US Army

ordnance maintenance company, had been part of a convoy that had taken a wrong turn in Nasiriyah and had ended up being ambushed by the Iraqi fedayeen. In the firefight that followed, nine of her colleagues were killed. Over a week later, the Americans had learnt that she was still alive and being treated at the general hospital in Nasiriyah. Grasping the propaganda value of a dramatic rescue, the Pentagon mounted a full-blown raid on the hospital, spearheaded by Navy Seals and US Rangers, even though intelligence reports made it clear the Iraqi Army and fedayeen had fled the day before.

The mission, punctuated as it was by shouts of 'go, go, go' from the rescue team and filmed in the jerky, handheld style of a Jason Bourne movie, made for enthralling television, which was precisely the intention. From its purpose-built, multi-million-dollar media centre in Doha, the Pentagon released an edited version of the luminous green night-time video along with a still photograph of Jessica on a stretcher clutching an American flag that had been handed to her by a soldier.

Needing both a hero and a good-news story at a time in the war when the Pentagon was facing questions about the sluggish pace of its advance, young Jessica had become the perfect muse. To further embroider the story, the Pentagon turned the diminutive former supply clerk into some kind of Rambo. According to leaks handed to selected reporters, she had fought to near death and been stabbed and shot 'multiple times'.

'Saving Private Lynch', as the rescue was inexorably dubbed, certainly had cinematic potential. Alas, it had a counterfeit plot. Though held captive initially by Iraqi soldiers, she was later cared for at the hospital by local doctors, who protected her from government agents and had offered up their own blood for transfusion because of a chronic shortage of supplies. The doctors had even arranged to deliver Jessica by ambulance to the Americans.

By the time we got to Palestine – a community festooned in yellow ribbon – the usual armada of satellite trucks already filled the paddock outside the tin-roofed cottage where the Lynch family had kept vigil. The enamel-lapel-badge brigade was also doing its thing, turning a shy teenager into an icon. Arriving with less than an hour to go before the evening news in Britain, we just about managed to get a report to air that was dispatched, I would like to think, with the necessary dose of scepticism. However, I came away from Palestine the next day thinking myself the world's worst journalist.

That morning, the *New York Times* published a quite superb colour piece from Palestine, packed with local characters and atmospherics, most of which I had completely missed. In my defence, our deadlines had been even more testing than usual, and there had not been much time to survey the scene adequately. But I had always prided myself on being something of a 'colour man' and felt awful that the *Times* had done such a better job at capturing the mood.

It was only the following month, when the newspaper published a front-page, 7000-word article chronicling the writer's deceptions, that I realised why. The author of that report had been Jayson Blair, a serial fabricator and plagiariser, who wrote much of his copy from his apartment in New York in a cocaine-fuelled haze. On this story, like many others, he had not even left Manhattan Island. I mention it now to highlight the hazards of reporting during this disorientating phase. Not only did we have to sift through the Bush administration's spin, obfuscation and misinformation, but also we could no longer rely on our usual bedrock, the *New York Times*.

By the end of the war, our professional scepticism and cynicism started to reassert itself. On the day of Baghdad's 'liberation', we suggested from our rooftop vantage point that running Saddam out of town had been the easy bit and that far greater challenges lay ahead.

When museums and businesses in Baghdad started being ransacked under the idle gaze of US forces, we were quick to jump on Donald Rumsfeld's famed 'Stuff happens' line. Then came Bush's *Top Gun* moment, when, dressed in a shimmering olive jumpsuit, the president flew in for a tail-hook landing on the deck of an aircraft carrier ordered to anchor off the coast of California.

'Militainment,' someone said of a photo opportunity that screamed conquering commander-in-chief. And what of *that* banner: 'MISSION ACCOMPLISHED'? To celebrate what Bush had described as the end of major combat operations in Iraq, the press was invited to a hoedown in the central courtyard of the Pentagon, a tree-dotted paved area long known as 'Ground Zero' because it was thought to top the Soviet Union's ballistic target list. Amidst a mood of demob happiness, a country and western band serenaded the military top brass, which toasted its success with lemonade in the late-afternoon sunshine.

In my piece to camera, delivered front of the stage and to disapproving glances, I asked how the Bush administration could claim bragging rights when Saddam Hussein remained at large and not a single weapon of mass destruction had yet been located. Perhaps for the first time since 9/11, I felt like a fully functioning journalist and that my faculties had been restored. After the fall of Baghdad, there was a sense that we had been liberated as well.

Looking back, what I should have done immediately after

the Iraq war was to head straight for Baghdad. Instead, the weekend after the toppling of Saddam's statue I boarded a plane to Augusta, Georgia, for the US Masters. A feminist group calling itself the Pink Ladies planned to picket the tournament in protest at the refusal of a golf club where all the holes were named after flowers to admit women as members. It was an inconsequential story, a real 'And finally' number tagged onto the end of the sports bulletin. But that was the point. After the war and its elongated build-up, this was my own kind of exit strategy.

Shamefully, I never did make it to Iraq, and to this day it remains the biggest lacuna on my résumé. Perhaps it was sheer spinelessness that kept me from going, although I would like to think it had more to do with the difficulties and frustrations of reporting post-war Iraq. So violent was the insurgency, and so strong was the risk of kidnapping and beheading, that our news teams found it hard to venture out beyond the front door of our heavily protected Baghdad bureau. Most of all, I suspect, it was simple mental fatigue. As with that trip to Augusta, Georgia, I needed a holiday from post-9/11 news.

—

From that first moment of semi-consciousness and semi-understanding in Seattle to the time more than two years later that I boarded a plane at Dulles International Airport at the end of my posting in Washington, virtually everything came to be viewed through the lens of the war on terror.

My lasting recollection from a drop-everything-and-go dash to Chicago was that we ended up kipping down for the night in what had once been Hugh Hefner's hotel suite, which partly compensated for the Saturday night on the eve of the Democratic national convention when I turned down the Playboy Mansion invite. But the reason we had rushed there was to cover the arrest of an al-Qaeda suspect accused of plotting a dirty-bomb attack.

Even after the second shuttle disaster, when the *Columbia* disintegrated high above Texas on 1 February 2003 on its approach to Cape Canaveral, the Department of Homeland Security had to play down fears of sabotage by terrorists. The shuttle had exploded over Palestine, Texas, and carried its first-ever Israeli astronaut. People jumped to conclusions. Ground Zero itself remained the source of an endless torrent of stories. There was the ongoing controversy over what should fill the gaping hole left in Lower Manhattan, and the bitter disputes over how victim-compensation payments should be dispensed. The last two involved large sums of money and large numbers of lawyers – an unmistakable sign that America was on the mend.

To start with at least, we suspected that the Washington sniper attacks could be the work of jihadists. Certainly, they brought terror back to the capital. During the 23 days in October 2002 that the killings continued, almost everyone in Washington imagined themselves framed in the crosshairs of a marksman's rifle. As I walked to and from work at a much hastier pace than normal, and relied much more heavily on cabs, I knew I did.

A man mowing his lawn. A woman vacuuming her Dodge caravan. A 55-year-old government bureaucrat picking up groceries at Shoppers Food Warehouse. An FBI intelligence analyst outside Home Depot. A boy, just 13 years of age, arriving at middle school. A bus driver at the end of his morning run. The simple fact that the sniper struck in such banal suburban locations made the attacks all the more terrifying. The Tarot death cards left at the murder scenes, with macabre messages such as 'Call me God' and 'Your children are not safe, anywhere, at any time', also made them surreal. Stranger still was the coded dialogue used by the police to communicate with the sniper, one side of which played out on television as the officer leading the investigation addressed the murderer through the media.

A barrel-chested African-American with a trance-like stare, Chief Charles Moose, could hardly have been better cast, and even his name seemed fictionalised. 'You have indicated that you want us to say and do certain things,' said Moose at a particularly mystifying news conference. 'You have asked us to say "We have caught the sniper like a duck in the noose."' The story defied analogy, and London could not get enough of it.

For three weeks, we chased the sniper from one suburban murder scene to the next. One night, we even caught up with him, after checking into a cheap motel over the road from the scene of his latest killing, a Ponderosa Steakhouse just north of Richmond, Virginia. Kicking back with a beer on the walkway outside our rooms after filing our report over to London, we toasted our luck at staying in what must have been the safest place in the entire metropolitan area.

Afterwards, however, we discovered that the sniper had checked into the very same motel. His car, a blue 1990 Chevrolet Caprice with a boot adapted into a makeshift sniper's perch, was parked outside. As stakeholders in this story, we were all relieved and delighted when John Allen Muhammad and his 17-year-old accomplice, Lee Boyd Malvo, were arrested.

As we learnt more of their biographies, the circumstantial evidence suggested that Muhammad had launched a one-man jihad. A member of the Nation of Islam, who had changed his name to Muhammad a month after 9/11, he had purchased his blue Chevrolet on the first anniversary of the attacks and openly expressed admiration for Osama bin Laden. Prosecutors, however, preferred the theory that he had intended eventually to murder his wife, and that the killings were designed to make her death look random.

A week after his arrest, the *New York Times* carried a riveting piece about the interrogation of Muhammad, which suggested that he was about to explain 'the roots of his anger'. But just as he was about to reveal all, the Feds came barging into the interview room on the orders of the Justice Department and the White House, thus halting him in his tracks. Alas, the story was complete fiction. Another Jayson Blair special.

Beyond the Beltway, the most fun that I had in those final months came covering the New York blackout, which became both a testament to how firmly bin Laden had imprinted himself on the American mind and how quickly New Yorkers wanted to erase him from their thoughts. The lights went out as we were filming in the chamber of the United Nations Security Council and coincided with the precise moment that my cameraman, Chuck, bent down to plug his Klieg lights into a power socket behind the famous horseshoe conference table.

Initially, we thought we were about to be the cause of some diplomatic incident, but a UN security guard wandered into the darkness to announce that the lights in the entire building were out. In the super-slow-motion way that these events tend to unfold, we all looked down at our mobile phones and saw that they had no service. Our immediate, unspoken reaction was 'here we go again'. Then the Manhattan human telegraph cranked into action, and we realised that the lights were out all over New York. The fear everywhere was of another 9/11, that al-Qaeda was in the process of launching another attack on America's eastern seaboard.

What followed, however, was a carnival. As soon as word spread that the blackout was the result of nothing more sinister than a decrepit, third-world power grid, New Yorkers reverted to type. In merry defiance of the city's bylaws, they held impromptu drinking parties on the sidewalks. With all the lights out, and the roads jammed with rush-hour traffic, many New Yorkers anointed themselves as traffic cops and leapt into the streets to help relieve the gridlock. In a city with an eye for the theatrical, the more exuberant the volunteer the more quickly they moved the traffic. Close to Central Park, Chuck and I ran into a balding Italian-American who was orchestrating the cars and trucks with the operatic exuberance of a conductor reaching the finale of *Turandot* at the Met.

'You look like you've done this before,' I ventured.

'Well, I play a cop on TV,' he shot back, as, with a snap of his wrist, he unleashed his white flag into the air. I should have recognised him. It was Matt Servitto, or, as he was better known, Special Agent Dwight Harris from *The Sopranos*.

As I prepared to leave Washington, and to swap suits for boots in South Asia, I filed my wistful 'how America has been transformed' farewell despatches and pretty much followed the well-trod analytical path that the country had been overtaken in an instant by massive and irreversible change. Reshaped and distorted forever, from the erosion of civil liberties to the delays and irritations at airports, from the pervasive sense of gloom that America's best days were yesterdays to the fear that hope would never fully reassert itself, the country seemed mired in a sloth of anxiety and negativity.

While all that was true, I should have reflected more on the extent to which the country remained unaltered, how *little* it had changed. For a long time, one of the central tenets of new normalcy theory was that Washington and New York would come under intermittent, possibly even regular, attack. So, too, cities such as Los Angeles and Chicago. They would be targeted with an ever more sophisticated menu of terrorist weaponry and suffer even greater loss of life. The detonation of a dirty bomb, packed with radioactive material, was seemingly impending. However, for all the warnings about a home-grown terror threat and the potential disloyalty of young male American Muslims, there has been no American jihad. If anything, the US has actually come to be seen as a model of assimilation, which Britain and other countries have sought to copy.

Americans have been asked to put up with mildly annoying workaday inconveniences, but no great sacrifices have been demanded of them. Even though the country simultaneously fought two wars, in Iraq and Afghanistan, placing huge manpower demands on the US military, there was never any serious debate about conscription. 'Ask not what your country can do for you, but what you can do for your country' was an idea from the Cold War that was not refurbished for the Bush administration's war on terror. Instead, its domestic agenda was marked by giveaways, in the form of huge tax cuts and prescription drugs for the elderly. Materially, Americans pretty much went on as before. Indeed, they were encouraged to do so: to shop, to dine out, to take to the skies again. In other words, to keep the economy from stalling.

After 9/11, it would have seemed ridiculous, fantastical even, to suggest that historians and my successors in Washington would one day debate whether the collapse of a bank, Lehman Brothers, on 15 September 2008, had more impact on the American way of life than the destruction of the World Trade Center. Nonetheless, the question of whether the sub-prime-mortgage crisis represented a more serious risk than al-Qaeda to everyday Americans, and more of an impediment to their dreams, is far from settled.

The reason, of course, is simple: much more so than the global war on terror, the global financial crisis affected Americans' purchasing power – the bottom line. All this is not to minimise the effect of 9/11, nor to deny that the changes afterwards were profound. However, 9/11 was not nearly as transformative as we forewarned at the time. Quick though we were to plumb the darker recesses of our imaginations, and to talk in apocalyptic terms, the new normalcy is nowhere near as bad as we predicted.

Everyone has a 'New York returns to normal' story. Mine had actually come in the run-up to Christmas in 2001, when I got off the train from Washington and started walking to my nearby hotel. It was the thick of rush hour. Commuters were shoulder-barging through the sidewalks on their way to Penn Station, and at the kerbside a trumpeter stood with an open instrument case at his feet, blasting out a few raspy melodies. Struggling to both hold a tune and make a dime, he was absolutely useless. Unable to put up with his busking any longer, a female passer-by, with a voice as penetrative as his bugle, stormed up, stood directly in front of him and launched into a baseball-style face-to-face tirade. 'Just shut the fuck up!' she blasted. 'JUST SHUT THE FUCK UP!' That, I suspect, came as music to most New Yorkers' ears. I know it did to mine.

Chapter 6

Afghanistan: America's Forgotten War

With her mournful green eyes and bewitching stare, Kamila had the kind of ravaged beauty common in Afghan children, and a face that could easily have been staring out from the cover of *National Geographic*. Wearing a crimson dress embroidered with shimmering green thread, she had spent the afternoon chasing a herd of goats high in the mountains near to the border with Waziristan, but she had made the mistake of darting from the pathway in an area littered with anti-personnel landmines, the deadly detritus of 20 years of almost continual war.

Her right foot landed on a mine with sufficient force to detonate its hidden explosive charge. Shrapnel ripped upwards, tearing off part of her foot, maiming rather than killing instantly – which was precisely what its designers had intended. Kamila was now losing so much blood at such a rapid pace that she was struggling to cling to life.

When first we encountered her, she was cradled in the arms of a beefy US Special Forces soldier with a scraggy black beard, wraparound shades and weaponry strapped to his torso and legs, who carried her as if she were his own daughter. Just a short while earlier, he had rescued her from the mountains and tried to staunch the flow of blood. Among the US military's most highly trained warriors, he was stationed in the forbidding border region as part of the hunt for Osama bin Laden. Here, though, he relied on one of his more elemental skills: basic battlefield first aid to try to save a young girl's life.

Now, he gently loaded her into the belly of a Black Hawk medivac helicopter, one of the army's ambulances of the skies. In a region where the fight against the Taliban and al-Qaeda was at its fiercest, Kamila's brother worked as a translator for the Americans and had managed to summon help quickly. Yet even though the Black Hawk had taken only 20 minutes to arrive, the medics crouching over her disfigured body feared they had not reached her in time. Already, she had lost a third of her blood, and the bandages wrapped around her mutilated foot were almost completely saturated. Kamila was so listless that medics struggled to detect a pulse. With an oxygen mask covering much of her small face, her eyes blinked slowly as she drifted in and out of consciousness.

On arrival at an American forward operating base to the north, she was borne by stretcher from the helicopter and rushed into a field hospital, where the Stars and Stripes was draped over the operating table. Kamila was sedated, pumped with more oxygen and given an urgent blood transfusion. A US military doctor examined her mangled foot and made an immediate diagnosis. 'Just prep from above the knee,' he said matter-of-factly, knowing that her foot and lower leg could not be saved. She was given anaesthetic, and the medical team prepared for an amputation. With Kamila now fast asleep, the doctor took out an electric saw, pressed its jagged stainless-steel blade against her bloody flesh and began cutting at the skin. The noise was indescribable, and when later we sent over our television report to London the editors found it so disturbing that they asked us to reduce the volume by more than two-thirds. Even then, it was excruciating.

When she came round after the operation, the medics told Kamila that she would have to confront life without her right foot. Fighting back tears, she replied that she was an orphan who had no friends and that her only fun in life came from chasing mountain goats. Thought to be just eight years old – she wasn't sure of her birthday – at least she was still alive. Had Kamila been taken to the nearest hospital, on the Pakistan side of the border, the journey through the mountain passes would have taken more than eight hours. Without doubt, she would have died en route.

Over decades of conflict, landmines killed or injured 70,000 Afghans, and around 30 per cent of the victims were children. Red-painted stones, barbed-wire fences and hazard signs marked with the skull and crossbones served as warnings, but each month some 60 people continued to be killed or maimed by landmines or unexploded ordnance. For the next 12 hours or so – the time it would take until another Afghan was maimed or killed – Kamila was the latest.

Two days later, Kamila's doctors carried out a second amputation, this time folding over the remaining muscle in the hope of forming a 'nice stump', as the surgeon described it, which would accept a prosthesis. In six months' time, he reckoned, she might be able to get an artificial leg – a lengthy process of fittings, consultations and rehabilitation, which, alarmingly, one in eight Afghan families have experienced.

The final time we saw Kamila was at a dilapidated hospital in Khost, the regional capital, where she was lying on a filthy bed in a dank, windowless room, wearing a bright-orange dress patterned with pink and white flowers. Towering over her was a barrel-chested Afghan doctor with a booming voice and a thick black beard. 'Do you feel any pain in your legs?' he bellowed.

'No,' came her fragile reply.

'Your leg is injured but you will be able to walk soon,' he said blithely. 'Then you can go to school and look forward to the future.'

Kamila looked mystified. Then she tried to sleep.

—

Floor by floor, the Kabul Intercontinental was being renovated, and although the swimming pool was still a turgid green pea-souper, most of the heaters now came with three-pinned plugs and the room interiors had the kind of bland furnishings you would expect to find in a Travelodge on the outskirts of Luton – a dubious sign of progress. More persuasive as a selling point was the simple fact that the hotel had not come under fire from the Taliban for the past 18 months.

If anything, the omelette chef at breakfast, an elderly man with a claret tunic and inscrutable smile, posed a more serious threat to the well-being of guests. Perhaps unfairly, I blamed him for the most violent bout of food poisoning I had ever suffered, one that caused me almost to vomit mid-question during an interview with a Tajik warlord, and which to this day continues to trouble my lower intestine. Whenever I see an omelette chef, I do the Continental.

Whereas the Intercontinental remained the residence of choice for visiting correspondents, other establishments had opened their doors to guests. Foremost among them was Afghan Garden One, which was billed as Kabul's first boutique hotel. It had velvet cushions, soft, peachy lighting, four-poster beds in the rooms, and bathrooms decorated in turquoise mosaic glass tiles trucked in from Herat, which would not have seemed out of place in an interior-design store in Fulham but looked absurdly incongruous *in situ*. Whatever, this ethnic chic had appeal for the more bohemian reporters who considered themselves a cut above the khaki multi-pocket-jacket brigade.

In the race to become Kabul's first boutique establishment, Afghan Garden One had just managed to edge out a rival guest house set up by an Afghan-American from Las Vegas. Denied first-boutique status, it marketed itself instead as the only hotel in Kabul with a pool in the shape of a Martini glass. Occasionally, we stayed at the BBC house that could also boast a swimming pool in the back garden, though it was shaped like a kidney and nobody could recall when they had last seen it filled with water. Among its many home comforts was a cook who prepared *kafta* (meatballs), *badenjah* (aubergine) and braised lamb shanks, but whose crowd-pleasing signature dish combined fried slenderly cut potatoes, tandoor-baked Afghan bread and dripping butter: the Kabul chip butty.

Even if the opening of the first branch of Afghan Fried Chicken suggested otherwise, the food all over the capital was vastly improved. There was a decent Thai restaurant, Lai Thai, which had been opened by a Bangkok-born woman who specialised in post-conflict eateries in hotspots such as Kosovo, Cambodia, East Timor and Rwanda. Preferring to operate in cities where there was little in the way of competition – her only venture in a peaceable country, Australia, ended in failure – she was already eyeing up Baghdad.

A French restaurant, Le Bistro, was another welcome addition, which served hearty food, a decent bottle of red and even staged the occasional art exhibition in its walled garden. Still, the night that my coq au vin arrived accompanied by a rock hurled over the wall from the adjoining street was the last time I dined there. Thinking that the next time it could just as easily be a grenade or home-made bomb, we decided to eat elsewhere.

For late-night drinks, Kabul could also boast a Manhattan-style cocktail bar and an Irish pub, but we steered clear of both. Not only were they a prime target for the Taliban but also they attracted American mercenaries from the US-based security firm DynCorp International, who were not renowned for their conviviality.

Once wrecked by fighting, now concrete blast walls, coils of razor wire, gun emplacements and stained sandbags around every major building disfigured the Afghan capital. Visits to the presidential palace, the Arg, for press conferences or interviews with Hamid Karzai would take hours, if only to negotiate the multiple tiers of security that lay between its outermost entrance and his office overlooking the central courtyard. Here, it was impossible to avoid the boneheads from DynCorp, who were trained to treat each visitor like a potential killer and made sure everyone felt like one. After being frisked, barked at and frogmarched, like fresh recruits at boot camp, even the most mild-mannered reporter could end up with the most murderous of intentions. Journalists were often so hostile towards Karzai, I came to think, because DynCorp had been so hostile towards them. The security consultants turned them into character assassins.

Almost everywhere in Kabul, the mood was darkening. Chicken Street, the once trendy stopping-off point on the hippy trail from Europe to India, had fallen into disrepute. Other than off-duty soldiers, its shops were largely empty of customers, though they were stocked still with antique muskets, knives with ivory handles, onyx chessboards, lapis-lazuli bracelets and magnificent Afghan coats, which made perfect sleeping bags. Soviet-era kitsch, such as Red Army medals, discarded bullet casings and winter ushankas, now vied for shelf space with 9/11-era kitsch. A favourite among US servicemen were Afghan rugs embroidered with the slogan 'George W. Bush Operation Enduring Freedom'.

The bookshop on Chicken Street now stocked cheap rip-offs of books on Afghanistan that had become instant global bestsellers: Åsne Seierstad's *The Bookseller of Kabul*; Khaled Hosseini's *The Kite Runner*; Yasmina Khadra's *The Swallows of Kabul*. Much of the foreign-correspondent corps found them hard to read with complete satisfaction. This was partly out of intense professional jealousy that the authors had enjoyed such literary and commercial success, but also because their own adventures occasionally threw up real-life stories that were just as extraordinary.

In hunting down these stories, I worked alongside the BBC's finest. Nik, my Australian cameraman, who grew up on a sheep farm near Albany, had not only worked in virtually all of the world's trouble spots – Bosnia, Sierra Leone, the first Gulf War, Kosovo – but also done so with marvellous distinction. Six foot six inches tall, he was something of a human tripod, and he could pull off shots that were beyond most cameramen, both physically and creatively. Starting from ground level and extending to his maximum height, Nik made it look like we had hired a cherry-picker. Not only was he the most technically gifted cameraman with whom I worked but he was also the best read. For my money, the BBC had no finer news cameraman, which arguably made him the best in the world. Certainly in South Asia, his work was the gold standard.

Vivek, my roving Indian producer, was wired very differently, but again quite exceptional at his job. Whereas Nik's towering height was usually enough to bend people to his will, Vivek would gently charm, cajole and tickle. Like Nik, he thought in pictures, and he not only knew how to track down stories but he also grasped immediately how best they could be brought to life. Like most upwardly mobile Indians of his generation, he seemed to absorb new technology and was also especially good at tracking down the finest local cuisine, whether it was momos in Kathmandu, the biryani in Lucknow, or Bengali fish curry in his home town of Calcutta.

Finally, there was our fabulously gruff South Asian bureau editor Paul, a journalist fiercely protective of those who worked under him. In Afghanistan and elsewhere in South Asia, I lost count of the times that politicians or diplomats complained about our coverage, but Paul's first impulse always was to return fire – at that time an unfashionable approach in the BBC, which was prone more to self-flagellation. A veteran of the Iraq war, who ran our Baghdad operation throughout the conflict, he was not only brave but also exceptionally good at finding ways of broadcasting from the most unpromising of situations, whether they be war or disaster zones. Again, I reckon he was the best in the business.

Kabul was normally the stepping-off point for our assignments, and the American military media-liaison office in the embassy precinct served as a kind of concierge service. It was here that we signed up for embeds with the US military. These excursions came with varying degrees of difficulty and danger, and granted access, pretty much, to all but the most secret of missions. Our aim always was to get as close to the tip of the spear as possible, and although it denied access to the Special Forces units hunting bin Laden, the Pentagon usually accommodated virtually every other request. The embed guidelines of US Central Command were very clear on this point. 'Commanders will ensure the media are provided with every opportunity to observe actual combat operations,' they noted. 'The personal safety of correspondents is not a reason to exclude them from combat areas.'

After making our bookings at the military-liaison office, and filling out the necessary disclaimers, we would drive out of the capital to Bagram Air Base, the Americans' main base in Afghanistan and also its busiest transportation hub. Bagram is to war nerds what Clapham Junction is to trainspotters, and the airfield was a constantly shifting swarm of warplanes: C-130 Hercules, which provided much of the Pentagon's rapid airlift capability; A-10 Thunderbolts, or Warthogs, with engines mounted on either side at the rear and noses customised with shark's teeth; Chinooks and Black Hawks, which ferried troops to the front; Apache attack helicopters, war machines with a chain gun configured to track the movements of the pilot or gunner's head.

Usually, we would be billeted in dormitories for a night or so, until space opened up on an aircraft carrying soldiers to the further reaches of the combat zone. Then we would wait in what looked and functioned like a commercial departure lounge, with vending machines packed with Mountain Dew, rows of cushioned chrome seats and banks of plasma screens tuned to the American Forces Network, a round-the-clock melange of 'touch of home' programming that included Hollywood action movies, NFL football, major-league baseball, and bulletins from Fox News and other US networks that were not so slavishly loyal.

The Pentagon produced its own five-minute daily in-house newscast called 'Freedom Watch Afghanistan', which was uniformly upbeat in tone, along with a batch of morbid advertisements warning soldiers about the hazards of smoking and letting their car insurance expire – lesser apprehensions, one would have thought, for men and women about to confront the Taliban.

In the lottery of seat allocation, first prize was to hitch a ride with a four-star general, since it meant zipping over the mountains and terraced canyons in speedy Black Hawks. The runners-up flew on Chinooks or military-transport planes, which belched out plumes of ballooning chaff as they flew out of Bagram to thwart attacks from the ground. Then, as Kabul disappeared into the distance, we prepared ourselves mentally for the conflict down below.

—

The last time the Afghan Government had tried to establish a foothold in the Bermel Valley, a lawless expanse of terrain adjacent to the Pakistan border, the local police chief had his head hacked off by the Taliban. Now, as it tried again midway through 2005, the newly hoisted Afghan flag shared the same airspace as an American B-52 bomber that flew in a sweeping arc high in the cloudless sky, and a tank-busting A-10 Thunderbolt ground-attack plane that screamed past not much above ground level, with an underbelly packed full of weaponry.

In recent weeks, the Americans had established a remote outpost, a scruffy bastion surrounded by blast walls and gun emplacements, strewn with tents and metal containers that doubled as toilet blocks and barracks. With Old Glory fluttering over the battlements, the Americans preferred to liken them to cavalry forts from the Wild West, but they looked more like gang redoubts from some dystopian fantasy – a kind of Pashtun *Mad Max*. In a boast that doubled as a warning, the local US commanders told us they inhabited the most dangerous corner of the country. But that was the point. They were 'bringing the battle to the front door of insurgents'.

It was midsummer, at the height of the Afghan fighting season, and we had been flown into the Bermel Valley to view a coming-out ceremony of sorts. The latest batch of newly trained regulars from the Afghan National Army was about to be deployed and had been handed the unenviable introductory mission of patrolling the Bermel Valley. Baptisms rarely come with more fire, and that week Afghanistan was even more volatile than normal. Reports had come from Guantanamo Bay, first published in *Newsweek* and later retracted, that US interrogators had flushed a copy of the Koran down the toilet. Across Afghanistan, anti-American demonstrations broke loose with a scalding fury, the most angry since the fall of the Taliban in late 2001. Jalalabad was already aflame, and at least 17 people had been killed in rioting nationwide.

For the US commanders on the ground in the Bermel Valley, the reports from Gitmo could hardly have been more ill-timed. During weeks of negotiations with local Pashtun elders, they had offered the usual carrots of new roads and schools. However, in a region of continually switching tribal allegiances, it was the stick that normally held sway: did the tribesmen want to side with the coalition forces against the Taliban or risk America's wrath? Confronted with so stark a choice, and with so much US firepower, local chiefs had agreed to line up behind the Kabul government. The question that morning was whether the pact would survive the wave of anti-Americanism sweeping the country.

The answer came outside the gates of the American base in a colourful welcome ceremony for the newly commissioned Afghan troops. As the warthog completed another howling fly-past, elders sat cross-legged on the stony ground in their finest *longis* – lavish turbans fashioned out of shimmering gold and silver fabric. To the clatter of drums, young men with wispy beards performed dance moves that were swirling and seductive, a long-time favourite of Pashtun tribesmen. There was also something deliciously camp about the Afghan soldiers, clasping their US-made weapons diagonally across their chests and running, frenetically, on the spot to the same fast-paced drumbeat, as if performing the show-stopper in a Berlin cabaret.

The brief ceremony over, we jumped aboard a convoy of Humvees and edged into the centre of town, where hundreds more tribesmen had congregated in the bazaar. Given the anger unleashed by the Koran-desecration allegations, the mood was harder to predict, and the fear was that they might lash out against the blasphemy. To calm the crowd, the US commanders had the good sense to allow a State Department official to speak first, and the man from Foggy Bottom rose magnificently to the challenge.

Wearing his own golden turban, made up of enough material to cover a tennis court, he gestured towards his white beard, which he said attested to his age if not his wisdom – a line that, when relayed by his translator, got a gentle ripple of laughter. A promising start.

Emboldened, he then waged a war for hearts and minds with disarming honesty. The reports from Gitmo may be true, he admitted. He simply had no way of knowing. But this was not how America should be judged, nor its mission in Afghanistan. It was not a religious crusade. 'If there was a Koran on this stand today, and the devil came to set fire to it,' he shouted, 'I would throw my own body on the Koran to protect it from the devil's fire.' Then, in an even louder voice, like a Pentecostalist preacher reaching the climax of his sermon, he exhorted, 'With my last drop of blood, I would stop this thing from happening.'

The elders looked stunned but impressed nonetheless by this bravura performance. In the most unpromising of situations, where the fury of Muslims could easily have been expressed violently, he had somehow turned a negative into an undoubted positive.

Then, as the convoy moved further up into the valley, he delivered, word for word, an identical speech with the same show-stopping panache. With representatives of this calibre, America at least stood a chance. Alas, our State Department whitebeard was on his last tour of duty and just on the verge of retirement.

This small episode showed how the unrivalled masters of mechanised and computerised warfare had started to become much more adept at counter-insurgency strategies. A greater number of patrols were conducted on foot, with Afghan translators always in attendance. The cannier commanders had come to appreciate the benefits of getting out of their Humvees, sitting down with tribal elders and doing something as banal as sharing some freshly brewed tea. Even the grunts could now greet locals with a cheery *As-Salamu'Alaykum.*

The incursion into the Bermel Valley also attested to the benefits of the Pentagon working in tandem with the State Department. Back in Washington, where institutional rivalries and an ongoing feud between Donald Rumsfeld and Colin Powell had bedevilled the reconstruction effort in Afghanistan and completely hobbled it in Iraq, this was still not happening.

As opposed to their uniformed cohorts, State Department

officials had the advantage of often being older, wiser, and more emotionally intelligent and culturally sensitive. By definition, they were more diplomatic, and they grasped the value in projecting American soft power rather than its armour-plated alternative. Though marginalised still in Washington, they were becoming increasingly central players on the ground in Afghanistan.

Also striking in these far-flung corners was the extent to which local US military commanders fought their own wars, relying on their own strategies, tactics and instincts. Back at headquarters in Kabul, the military top brass remained faithful to the doctrinal strictures coming from the Pentagon, which prohibited nation-building and a more ambitious reconstruction effort. Yet that was precisely what was happening in the very areas of Afghanistan where the Americans were making inroads, even if the colonels and majors responsible performed verbal contortions to come up with more Rumsfeld-friendly euphemisms to describe the rebuilding process. Here, they were architects of genuine landmarks to progress.

The town of Khost, the one-time stronghold of Osama bin Laden, could now boast a newly renovated technical college, where young Afghans were taught mathematics and geometry in classrooms that had blackboards, desks and textbooks. Before 9/11, the same building had been a training school for al-Qaeda. The governor's mansion nearby had also been refurbished, and a team of gardeners tended to the gubernatorial flower beds outside. Its first occupant was a newly returned Afghan-American, who only a few months before had been running a weightlifting gym in Arlington, Virginia – admittedly not an ideal job swap, but at least he was hard-working and incorruptible.

In a safe house in a quiet side street in Khost, we also

encountered a one-time comrade of bin Laden's, who had recently become the most senior Taliban commander to switch sides under a new amnesty programme. Still wearing the scars of conflict – the top of one of his fingers had been blown off – Malanjam sounded drawn and battle-weary, as he sat in a leather armchair in the late-afternoon sun on a veranda decorated with small pot plants. 'I used to enjoy fighting in the past. I was a battlefield commander for twenty years,' he said, with two of his former henchmen looking on. 'If someone like me can give up fighting, then I'm sure others based in Pakistan will soon come home.'

At that point of the Afghan war, US commanders in the troubled eastern provinces claimed to have the upper hand, and they flew us low over the border with Pakistan to underscore how incursions from Taliban fighters had slowed to a trickle. Only the previous year, insurgents had flooded over the border in groups of 60 to 100. Now, purportedly, they arrived in fives and sixes. Tellingly, however, even the most optimistic commanders stopped short of predicting a definitive military victory. Most had read enough Afghan history to know that war was the status quo, and fighting was the national pastime.

Even a weakened Taliban continued to pose a threat. From the mountains and hills, insurgents were still capable of launching regular attacks on Camp Salerno, the forward operating base within artillery range of Waziristan, which served as our temporary home on visits to the border region. Salerno so regularly came under assault from incoming mortar and rocket fire that it became known as 'Rocket City'.

Friday was 'Surf and Turf' night, an end-of-week feast of lobster and steak imported from home, and GIs came dressed in helmets and full body armour. The Taliban had learnt the mess hall was crowded on Fridays and thus a perfect time to strike. However many times the Apache attack helicopters pounded the nearby hills in drills that also served as a deterrent, and however often artillery units fired ordnance into the nearby mountains to ward off attacks, the insurgents kept on returning.

Venturing out of the base in military convoys was far more dangerous, because of the threat of improvised explosive devices, the dreaded IEDs. In the past, Taliban fighters had tended to engage the Americans in gun battles using rocket-propelled grenades and assault rifles, considering it a more honourable and righteous form of combat. Now, however, they had learnt from the insurgency in Iraq that the best way to cripple an American patrol was to plant IEDs in the path of a convoy.

In face-to-face combat, the Taliban were thought to lose 15–20 men for every foreign soldier killed – a casualty rate that was unsustainable. Even though it generally took six IEDs to kill a single soldier, they were ideal for asymmetrical warfare. Their use had increased by 400 per cent, and the Taliban hoped they would have the same morale-sapping effect on the coalition forces as the mujahideen's use of Stinger missiles against Soviet helicopter gunships. With the invisibility of the enemy making excursions all the more terrifying, there was a lottery-like feel to going out on patrols with the Americans. Whether or not your convoy was hit by an IED was largely a matter of luck.

Sometimes, Apache helicopters would hover overhead on the lookout for insurgents waiting in ambush, and the Americans have since developed jamming technology and detection devices to combat improvised devices, along with stronger vehicles to withstand explosions, and better battlefield first-aid techniques. But in those days the Humvees in which we travelled were not particularly well protected, and our body armour did not offer much of a shield. Designed to cover the vital organs rather than the whole body, the bullet-proof plates in flak jackets felt fig-leaf small, and there was always a feeling that it made more sense to sit on them than wear them, since the explosion from an IED would generally rip through the vehicle from underneath.

Always, we wore our combat helmets – an indicator of maximum danger – and made sure to buy high-strength wraparound sunglasses with cushioning between the frames and skin, because so many soldiers were blinded by the intense flash at the moment of detonation. Then we would rumble into the mountains along roads that could almost have been designed with ambushes in mind, hoping they had not been booby-trapped and that the Taliban had not sketched out a kill zone.

One evening, I recall returning from a patrol to hear that an American convoy on a parallel road had been hit by an IED, which underscored the crapshoot effect of leaving the base. On the first trip that Nik took to Afghanistan after I had left the region, a Canadian convoy in which he was travelling came under suicide attack in downtown Kandahar. In a vehicle splattered with human flesh and the fragments of body parts, the only thing that had saved him and the correspondent sitting alongside him was ten inches of Canadian armour.

In these situations, the simple fact that our hosts doubled as our protectors exposed one of the main flaws of the embed system. If pinned down in a gun battle, our only hope was that US soldiers would get us out of trouble. If wounded by an IED, US medivac teams would hopefully save our lives. Truth was no longer necessarily the first casualty of war. Indeed, the embed greatly increased our access to the battlefield and our ability to decide for ourselves what was happening. Instead, it was our objectivity that was arguably at greater risk.

Fear was not the only compromising impulse. Be it the firepower, the hardware or the thrill of skimming over the countryside in Black Hawks, there was a risk of succumbing to 'embed fever', a variant of Stockholm syndrome. Journalists always ran the risk of going a little weak-kneed in the company of warriors. Still more impairing was the instant camaraderie that combat zones tend to nurture, and the congeniality of many Defence Department media-handlers, most of whom were white-collar reservists dragooned into service because of the manpower shortages in the US military. Jovial men, seemingly happier in the company of journalists than that of professional soldiers, often they lapsed into that battlefield habit of immediately surrendering their innermost secrets, which again had an endearing effect.

One Pentagon PR man, a middle-manager from Connecticut, dropped into dinnertime conversation, in a disarmingly unemotional way, that his wife had declared herself to be a lesbian and run off with another woman at work. Another, a square-jawed 50-something, still with good looks, told us he had been a jobbing actor in Hollywood and dropped heavy hints that he had enjoyed success in the porn industry. His frequent use of the word 'wood' appeared to say it all. Alcohol may possess powerful properties as a conversational lubricant, but it doesn't have anything on being cooped up on a military base confronting outside the daily possibility of death, and these kinds of conversations heightened the sense of allegiance.

There was sharing and, occasionally, there was over-sharing. On an embed in northern Afghanistan, we ended up in a billet for the weekend with a group of British soldiers, one of whom had an unhealthy fixation with how frequently we masturbated. 'Have you banged one out yet?' he asked in a thick Welsh accent before every meal, nodding eagerly as he waited for our answers. 'Have you? Have you banged one out?' What else could we call him but Onan the Barbarian?

There were other undoubted benefits to the embed system. Had we not been with the US military, the Bermel Valley would have remained little more than a place on a map. Had we not been given such free access to the medivac choppers, we would never have encountered Kamila and been able to bring much-needed attention to the problem of unexploded mines (many of which had been manufactured in America and Britain, as well as the former Soviet Union).

Granted such unfettered access, we also inevitably ended up with a much more nuanced view of the American military. Inevitably, we spent time with the buzz-haired grunts and jarheads who fitted the stereotype of the trigger-happy gunslinger with more bravado than brains. 'We should reduce this country to glass,' I recall one of them telling me.

But often the behaviour of troops was far from stereotypical. We saw how young and frightened many of the GIs could be. How, when out on foot patrols in the oppressive heat of the Afghan summer, they would wilt under the weight of their weapons. How, in the computer rooms back at base, they would stare lovingly at wives and children, whose bleary and stuttering images appeared on the screens via sluggish broadband. We had access to the top brass on the ground – the colonels and commanders with all the 'chest candy', as their multicoloured rows of medals were called. It meant we could press them on why US military operations so often ended up killing civilians, which, arguably more so than anything else, severely undercut the war effort. Certainly, the embed system never stopped us from making critical judgements, and I would like to think we were self-conscious enough not to fall prey to any subconscious feelings of alignment.

Unquestionably, embeds came with annoyances and frustrations. It was notoriously difficult to get access to the Special Forces soldiers trying to hunt down Osama bin Laden, who avoided the chow halls, slept in separate quarters and operated outside the normal military hierarchies. Sharing helicopter rides on occasions, they would rarely speak or engage in any way, other than to make doubly sure we were not filming their faces. Clearly, they hated us being there. They maintained this strict code of anonymity, one sensed, not only to protect their identity but also to guard their elite status. Similarly, their gruffness – like the long beards they were allowed to grow to blend in more with local tribesmen – was worn almost as a status symbol.

Occasionally, we would be aboard the Black Hawks that dropped them into the remote US outposts right on the mountainous border, from where we assumed they launched covert incursions into Pakistan. The official line from Washington was that US forces refrained from mounting such operations because they violated Pakistani sovereignty. But that just sounded like another post-9/11 falsehood. The working assumption was that bin Laden was hiding out in Pakistan's lawless tribal regions not far over the border – the Federally Administered Tribal Areas, or FATA, to give them their official name. The diplomatic niceties of respecting another country's sovereign soil surely offered him little in the way of protection.

What those helicopter rides along the border also rammed home was the vastness and inhospitableness of the terrain, where mountain ranges seemed almost to be superimposed on each other, one after the other, as if reflected in some giant hall of mirrors. Combined with Pakistan's North-West Frontier Province, FATA covered some 40,000 square miles, which was the size of New England. It also harboured a population of about 20 million, providing useful human camouflage. Whenever I was asked by friends about the hunt for bin Laden, I started by trying to describe this most unyielding of landscapes. Once, it had served as the perfect staging post for the CIA-backed mujahideen in their fight against Soviet occupation. Now, it offered a haven for al-Qaeda.

When it came to discussing the whereabouts of bin Laden, the reticence of the Special Forces was shared by their senior commanding officers. Nobody wanted to speak about him, and instead they pursued a deliberate policy of downplaying his significance. They had taken their lead from the US commander-in-chief, George W. Bush, who strongly implied that the famed Wild West poster 'DEAD or ALIVE' no longer loomed so large in his mind. 'Who knows if he's hiding in some cave or not?' the president said from the lectern of the White House briefing room in March 2002. 'I truly am not that concerned about him.' Thereafter, bin Laden became a taboo, since his name reeked of mission failure. In any case, the suspicion always was that the Americans preferred him dead or dead.

Just about the only thing US commanders would tell us was that they thought bin Laden was somewhere in Pakistan and that the trail had gone cold. It became their default response. In the end, I heard that answer from so many officers over so many years that I believed it to be true.

—

If a corrective were ever needed after an embed with the Americans or the British, normally all it took was a dinner party back in Kabul. Over cheap Australian wine and meals prepared by Afghan chefs using recipes from Delia Smith cookbooks, the conversation among off-duty diplomats, UN officials, NGO workers and other journalists invariably came round to how a 'good war' had gone bad.

Rarely was there much debate over the failure of the Americans to devote more forces at the start of the conflict. It was a given. From the outset, Donald Rumsfeld was determined to fight a small-scale conflict with the fairly narrow aims of toppling the Taliban and rooting out bin Laden. As a matter of principle, he showed no interest in remedying over a decade of international neglect that had started in 1989 with the withdrawal of Soviet forces.

The defence secretary was also determined to prove that the Powell Doctrine, which relied on overwhelming force, was a relic of twentieth-century warfare. He therefore committed just 316 Special Forces personnel to overthrowing the Taliban, with the CIA providing an additional 110 field officers. Rigid and doctrinaire, Rumsfeld continued to insist thereafter that a small force could maintain the peace, and that Kabul should be the main focus of its operations.

Although Colin Powell argued for a repeat of the Panama Model, where American troops fanned out across the country after ousting the Noriega government in 1989, Rumsfeld remained determinedly Kabul-centric in his thinking. Not until September 2003, almost two years after the fall of the Taliban, did he allow the UN-mandated International Security Assistance Force (ISAF) to expand its remit beyond the capital, thus preventing it from establishing much-needed bridgeheads in regional centres earlier on.

He also placed strict limits on the size of the troop presence, and, as a result, the multinational force was just 8000-strong. In Bosnia, by comparison, there were 40,000 peacekeepers. In terms of international donor money, Afghanistan also received significantly less assistance per capita than Bosnia or Kosovo, even though the challenges were arguably much greater. Four months after the 'liberation' of Kabul, in a set-piece speech at the Virginia Military Institute, George W. Bush spoke boldly of a Marshall Plan for Afghanistan modelled on the US-financed reconstruction programme that rebuilt post-war Europe. However, Rumsfeld blocked it.

His insistence on 'light footprint' military missions was also widely blamed for Osama bin Laden's escape in December 2001 from Tora Bora, the network of caves adjacent to the Pakistan border – another great juncture of the post-9/11 years. Believing he was surrounded and fearing he was about to be killed, the al-Qaeda leader had even written his own will, in which he enjoined his wives never to remarry and apologised to his sons for pursuing a life of jihad.

On the express wishes of Donald Rumsfeld, however, fewer than a hundred US commandos were deployed in the operation, despite calls for reinforcements. Instead, the Pentagon relied primarily on air strikes – at one point a massive 15,000 lb bomb that had to be rolled out of the back of a C-130 transport plane was dropped on the caves complex – and untrained local militiamen. Had the Americans performed a classic sweep and block manoeuvre, involving the marine units and sniper teams that remained on the sidelines, bin Laden might not have escaped. As it was, he slipped through the mountains into Pakistan completely unimpeded.

Just as there was general consensus that Washington had not committed anywhere near enough troops or reconstruction money, diplomats and aid workers rued the diversion of resources and attention to Iraq. In December 2001, even as the siege of Tora Bora continued, President Bush had ordered General Tommy Franks, the commander of the US Central Command and the soldier tasked with 'liberating' Kabul, to draw up war plans for Iraq. Soon after, Special Forces units and the CIA's most experienced field agents were ordered to concentrate on overthrowing Saddam Hussein. Much of the US military's heavy airlift capability, along with the new Predator spy planes rolling off the production lines in America, were sent to the Gulf. Even the Afghan-born US ambassador in Kabul, Zalmay Khalilzad, who was uniquely well qualified to deal with the problems of his homeland and often called 'the second president', was reassigned to Baghdad.

In Afghanistan, deprived of troops and resources, the Bush administration continued to rely heavily on proxies. This meant vesting an inordinate amount of power in the hands of the warlords. In the fight for Kabul, the Americans had relied on the anti-Taliban warlords from the Northern Alliance, whose main commander, Ahmad Shah Massoud, the famed Lion of Panjshir, had been killed on 9 September 2001 by an al-Qaeda hit team disguised as a television crew. After the fall of the Taliban, Washington called on them to maintain the peace.

Proud of getting good bang for his buck, George W. Bush boasted of the great 'bargain' in handing out over $70 million in $100 notes to the warlords who headed up the private militias: men such as General Mohammed Fahim, Ustad Atta Mohammad and Ismail Khan. But it was Faustian in the extreme. Of all the warlords, none was more notorious than General Abdul Rashid Dostum, a formerly pro-Soviet warlord famed for continually switching sides, whose Uzbek militiamen were not averse to dealing with enemies by fastening their heads to their Russian-made tanks then driving them around in circles to crush their skulls. During the war against the Taliban, his men had also been accused of locking up hundreds of captured Taliban fighters in shipping containers then leaving them to asphyxiate.

Investing in these warlords had the effect of devaluing Hamid Karzai. Not only did Karzai have to accommodate them in the first Cabinet – General Dostum served as deputy defence minister – it meant his writ rarely extended beyond the capital.

To get a sense of who was truly in the chair in post-war Afghanistan, all one had to do was spend a morning with the police chief of Mazar-i-Sharif, the major city in the north of the country some 40 miles from the border with Uzbekistan. A heavily bearded man, who looked like the potentate of a small Latin American republic when dressed in his olive-green uniform with its outsized crimson epaulets, Akram Khakrezwal was one of Karzai's close associates. Yet the patronage of the then interim president was pretty much worthless across much of the north, which had always been the bailiwick of the Northern Alliance. The new police chief was determined to change this and seized a consignment of illegal opium to mark out his turf.

So furious were the local warlords that they retaliated by effectively keeping him under house arrest for weeks on end. If he ventured outside, they would kill him. And neither the Afghan Government, a nearby contingent of British soldiers nor even the Americans were able to gain his quick release. Eventually, the warlords relented, but with conditions. Just about the only journey the police chief was allowed to make was from his heavily fortified home to his heavily fortified police compound. Even then, his morning commute became a mad scramble of blaring sirens, screaming tyres and protruding AK-47s, for fear that he might be assassinated en route.

Inside his police headquarters, he showed us where the warlords' gunmen had broken open the locks and seized his investigative files – a raid his officers were powerless to stop. 'Without disarming the warlords,' he told us, in frustration, 'we can't have security, legality or a fair and democratic election.'

The following day, we interviewed the man who had effectively kept the police chief imprisoned, the Tajik warlord Ustad Atta Mohammad, who now gloried in the title of the governor of Balkh province. At his plush governor's mansion, Atta seemed to be enjoying the perks of his new office, and as we arrived workers were putting the finishing touches to his swimming pool.

Once inside, after his security guards had checked that our camera had not been booby-trapped with some kind of gun, we were ushered into a gigantic office, which had a small Afghan flag on the coffee table and a much larger one behind the governor's throne-like armchair. Then came Atta himself, a hulking man dressed in a suit and tie, his civvy-street garb.

Interviewing Afghan warlords is always something of a delicate dance. To mildly upset them runs the risk of being ejected. More serious aggravation runs the risk of something altogether worse. So I lobbed up the mandatory softballs about the challenges and progress of reconstruction, before turning to the business at hand: why had he bullied the local police so mercilessly, and why were warlords still acting like gangsters?

Atta looked at me with exquisite disdain and delivered what he thought was a bullet-proof justification. 'We fought for the freedom of Afghanistan, and our soldiers became heroes,' he growled. 'They fulfilled their human and Islamic obligation.' He did not have to finish the thought. It was the mantra of triumphant warriors down the ages: to the victor, the spoils. Then, we were shown the door.

After the fall of Kabul, the warlords had entered into a tacit agreement with the Americans: in return for the maintenance of order, the drugs trade could continue and even flourish. All part of the same Faustian deal. By far the country's most profitable business, it was thought to account for 60 per cent of the economy and to employ 2.3 million Afghans. With American efforts focused on preventing Afghanistan from becoming a safe haven for terrorists, it was in danger of becoming a narco-state that was a safe haven for drug traffickers. Already, it was the source of 93 per cent of the world's opium, the raw ingredient of heroin. Only when reports emerged that the Taliban was also making more than $100 million a year from narcotics, the profits of which bankrolled the insurgency, did the Americans pay more attention to disrupting the trade.

One of the few genuinely hilarious sights in Afghanistan at the time was the madcap efforts of the US-trained eradication teams who toured the countryside, like marauding armies, scything down the thin stems of the opium poppies. They screamed, laughed and hollered as they sprinted through the fields hurling their wooden batons, as if they themselves were high on drugs. Yet for all the efforts of eradication teams, poppies were being grown in 28 out of the country's 34 provinces.

Certainly, it was doing little to disrupt the supply chain of a local opium dealer, whose back-street drug den was reached with little effort – a few mobile calls from our local fixer – and minimum subterfuge. Inside, bulging translucent sacks of thick, sticky black-tar heroin awaited shipment to nearby processing plants. If the bags had been full of wheat, they would have been worth about 50 cents each. Stuffed with black-tar heroin, they commanded a price of $800. So uneven were the economics that they made a mockery of one of the central pillars of the eradication programme: the promise to farmers of alternative incomes from crops such as pomegranates if they shunned the drug trade. 'You figure it out,' said the opium dealer, as one of his young charges slowly scraped globules of heroin off his blackened fingers with a blunt knife.

Again, the openness of the operation was astonishing. Often, we agree to hide the identities of interviewees – a technique that involves shooting into a bright light so as to blacken their faces. Here, however, the dealer happily spoke on camera, with his craggy face in open view. He had the backing of the warlords, and the warlords could usually rely on the Americans averting their gaze.

—

As if to underscore the hazards of conducting a national election in the midst of a civil war, Hamid Karzai's first campaign swing outside of Kabul suddenly became a panicked scramble back to the comparative safety of the capital. With just a couple of weeks to go before polling day, the plan had been for him to address a rally attended by tribesmen and local schoolchildren in Gardez, a town in the south-east of the country. As his American Chinook started to land, however, it came under rocket attack from Taliban insurgents on the ground.

After his chopper banked violently and started its hurried journey homeward, Karzai pleaded with his DynCorp personal-protection detail to allow him to land. But he was no more in charge of the pilot than he was of the country. Thereafter, his electioneering was restricted to one solitary rally outside of Kabul's city limits. Although his American sponsors were determined for him to win the election, their first priority was to keep him alive until polling day. (There was an irony in this. Karzai had almost been killed by a stray American missile on the day in December 2001 when he found out the Bush administration had selected him to become interim president.)

It meant that his first major campaign event outside of the capital, just four days ahead of the poll, also doubled as his last. At a public park in the town of Ghazni, some 5000 of Karzai's fellow Pashtun tribesmen gathered in their turbaned and often toothless glory. With the streets of Ghazni placed in virtual lockdown, truckloads of soldiers were drafted in to provide an outer rim of protection, while everyone was frisked as they entered the park – a novelty for Afghans unused to airline-style security.

Karzai was in irrepressible form and spoke passionately about the possibility of ending decades of war. 'Brothers and sisters, I ask you to vote for me freely, with no pressure,' he declared. 'We want a proud Afghanistan, a stable Afghanistan, a peaceful Afghanistan.' Then, bravely, he thrust himself into the front row of the crowd, like an ageing rock star diving into a mosh pit.

Emboldened by the experience, he even felt confident enough to admonish his guards when they manhandled an elderly tribesman who clawed at his clothing. 'Don't push him! Don't push him!' shouted Karzai, for once dishing out orders to his grim-faced protectors. 'This is democracy. This is emotion!' The unscripted drama of the moment provided terrific pictures, which were far superior to what Karzai's media-handlers had laid on. At the climax of the rally, he released a flock of snow-white peace doves into the bracing morning air, but as the cameras followed the birds skywards they captured the American helicopter gunships circling high above. Despite that small snag, the event was deemed a stunning success, if for no other reason than Karzai had escaped without being assassinated.

Already postponed twice because of concerns over security, the official launch of the 2004 presidential campaign had come a few months earlier. In a Soviet-era auditorium in the centre of Kabul, election officials held a raffle-like draw to decide the order on the ballot papers in which the names of the 18 presidential candidates should appear.

Among the candidates plucked from the rolling tombola was a poet, an amateur boxer, a Sufi intellectual, an avowed monarchist who wanted the country to once more become a kingdom, a paediatrician physician and a female doctor, Dr Massouda Jalal, who was the sole woman in the race. Aside from Karzai, the most familiar name in the drum belonged to General Dostum, who was among at least five candidates considered to be a warlord because they controlled their own private armies.

Nobody was in any doubt, however, as to who would win the upcoming election. Karzai, or 'Uncle Sam's Choice', as he was often known, was such the clear front-runner that it risked discrediting a process designed by the Americans and the United Nations to legitimise his rule. 'Karzai is an American appointee,' shouted a heckler from the stalls of the auditorium that afternoon. 'He will be elected with American money.'

Days later, Karzai did little to dispel this widespread impression when he appeared alongside Donald Rumsfeld at an open-air press conference in the dappled late-afternoon sun of the Arg. Throughout, he looked and sounded very much the junior partner. Fielding questions, he claimed to be untroubled by a new report from the United Nations that showed that nine million people had registered to vote in a country where only 9.5 million were eligible to do so. Given that less than half of the country's women had registered, this meant that significantly more men were now entitled to vote than there were men.

A number of factors explained this incongruity. Some of them were sinister, such as the acquisition of multiple cards by warlords determined to rig the entire ballot. Others were quite charming and brought home the newness of democracy. Each voting card came with a laminated photograph – a prized possession in a country where cameras had up until recently been banned and where the Taliban used to carry out public hangings of television sets and stereo systems. It meant that thousands of voters returned to register several times, keen to maximise their own campaign photo opportunity.

When called upon to ask my question, I wanted to tackle Karzai on these multiple registrations but also to challenge Rumsfeld on a recent statement in which he had likened the level of violence in Afghanistan to crime levels in Berlin. 'Some six hundred people have been killed since your last visit,' I said, as the defence secretary fixed me with his squinty stare. Then I swivelled to face Karzai. 'There is clear evidence, President Karzai, of multiple registrations – people registering over and over again out of coercion from the warlords. Given the volatile security situation, given the unchecked power of the warlords, how can these elections be free and fair in any way?'

After a long pause, Rumsfeld replied, and his first words came as a surprise: 'You're right.' Still, he did not regret drawing parallels with Berlin. 'In important countries, violence occurs,' he said, in a line that echoed his famed 'stuff happens' comment after the fall of Baghdad. 'It occurs in European countries. It appears in western-hemisphere countries and it is occurring in this part of the world.' Normally so unflappable in front of reporters, the defence secretary looked and sounded ruffled, and it produced a definite charge in the air.

Then Karzai weighed in. 'With regard to multiple registration of voters, we don't really know if a thousand people or two thousand people or three thousand people or a hundred thousand people have two registration cards. And, as a matter of fact, it doesn't bother me.' Then, with exuberant incoherence, he added, 'If Afghans have two registration cards because they like to vote twice, well, welcome!' As Karzai careered off message, Rumsfeld started to fidget visibly behind his lectern, like a puppeteer who has lost control of his marionette.

At this point, I jumped in with the obvious follow-up. 'But you are describing a farce not an election,' I suggested.

'No, no, no,' said Karzai. 'We are just beginning an exercise. People are enthusiastic. They want to have cards. They have taken cards. Maybe some have taken one or two cards. We don't know. It's speculation. I have not seen anybody that has taken two cards or three cards.'

Anticipating this problem, election officials had put safeguards in place. As in India, voters' fingernails would be etched with a thin mark of indelible ink. Yet Karzai overlooked this salient detail. It was only later in the press conference, when an aide whispered in his ear, that Karzai finally remembered the indelible ink. By now, however, the damage had been done, and he just wanted to get the hell out of there. 'We're looking forward to the elections,' he said with another flourish. 'We are not worried. Have a good heart, and let's go to the elections.'

At the risk of immodesty, the headlines that day came from my exchange with Karzai and his garbled logic. So, as the press conference came to an end, and Rumsfeld could be seen gently berating him as they walked back towards the presidential palace, I felt a small pang of professional pride. Even a few fellow correspondents – a notoriously ungenerous bunch in evaluating the work of rivals – were complimentary. London also seemed delighted when, late that night, we filed a report for the ten o'clock news that carried an abbreviated version of the exchange with Rumsfeld. It also ended with the question of whether Afghanistan was seeing a rush to democracy propelled by the Bush administration's need to score a foreign-policy success ahead of the US presidential election in November, especially when so much miserable news was coming out of Iraq. All seemed well with the world when finally we turned in, with the praise of London ringing still in our ears.

Regrettably, our delight was short-lived. At the following morning's editorial meeting in London, which serves both as a look-ahead and a post-mortem on the previous day's coverage, the view was that I had come across as a bit of a smart-arse and skirted too close to editorialising on the question of whether Afghanistan was ready for democracy.

On the first complaint, I accepted guilt. In a medium that rewards understatement, a note of hubris had crept into my report. As for making judgements about the Bush administration's

Afghan-freedom project, I considered myself harshly done by. Rather than deliver a blanket condemnation, I had merely posed the question that was on everyone's lips.

Over the next few days, admonishing calls came in over the satellite phone from London. My card was well and truly marked. Seriously out of favour for the first time in my career, it was not even certain whether I would get the chance to cover the forthcoming elections. As it was, I did return to Kabul for polling day but was given a fairly peripheral role and kept well away from the premier television bulletins – the BBC's cruellest put-down.

When election day arrived, it came with a spectacle both stirring and cinematic. From early morning, women lined up patiently outside polling stations to vote, some with the pride of suffragettes. Most were wearing burqas but many had put on their finest clothes and spent time doing their hair and make-up. With female turnout high, there was the strong suspicion that many would have been instructed how to cast their ballots by their husbands, who in turn would have received instructions from imams, tribal chiefs or local militia leaders. For many Afghan women, however, the act of voting was also an act of liberation, and watching them lift their blue veils so they could identify themselves to voting officials was breathtaking.

The men lined up in a separate queue, clasping blankets tight around them and gripping their laminated voting cards. In many parts of the country, the voters had to brave unseasonably chill winds; in others, dust storms. But everywhere, millions of Afghans stood up to threats from the Taliban.

As voting got underway, I was at a school near Kabul Airport, whose crumbling, mud-brick walls were pockmarked with bullet-holes. Polling booths fashioned out of cardboard were laid out in two classrooms, the war-wrecked state of which offered the most powerful reminder of what precisely was at stake. Some parents brought their infant children along to witness the birth of democracy. Then they cast their vote on long ballot papers that listed the candidates and included a small passport-style photograph of each one, along with their adopted symbols. Karzai had chosen the scales of justice and told voters in the final days of campaigning that they should look out for his Karakul, his trademark sheepskin hat. Since only a third of Afghan men could read, and just eight per cent of women, the process was designed to be as simple as possible.

Beforehand, the Taliban had threatened to wreak mayhem across the country, but as yet there were few reports of violence on anywhere near the scale previously feared. Instead, the first indication that anything was awry came when a young woman, who had ventured out without her burqa, approached us in a state of teary agitation, thrusting a finger towards our camera.

Moments earlier, voter officials had marked her nail with indelible ink to prevent her from voting twice. Now, all that was visible was the faintest of blotches. A few seconds later, it had all but disappeared. Sensing immediately the potential for fraud, she was distraught. Other voters merely thought it hilarious that they could rub the ink from their fingernails so effortlessly. What we needed to establish, and fast, was whether this polling station had simply been given a duff batch of ink or this was a nationwide problem that could result in thousands of Afghans voting twice or even more times.

To find out, we turned to our local Kabul producer, Bilal, a gem of a young man and a quite brilliant news-gatherer, who was sitting outside our satellite truck and served as a one-man search engine, a human Google. For months in advance of the election, he had travelled all over Afghanistan hooking up with our network of stringers, or local reporters, and now, working two mobile phones at once, he rang around to find out if there were similar problems elsewhere.

Within minutes, we had the answer: everywhere, the supposedly indelible ink had dangerously delible properties. Now, there was no safeguard left against multiple voting and mass fraud. As the ink disappeared, so, too, did confidence in the process, and rival news organisations, which could not boast a Bilal, started picking up on the same irregularities. One after the other, candidates shunned the election. By lunchtime, their boycott was all but complete. Only Karzai and two others continued to argue that the election could be free and fair.

A campaign without a trail. An election without much electioneering. A vote that by lunchtime had been boycotted by 15 of the 18 presidential candidates. For all its historic trappings and unforgettable imagery, the poll still left unanswered the central question asked of the country at that first *loya jirga*: was Afghan democracy a contradiction in terms?

Cutting the first television report on this now disputed election posed all sorts of editorial dilemmas, and the pressure of deadlines meant there was little time to resolve them. Clearly, we wanted to reflect the history of the moment – a chronically overused word in the news business but one that automatically attached itself to this election. The queues, the obvious enthusiasm, the deep hankering of average Afghans for a non-violent future. We also wanted to chronicle another undoubted success: the failure of the Taliban to cause much fatal disruption.

213

For balance, we needed to put the boycott in context. After all, all but one of the candidates who had withdrawn were complete no-hopers. But the problems with the ink had clearly compromised the process, even if there was not much evidence, as yet, that people had cast more than one ballot.

Something else we had to weigh was the possibility that the spat over the disappearing ink had diverted attention from more serious electoral abuses, such as the widespread intimidation of voters, which, in hindsight, was arguably the most glaring weakness of our report. What we essentially had to decide was to what extent the technical failings of the election had eclipsed its spirit and historical import.

Personally, this was especially tricky, because if I went with the line that the election had been compromised hopelessly it might have looked like score-settling from the summer. Given that the whole exchange with Karzai at that open-air press conference had centred on the safeguards against multiple voting, *Schadenfreude* was an obvious temptation, though to indulge it now would have suggested an unhealthy fixation.

Honestly, I thought we produced a fair-minded report, balancing the history and the hitches, which ran on BBC World News in Afghanistan for most of the day. Hamid Karzai most certainly did not. That evening, as chaos continued to engulf the election and he faced the usual accusations about being America's stooge, he opened his press conference with an attack on our coverage. With uncharacteristic scorn – Karzai is usually the most good-humoured of men – he argued that our reports had been unnecessarily sensationalist and had attached far too much importance to the disappearing ink. Here, I run the risk of inserting ourselves into the story – that common pitfall of correspondent memoirs. However, all we had done that day was to report on the nationwide scale of the problem, which our far-flung stringer network made us uniquely well placed to do.

Indelible ink or not, Karzai was quickly declared the winner, with 55.4 per cent of the vote, which meant the election did not have to go to a second round. The United Nations validated his victory, and the whole sorry mess was blamed on the company in India that had supplied the ink. (Pakistani diplomats, of course, suspected skulduggery from Delhi.) The whole flap was explained away as the inevitable birth pangs of democracy.

Instead, the UN, which had organised the entire poll, asked the media to reflect on the lines of burqa-clad women outside the polling stations and the fact that the Taliban had failed to cause serious disruption to the election. Fourteen people were killed that day – a much smaller number than had been feared. US commanders went even further, claiming that the presidential election had brought about 'the psychological defeat' of the Taliban – a statement that sounded optimistic at the time, and even more so with each passing fighting season.

The problem for America and its allies was that the insurgents spoke of Afghanistan not as a cradle of democracy but as a graveyard of empires – a cliché in the hands of journalists but an article of faith in the minds of the Taliban. Its fighters believed that endless conflict was Allah's way of testing them and that, whether it took decades or centuries, they would ultimately achieve a God-given victory – hence the old adage 'the West have the watches but the Afghans have the time'. Looking back on the first presidential election, whether Afghanistan was ready or not for democracy was never really the most pertinent question. Then and now, it was whether America and its allies could ever conquer the Taliban.

As for that other bothersome question, where was Osama bin Laden, surely the answer lay over the border in neighbouring Pakistan.

Chapter 7

Pakistan: The Land of the Double Game

akistan was probably the most impenetrable country I had ever covered. This was largely because of the difficulty in divining the true motivations of its key players, whether they be politicians, army chiefs, diplomats, spooks or even cricketers.

Sometimes, I felt that the people of Pakistan were in on some giant secret, like conjurers inducted into the magic circle, which they had successfully concealed from the rest of the world. Then I would speak to some of the country's most well-sourced journalists and erudite intellectuals, who often struggled to make sense of their own country. What made Pakistan even harder to comprehend, especially after 9/11, was the enormous discrepancy between what the West thought should be its most urgent national priority – which is to say the hunt for Osama bin Laden, along with the defenestration of al-Qaeda and the Taliban – and its own national obsession, which was the historic rivalry with India.

It was important to understand that Pakistan had been founded on a grievance and a grudge: that as the Union Flag came down on the British Raj, the last reigning maharaja of the princely state of Jammu and Kashmir – who had initially favoured independence – decided eventually to side with India instead of with Pakistan. The

Kashmir Valley was overwhelmingly Muslim, and Muhammad Ali Jinnah, the father of Pakistan, had supposedly described it as the jugular vein of his newly created country. So a question became lodged firmly in the national psyche, where it festered for decades: how could the nation prosper when such a vital artery was under the sword of its great rival? With the 'k' in Pakistan standing for Kashmir, the letter served as a portmanteau reminder of the country's continuing humiliation.

For any new arrival hoping to map Pakistan's DNA, as good a starting point as any was to make the drive across the plains of Punjab from Lahore to Wagah – the only official border crossing with India. The trick was to arrive just before dusk to witness Wagah's great sunset ceremonial, the Beating the Retreat.

For 30 minutes each evening, soldiers from India's Border Security Force and Pakistan Rangers would high-kick, stamp, speed-march and flash downward thumbs at each other in perfect and well-rehearsed synchronicity. Picked for their towering height, limb flexibility, extravagant facial hair and ability to carry off fan-shaped headdresses that gave them the appearance of strutting peacocks, they engaged in a burst of military machismo that rivalled the All Blacks' haka in terms of its controlled fury and dignified rage.

What made it even more entertaining was that it had shades of Baz Luhrmann's *Strictly Ballroom*, Basil Fawlty's acrobatic goose-steps and the sort of harrumphing, head-turning high-camp that one might expect to see in a West End bedroom farce – normally at the point where the wife returns home to find her husband in bed with the Swedish au pair.

The soundtrack came from two note-splitting buglers and the pantomime cheers of Pakistanis and Indians packed into bleachers on either side of the border. The ceremony would end with a brief exchange of handshakes, the slamming of gates and the lowering of flags. Honours were intended to be even. Yet, having watched the ceremony from both sides of the border, my guess was that it meant more for Pakistan than for its bigger, richer and more internationally lauded neighbour. Though it still considered Pakistan a major irritant and intermittent threat, India was starting to view China as its main twenty-first-century rival. Fifty years after partition, and three wars later, Pakistan still had an India fixation.

This helped to explain why Pakistan was the principal sponsor of the Taliban when it rose to power in Afghanistan in September 1996 – providing food, fuel, financing, munitions and military assistance from its Frontier Corps. In South Asia's modern-day Great Game, an Islamabad-friendly regime in Kabul was not only an essential bulwark against Delhi but it also meant that Pakistan could amass its forces on the border with India rather than worry about Afghanistan. Only three countries granted diplomatic recognition to the Taliban government in Kabul: Saudi Arabia, the United Arab Emirates and, of course, Pakistan.

The India fixation explained why forceful action was not taken against militant Islam by dismantling Lashkar-e-Taiba (Army of the Righteous), its home-grown jihadists, or al-Qaeda, whose leaders had taken up residence in Waziristan, parts of the North-West Frontier Province and many of the major cities, such as Karachi. Viewed as useful proxies, these militant groups carried out attacks in Indian-administered Kashmir and major Indian cities, such as Delhi and Mumbai, which had a destabilising effect on Pakistan's arch rival. This not only meant that the jihadists often avoided censure but also that they came to enjoy the active backing of high-ranking generals in the Inter-Services Intelligence (ISI), Pakistan's shadowy intelligence service, as well as senior figures in the army.

Operationally, the ISI was thought to be divided now into two sections: one that offered assistance to the Bush administration in its search for high-value al-Qaeda targets and one that maintained its patron–client relationship with the Taliban and other militant groups. Towards jihadists, the ISI was believed to have adopted an à la carte approach: assisting some while attempting to thwart others, even though ISI spies had been beheaded in the tribal areas and scores of its officials had been killed in suicide attacks.

Pakistan was playing a double game, which also explained why the military continued to divert US funds earmarked for the war on terror – we are talking here of a gargantuan sum of money, now in excess of $20 billion – to finance its arms build-up against India. This, even after the Pakistani Taliban tried to take control of the Swat Valley, close to Islamabad, and al-Qaeda mounted attacks within the capital virtually at will. Militant Islam now posed an existential threat to the state – the talk was of the Talibanisation of Pakistan – but the army and ISI continued to sponsor jihadists.

Trying to fully comprehend Islamabad's double game was difficult enough, but making half-decent television out of it was immeasurably harder. Finding a diplomat or a former Pakistani spook to repeat on camera what they would tell you off the record was next to impossible. As for getting pictorial evidence of the ISI's complicity with jihadists, it was not as if they offered embeds. On issuing journalist visas, the Pakistan authorities also placed quite heavy restrictions on where we were allowed to travel, limiting us for a long while to the major cities. Suffice to say, the areas of our primary interest, such as the North-West Frontier Province, where the militants were most active, were out of bounds and guarded with military checkpoints. Alas, this was a story best told in heavily classified intelligence cables rather than in the form of broadcast journalism, because so few people would speak honestly on the record.

Often, I would come away from Pakistan – a country I looked upon with great affection – thinking I was probably too naive to cover it properly. Journalistically speaking, it was a place that favoured the deeply cynical – wizened old hacks who never believed a word that anyone told them, on or off the record. Being something of a conspiracy theorist was also useful – a spy novelist even – because of all the secret plots that were actually playing out. It was more a case, however, of being a conspiracy reporter: of working clandestine contacts, over and over, to chronicle what was happening in the shadows, where the fantastical so often doubled as fact.

From 2003 onwards, the country's deteriorating security situation came to be reflected in our choice of accommodation. On trips to Islamabad, we traditionally stayed at the Marriott, the long-time haunt of visiting correspondents, where waiters served wine in teapots to break the Islamic prohibition on booze and where beers ordered through room service arrived with forms for guests to sign admitting to a medical dependence on alcohol – a signature that many a correspondent could deliver with an entirely clean conscience. By 2004, we had started staying in small guest houses, which were less of a target. The allure of a middling pinot noir served in bone china or a locally brewed Murree lager – which was something of a crime against beer – was no longer worth the risk.

In October that year, I happened to be staying at a nearby guest house when the Marriott was bombed for the first time, destroying much of the lobby and restaurant area on the ground floor, where 11 members of staff from the US embassy were dining. Downplaying the incident, Pakistan's inaptly named information minister told us that the explosion was caused by an electrical short circuit. But the official explanation was risible given that the foyer was strewn with wrecked furniture and broken glass, and that seven people had been injured, including an American diplomat. Here, the phrase 'it looks like a bomb has hit it' was a statement of the blindingly obvious. Still, the information minister refused to recognise the evidence right before his eyes. In common with so many officials in Pakistan, he was in a state of public denial about the dangers posed by jihadists. Sure enough, an investigation quickly found that the explosion had been the work of a bomber, who had tried to smuggle a laptop packed with explosives in through the front door.

That attack on the Marriott came just days before the 2004 American presidential election between George W. Bush and Senator John Kerry, and I had flown to Islamabad just in case the Bush administration pulled off a genuine October surprise by announcing the capture of Osama bin Laden. With the election deadline looming, everyone knew that the CIA and US military had redoubled their efforts to capture the al-Qaeda leader, although there was nothing to suggest that the trail was anything other than wintry.

Not for the first time, however, it was bin Laden who pulled off the coup, by getting his couriers to smuggle an 18-minute tape to the offices of the Arabic news network Al Jazeera in Islamabad – yet another indication that he was hiding out within the borders of Pakistan rather than Afghanistan.

Dressed in a snow-white turban and a golden robe, looking noticeably older and greyer than in his previous appearances, he presented himself as the untitled leader of the Islamic caliphate he so desperately wanted to restore. There was even the quasi-presidential flourish of being seated behind a desk with his script laid out before him, as if he were mimicking an Oval Office address. Even more so than in his usual recorded messages, he heaped scorn on its present occupant and admitted responsibility for the attacks of 9/11 – the first time he had done so publicly. 'It never occurred to us that the commander-in-chief of the country would leave 50,000 citizens in the two towers to face those horrors alone,' he scoffed, in what sounded very much like a riff from Michael Moore's *Fahrenheit 9/11*, 'because he thought listening to a child discussing her goats was more important.'

Rather than hurting George W. Bush, however, bin Laden was giving him an election-winning boost, which CIA analysts believed was precisely his intention. John Kerry – for all his weaknesses as a candidate and for all Karl Rove's attempts to portray him as a closet Frenchman – had gone into the final weekend of campaigning ahead of the president in a number of polls. But to attack George W. Bush now that the tape had been broadcast gave the appearance almost of siding with bin Laden or of being unpatriotic. Indeed, the Massachusetts senator, who had once lambasted Bush for not doing more to bring the al-Qaeda leader to justice, had decided months before to drop references in his speeches to how bin Laden remained at large. Internal polling showed it was badly hurting him with voters.

The proof of this came when Bush received an Osama bounce on that final weekend, which meant that going into the last two days of campaigning the wind was behind his back. In another photo-finish election, Bush won with 50.7 per cent of the vote compared with Kerry's 48.3 per cent. It remains one of the great political paradoxes of the post-9/11 years that George W. Bush's failure to capture his number-one enemy actually helped him win re-election.

More obliquely, what bin Laden was also delivering in that tape was a crushing indictment of the Bush administration's war on terror. Al-Qaeda clearly believed that the invasion of Iraq, and the scandals coming out of Abu Ghraib and Guantanamo Bay, had invigorated the global jihad. Its leader, who seemingly relished his eye-to-eye struggle with George W., was essentially saying that he viewed America's commander-in-chief as al-Qaeda's leading recruiting sergeant.

—

Long before 9/11, and soon after the end of my traineeship with the BBC, Pakistan had provided an early rite of passage for a wannabe foreign correspondent: my first election abroad. It was February 1997, and a few months earlier the president had dismissed the government of Benazir Bhutto on charges of corruption and misrule. Not only were Cabinet ministers alleged to be looting billions from the national exchequer, but also the prime minister herself was accused of leading a cover-up into the death of her elder brother and dynastic rival, Murtaza, whom the Karachi police had mowed down a few months earlier. These allegations seemed jaw-dropping for a fledging reporter just in from London, but they were fairly run of the mill for a Pakistani press corps that had witnessed almost every kind of scandal.

When I encountered her at an election rally in Lahore, Bhutto came across as a deeply embittered figure, fuming with acid, whose once-beautiful face was haggard and white like a geisha's. Though still only in her early 40s, the ravages of Pakistani politics had made her look ten years older. No great fan at that time of the BBC, she launched a scolding tirade at what she perceived as our bias when I approached her for an interview. Seemingly, we had been added to an enemies list in her mind that included the president, the army, the ISI and her main election rival, Nawaz Sharif, the leader of the Pakistan Muslim League.

Sharif, a podgy-faced industrialist from Lahore – who, like Bhutto, had once been sacked as prime minister following the usual accusations of corruption and misrule – was much more accommodating. As the clear favourite in the election, he was more than happy for us to join him on his helicopter as he launched into a campaign swing that felt like a round-Pakistan whirlwind intended to show the country's topographical and meteorological extremes.

First, we flew into a mountain community in the Swat Valley, where the craggy ledges formed a natural amphitheatre, as Sharif delivered a limp speech met by the local tribesmen with respectful puzzlement. From the bitter cold of the Swat Valley, we headed to the parched farmland of Punjab, where we stepped out of the helicopter into oven-like temperatures and a giant dust storm of our own making.

Next was a massive rally in Rawalpindi, the garrison city on the edge of Islamabad that is the home to the headquarters of the Pakistani Army. Here, a mob of screaming supporters rushed towards our helicopter with such force that for a time we were swept uncontrollably towards its still-whirling tail rotor. (Given the sheer size and passion of crowds on the subcontinent, one of the major regional hazards was of being crushed in a stampede at a political rally or religious festival.)

Finally, we made the short hop to the centre of Islamabad for a fast-breaking iftar supper at the Marriott, where, having observed his Ramadan fast since dawn, Sharif showed considerably more appetite for his plate of biryani than for his day of campaigning.

Fun though it was to fly with Nawaz and joust with Benazir, the main reason I was in Pakistan was to follow Imran Khan, the former cricketer whose newly formed party, the Movement for Justice, was making its political debut. All the fly-in correspondents who descended upon Pakistan arrived hoping to write the story of how a World Cup-winning cricket captain became the leader of his country in one giant leap. Once Pakistan's most flamboyant playboy, Imran was still remembered in Britain as a debonair cricketer, Oxford Blue and late-night fixture at Mayfair nightspots such as Annabel's and Tramp. More recently, the tabloids and celebrity magazines had feasted on his high-society marriage to Jemima Goldsmith, who had converted to Islam and borne the first of their two sons. Now, however, Imran was unrecognisable: devout, humourless and strangely melancholic.

His home in Lahore had the same joyless air throughout the hour or so we spent there, and his young bride, Jemima, looked thoroughly miserable. Less than two years into their troubled marriage, it was clear that she belonged still in *Tatler* rather than in Lahore. Neither did his political career merit the fairy-tale treatment. For all his supporters' fervour – 'He is still captain, he is still my captain,' yelled one of his fans at microphone-busting volume during a night-time rally in Lahore – Imran was a neophyte. So shambolic was his new party that it had not even organised for him to vote on election day – a political golden duck.

Rather than spend election night with the Imran camp, we set up shop on the lawn of Nawaz Sharif's Lahore mansion.

Sharif was celebrating the biggest landslide since Benazir's father, Zulfikar Ali Bhutto, in the late 1970s. Not that it meant much. Turnout across the country hovered around a pitiful 30 per cent – an indication of the lamentable health of Pakistani democracy. It was not the sort of mandate that the Pakistani military was likely to respect.

It is worth recalling what happened in the aftermath of the 1997 election, if only to underscore Pakistan's chronic democratic dysfunction. To avoid corruption charges, Benazir went into self-imposed exile in Dubai and London. By this time, her husband, Asif Ali Zardari – who was known as 'Mr Ten Per Cent' because of the kickbacks he was alleged to have received during her prime ministership – was already in jail. Then, in the way that these things often work out in South Asia, he won election to the Senate from his prison cell in Karachi.

After Benazir returned to Pakistan in 2007 in a bid to regain power, she was assassinated at the same municipal park in Rawalpindi where we had landed in Sharif's helicopter. In the elections that followed, her widowed husband, who had now been released from prison, rode the wave of public sympathy and anger all the way to the presidency of Pakistan.

As for the victor of the 1997 election, Nawaz Sharif soon found himself in a power struggle with the military top brass. This in turn contributed to the rise of a general, little known at that time beyond Pakistan's borders, who was about to become a central figure in the whole post-9/11 story. Back in 1999, during his flunked pop quiz ahead of the New Hampshire primary, George W. Bush had not been able to recall his name. Now, in the aftermath of the attacks on New York and Washington, General Pervez Musharraf became a vital ally.

—

In a garrison nation where the army had been in the chair for 24 out of the 53 years since independence, there was a certain brazenness in Nawaz Sharif's decision to mount his own personal coup. He seized his chance in October 1999 when he sacked the army's chief of staff, General Musharraf, who was on a brief visit to Sri Lanka, and announced that the head of the ISI, the country's leading spymaster, would take his place.

Musharraf was mid-air on his way back from Colombo when he learnt of his dismissal, and his plane, a commercial airliner with 198 passengers and crew on board, was prevented from touching down at Karachi Airport, where the landing lights were turned off and fire trucks blocked the runway. With fuel fast running out and his fellow passengers in peril, Musharraf was given the option of flying to India. 'Over my dead body will you go to India,' thundered the general, even though he had actually been born in Delhi. Instead, the pilot started heading to another airfield in Pakistan in the hope of getting clearance to land.

On the ground below, Musharraf's military underlings were already coming to his rescue, and in the time it took for his plane to climb to 20,000 feet the army seized control of Karachi Airport. When a soldier came across air-traffic control to assure Musharraf it was now safe to land, he thought it was a trick and that a Sharif plant was trying to lure him to his death. 'Can you tell me the names of my dogs?' asked Musharraf, fully expecting to expose the ruse.

'Dot and Buddy,' came the instant reply.

When the plane landed, with just seven minutes of fuel to spare, the general was in effective control of the entire country, and Dot and Buddy had become Pakistan's 'First Dogs'.

By the time I returned to South Asia, two years into the Bush administration's war on terror, Musharraf was not only Pakistan's undisputed ruler but could also lay claim to being among the world's five most consequential leaders. (My list at that time would have read George W. Bush, Hu Jintao, Tony Blair, Musharraf and Hamid Karzai, just edging out Vladimir Putin.) He was also one of the most likeable: unpretentious, clubbable and with a taste for finely blended whisky – a highly congenial dictator.

I interviewed him once on the day after the Kashmir earthquake in 2005, when he was touring the worst-affected communities aboard his military helicopter. Then, when our questioning was complete, I asked if he would mind conducting an interview with the studio in London via satellite phone that would be broadcast live around the world. Without hesitation, Musharraf agreed. Alas, our timing was slightly awry. In London, our global continuous-news channel, BBC World News, was broadcasting a recorded programme – a 'back half-hour' as they are known in the parlance of continuous news – and the rostered presenter had temporarily disappeared. It took an age for the producers to search the cafes, toilets and smoking dens of BBC Television Centre, and all the time the general's aides were looking edgily at their watches and angrily at me. 'Use him or lose him' was their unspoken message. Even on a normal day, I would have forgiven Musharraf for taking a rain check, even for getting huffy. Yet he stood for almost ten minutes happily chatting away until a breathless presenter finally appeared at the other end of the line.

The encounter suggested he was uncomplicated, obliging and the polar opposite of devious. However, rising to the very top of the Pakistani military does not come about through winning popularity contests. Even though Musharraf had been born in pre-partition India, he was a fiery nationalist, who broke down and wept when he heard of his country's surrender at the end of the 1971 Indo-Pakistani war, after which East Pakistan became the independent state of Bangladesh. For all his amiability, the general had also masterminded the famed and ultimately ill-fated Kargil incursion in 1999, when Pakistani-sponsored Kashmiri militants crossed over the Line of Control into Indian-administered Kashmir – a crisis that produced South Asia's first nuclear stand-off and brought the rivals close to the point of all-out war.

For all his undoubted charm, then, it was always worth remembering that Musharraf was a grandmaster in Pakistan's double game. The question of his true allegiances had troubled the Bush administration ever since it confronted the Pakistan leader after the attacks of 9/11 with the stark choice of being for or against its war on terror. His actions thereafter often suggested both.

In a speech to the nation on 19 September, eight days after 9/11, he stated that the capture of bin Laden could be achieved without the downfall of the Taliban and spoke ominously of a pro-Delhi government emerging in Kabul. Part of the double game. In December that year, Pakistan-based militant groups – Lashkar-e-Taiba and Jaish-e-Mohammed – carried out an attack on the Indian Parliament building in Delhi, which brought the two countries close to a nuclear exchange. It was hard to believe that such a bold and elaborate assault could have unfolded without the knowledge of Islamabad and even its active support. The double game squared.

When he came to publishing his memoirs in 2006 – tellingly, if predictably, entitled *In the Line of Fire* – Musharraf revealed that he had war-gamed the possibility of making America an adversary following the 9/11 attacks but had decided it would be near suicidal for Pakistan. However, while publicly he lent Pakistan's support to the war on terror, privately he hedged. His government even offered sanctuary to the remnants of the Taliban when they fled over the border after the Americans and Northern Alliance had liberated Kabul in November 2001. Thinking that America's presence in Afghanistan would be short-lived, Islamabad believed the Taliban should be kept on life support in anticipation some day of its eventual return. The double game times ten.

Many was the time, however, when Pakistan proved itself to be an invaluable ally. By 2006, it had arrested more than a thousand al-Qaeda suspects. These included Khalid Sheikh Mohammed, al-Qaeda's number three and the principal architect of the 9/11 attacks, and Ramzi bin al-Shibh, one of the founding members of the Hamburg cell that carried it out. For Musharraf, there was also a strong personal incentive to root out al-Qaeda. Twice in December 2003, Islamist militants had come close to assassinating him, and the former commando officer usually carried a laser-guided Glock pistol in a hip holster as his last line of defence.

For all that, the Bush administration thought the general could have done much more, but it gave him its support all the same – turning a blind eye to his suspension of democracy in the process – because it believed he was the only game in town. Here, once again, Musharraf displayed his Italianate cunning, for he had successfully persuaded Washington that he was an indispensable figure: the only Pakistani capable of holding his fractious nation together.

There were also unmistakable signs that Musharraf was trying to break his country's India fixation. Increasingly dovish when it came to Indo-Pakistani relations, he entered into peace talks with the Indians in 2004 and even raised the possibility of dropping his country's territorial claim on disputed Kashmir. A massive climbdown for any Pakistani head of state, let alone a military man, it was akin to a Palestinian leader relinquishing his people's demands for the return of the West Bank.

Here, Musharraf appeared to enjoy the support of the Pakistani middle class, which was increasingly prepared to let history be just that. There was great public enthusiasm for the new cross-border bus links, connecting Islamabad to Delhi, which allowed relatives separated by partition to be reunited with family members, some of whom they had never set eyes on. Business travellers especially enjoyed the resumption of air links, which finally meant one could fly from Delhi to Lahore without changing planes in Abu Dhabi – a detour that added 4000 kilometres to the journey. And then, in March 2004, there was the end of a cricket drought.

In South Asia, politics did not just intrude on sport, the two were indivisible, and not for 14 years had the Indian Government allowed the national team to embark upon a fully fledged tour of Pakistan. Cricketing ties had been severed completely after an attack on the Indian Parliament in 2001, which India blamed on Pakistan-sponsored militants, and thus the Pakistani Government, and the two sides had not met anywhere on the subcontinent since the beginning of the new millennium.

From the speed at which the 33,000 tickets sold out – there were riots in Karachi when they first went on sale – to the queues for visas outside the Pakistani embassy in Delhi, the pre-tour atmospherics – or mood music, as diplomats often call it – were encouraging to say the least.

On match day, fans transformed the terraces of the ground into a subcontinental fiesta. Rather than the usual face-paint nationalism, Pakistanis turned up with the flags of both nations daubed on their cheeks. Many carried aloft banners with messages such as 'We Wish Friendship Forever'. Someone had sewn together a massive flag combining the Indian and Pakistani colours, featuring the slogan 'One blood'. Exceptionally beautiful Karachi women, wearing tight-fitting white T-shirts and over-sized designer sunglasses, and carrying ripped-off Louis Vuitton handbags, found themselves sitting next to exceptionally beautiful Indian women in precisely the same get-up.

Most remarkable of all, perhaps, was the reaction to Rahul and Priyanka Gandhi, the scions of India's most famous political dynasty, who appeared in the stands joyfully brandishing the Indian tricolour. This in a city that their grandmother, Prime Minister Indira Gandhi, had bombed during the 1971 war. In years past, the Gandhis would have run the risk of being lynched. Now, though, they were received like idols. It was almost as improbable as watching the Bush twins turn up for a football match in Baghdad to a standing ovation.

To crown the day, the cricket was superb as well, with the drought between the two countries ending with a freakish cloudburst of runs, the most ever scored up until that time in a one-day international. Chasing a gigantic winning total of 350, Pakistan's flabby captain, Inzamam-ul-Haq, scored 122 off 102 balls – a characteristically nonchalant innings greeted in the stands with chants of 'Aloo, aloo', or 'Potato, potato'. Needing a six off the final ball of the match, however, the home side just fell short.

After the match, we adjourned to a rooftop barbecue joint overlooking the port, where open stoves were lined with Seekh, Reshmi and Afghan kebabs, and the walls adorned with photographs of the owner greeting General Musharraf, whose bouffant looked even more magnificent than normal. Kicking back with a non-alcoholic mocktail, I felt that Karachi had the carefree air of the Riviera, although the women were arguably more stunning.

What we had seen that day was Pakistan's often silent middle class asserting itself much more strongly. They were people who wanted to dress well, to eat in fashionable restaurants, to have the latest mobile phones and to match India's fast-rising living standards. The problem they were up against, however, was that violent nihilists wanted to shape the country's future and expressed themselves much more forcefully.

Our trip to Karachi, a city that the writer William Dalrymple pithily described as South Asia's Beirut, offered proof of that as well. In the run-up to the cricket match, the Pakistani police had turned Karachi's National Stadium into a citadel, encircling it with armoured vehicles, troops and sharpshooters, such was the fear of a suicide-bomb attack. As an added precaution, various decoy convoys fanned out from the Indian team's hotel in the hope of foxing militants who might be waiting in ambush for their coach.

Our hotel and theirs, the Sheraton, had been bombed during the New Zealand cricket team's last visit in June 2002, an attack that killed 11 French engineers and three Pakistanis. Next door was the US consulate, an outpost so heavily fortified that it resembled a cliff-top gun emplacement ready at any moment to repel an invasion. Twice since 9/11, it had been hit by jihadists, ranking it third on the list of America's most dangerous embassies or consulates, after Baghdad and Kabul. Only days after the cricket ended, it was targeted again, when militants tried to detonate a van loaded with 200 gallons of liquid explosives that was parked outside (which made sense of our precaution never to open the curtains in our hotel rooms, since they overlooked the consulate).

The host to a wave of anti-American protests since 9/11, in which US flags and effigies of George W. Bush were torched with paraffin, Karachi performed a dual role for al-Qaeda. It was a key recruiting ground and a frequent target.

Also close to the Sheraton was the street corner where the *Wall Street Journal*'s South Asian bureau chief Daniel Pearl had been abducted in January 2002. Nine days later, he was butchered by his captors, who hacked off his head and cut his body into ten pieces – an execution that they released with grotesque pride three weeks later as a beheading video entitled 'The Slaughter of the Spy-Journalist – the Jew Daniel Pearl'.

Pearl's successor at the *Journal* became a good friend and followed the procedure, whenever he was on the road in Pakistan, of regularly ringing New York to assure his editors of his safety. By now, however, all the foreign journalists in the region were much more risk averse in the face of al-Qaeda's barbarism. Again, this made Pakistan infuriatingly difficult to cover, because it was so difficult to get access to the key players: the jihadists themselves. Correspondents usually show a wilful disregard for the strictures of health and safety, but in Pakistan they truly were a matter of life and death. The beheading videos had made us pause.

As Karachi always reminded us, Pakistan was a country with a seemingly never-ending list of problems: the threat from al-Qaeda, other Islamist militants and more recently the Pakistan Taliban; the lawlessness of its tribal regions, where the writ of Islamabad did not extend; the dysfunction of its politics, where corruption was endemic and assassinations were routine; the regular bursts of sectarian violence between the majority Sunni Muslims and the minority Shias; a little-reported nationalist insurgency, which Islamabad claimed that India was bankrolling, in Balochistan, the country's largest province.

Under that sort of buckling pressure, the state should probably have failed. Yet Pakistan had this extraordinary ability to absorb whatever crisis or calamity befell it, and then to muddle through. However intense the national convulsion, however dire the warnings that it was staring into the abyss, whatever the fears that its nuclear weapons were about to fall into the hands of militants, Pakistan somehow withstood the shock waves. Just.

Flying into Islamabad to cover the latest bombing or political crisis, I was always slightly amused by the in-flight announcement aboard Pakistan International Airlines as we made our final approach: 'We will be landing in Islamabad in five minutes, *Insha'Allah* [God willing].' Admittedly, I would have preferred something more definite. But also it provided an essential clue to understanding the country down below. In their earthly lives, many Pakistanis seemed reconciled to living in an unending state of crisis and often were inclined to defer to their leaders as a result, whether they be elected prime ministers or military dictators. At times of crisis, this compliant, unquestioning faith had strong adhesive powers. It helped keep the country from falling apart. For all its manifold problems, Pakistan was as Allah intended it to be.

Chapter 8

India Shining

In the slums of Mumbai, where the stench of diesel oil and human excrement putrefied the air and stung the nostrils, we could smell the old India and see the new. We had flown in from Delhi to meet Hermat, a young father who sat almost motionless for hours on end in front of a colour television tuned to one of the 24-hour business-news channels, watching transfixed as a fast-moving ticker covered with corporate hieroglyphics raced from right to left across the bottom of the screen.

Every quarter-hour, the channel replayed a jingle in which a thumping bed of Bhangra music was overlaid with the words 'Indian Dream'. In his cramped, barely furnished shanty, Hermat was living out his own. With his tiny baby daughter in his lap, a cup of chai in his hand and a ring-bound brochure for the latest Initial Public Offering, or IPO, on his knee, he kept a constant check on the value of his share portfolio. Given the skyward trajectory of the Bombay Stock Exchange, it was rising with each infrequent blink of his eyes.

'I saw lots of people making money out of the stock market,' he told us. 'Now I'm doing the same.' Outside his open door, neighbours watched in wonderment, with looks of compliant faith that were reserved normally for holy men and doctors. Each of them had entrusted Hermat with small amounts of their own money and were waiting to see how quickly he could turn a profit. With India in the throes of a revolution of rising expectations, the feeling was now commonplace that tomorrow would be better than today. And here we were witnessing the oddest of oxymorons: a newly gentrified slum. In a country where hope had always fought a running battle with despair, even the poor were daring to dream.

Always a land of jolting disparities, never had they been more pronounced. The new collided with the old. The rich accelerated away from the vast majority of the poor. The beautiful averted their gaze from the wretched. And, rather usefully for the purposes of television, often the contrasts could be captured with a simple tilt, pan or zoom of the camera lens. Just down the road from Hermat's shanty in Mumbai, we filmed jetliners gliding in to land at the international airport, and then tilted down to the corrugated shacks just metres from the runway that lay on the fringes of Asia's largest slum.

In Hyderabad, the mirror-glassed citadels of hi-tech Cyberabad sat atop a hill, their satellite dishes angled upwards, while a Third World shanty occupied the valley down below.

In Calcutta, you did not even have to adjust the camera to catch in the same frame a chauffeur-driven Mercedes or BMW overtaking a rickshaw propelled by a willowy human puller.

At any major junction in any major city, you could film street urchins with hands outstretched and heads tilted pleadingly, then slowly pan across to the traffic jam of newly imported cars, with electric windows firmly shut and passengers peering implacably ahead. Useful as this particular footage often was, we used it sparingly. After all, we were often the ones sitting in the air-conditioned comfort of the BBC's fleet of four-wheel drives, with the glass unopened and the beggars blithely ignored.

In covering India's transformation from a near socialist economy to a fully fledged capitalist one, we operated out of a bureau that stood in stubborn defiance of these fast-paced times. Located on the top floor of an art gallery run by the All India Fine Arts and Crafts Society, with a sumptuous view of the pillared rotunda of the Indian Parliament building and the turrets of Lutyens' presidential palace just beyond, it was the kind of newspaper-strewn office in which you half-expected to see Graham Greene hunched over an Underwood typewriter or Ernest Hemingway sucking on a cigar.

In the absence of a water cooler or vending machine, a squadron of waiters spent the day ferrying trays of lukewarm water, chai and coffee from the kitchen to the newsrooms. In the absence of a lift, a team of porters dressed in pale-blue uniforms lugged our television equipment up two spiralling flights of stairs.

Three delightful receptionists manned the entrance, huddled together in a glass-fronted cubicle that looked like a soundproof booth from a 1950s quiz show. Inside, they answered the phones, sorted the mail into the wooden pigeonholes ranged behind them and sifted through all the bureau gossip.

Finally, there were 70 or so journalists, from the English, Hindi, Urdu, Bengali and Tamil language sections, who were crammed into a space that could comfortably accommodate about a third of that number. Theoretically, the overcrowding could have been worse, for there were 22 official Indian languages in which we feasibly could have broadcast. For years, we had been trying to move to new premises, but, on a matter of high principle, we refused to pay the mandatory bribes demanded by our prospective new landlords.

The correspondents' offices had the feel and musty smell of miniature museums, for over the years they had accumulated relics and artefacts from trips around the country that nobody had the courage to throw out. To do so not only felt like vandalising a heritage site but also ran the risk, in this most superstitious of countries, of being recklessly inauspicious. On arrival, then, I inherited a scale model of a steam locomotive mounted in a Perspex display case, an assortment of craft items from Nagaland, a leather-bound collection of budget estimates that appeared to stretch back to the days of Nehru, and, the collection's *pièce de résistance*, a metre-high chrome and plastic trophy that looked like it belonged in the hands of the Punjabi police department's weightlifting champion or, if not, his close runner-up.

What made our bureau feel even more antiquated was that the offices downstairs housed an Indian outpost of General Electric. Inside its boardroom, American executives had negotiated one of India's first major outsourcing deals, unleashing a white-hot technological revolution that had transformed vast tracts of the country. But it had not yet percolated through to the floor above. As a result, our stories on 'Before and After' India were compiled in an office that fitted neither description. It came from an entirely different epoch.

Still, modern India was all around us. Along with an Old Delhi and a New Delhi, a futuristic Delhi had risen up on the fringes of the capital in the newly developed suburbs of Gurgaon and Noida. It was there that we headed to cover the most modish story of the day: the headset-clad young Indians who manned the phones at outsourcing centres, all of whom received crash-courses in British culture in order to sustain the subterfuge that they were situated in, say, Stevenage or Hull.

Covering the full gamut, from Posh and Becks to Robbie Williams, from *Eastenders* to *Emmerdale*, I fear these master-classes said more about the decline of Britain than the rise of India, but they also illustrated how business-processing outsourcing, or BPO, was revolutionising the subcontinent. With British and American times and temperatures displayed permanently on their computer screens, young Indians were forced to show greater interest in the rest of the world. And the rest of the world had been forced to show a greater interest in India.

As well as being partisans of progress, most of these young Indians were fierce patriots, determined that India should regain its rightful place. The widespread presumption was that, by mid-century, the country would have become a global superpower rivalling America and China. The downside was that they had to work through the night in sync with their American and British clients, feign Western accents and even Anglicise their names in order to achieve it.

If the kids manning the call centres were the infantry in India's march towards greatness, the field marshals were the corporate tycoons, or the modern-day maharajas, as everyone had taken to calling them. Many had the showmanship and panache of their aristocratic forbears, and rarely needed much persuasion to show off their fabulous wealth.

For a profile on one of India's most swashbuckling businessmen, Subrata Roy, the head of the entertainment, real-estate and financial-services conglomerate Sahara, which sponsored the Indian cricket team, our producers thought it would be a terrific idea to film him playing cricket on the oval of his 100-acre Lucknow estate. What they had in mind was a gentle knockabout that, after editing, would probably make up at most about 30 seconds of the feature.

Roy, though, had a much grander production in mind. He put on a full-scale match under floodlights, for which he flew in a planeload of Bollywood lovelies and former Indian cricket stars, including the World Cup-winning captain, Kapil Dev. And I have a feeling that the finale of the game was stage-managed so that he would hit the winning run.

As if to prove that even the super-rich were impossible to stereotype, however, other Indian tycoons were much more frugal in their tastes and far more unassuming. Perhaps the greatest extravagance of the bespectacled N. R. Narayana Murthy, the founder and chairman of Infosys, the info-tech giant, was a classical-music collection that included the entire works of Mozart on 176 CDs. As for the country's richest man, Azim Premji, the chairman of Wipro Technologies and 'the Bill Gates of India', for years he had been driven around Bangalore in a Ford Escort, which he eventually replaced with a Toyota Corolla. Premji was also a Muslim, another sign of how the business world was disregarding time-honoured prejudices and hierarchies. The caste system finally faced a serious challenger: the flourishing meritocracy of India Inc.

New hierarchies were fast emerging, which were usually determined by spending power and commonly linked to one's means of transportation. What Indians drove, or were driven in, had become a telling social pointer. At the lower end, the Honda Hero motorbike had long been a sign of upward mobility. Now, though, the Maruti hatchback had become the gateway car for the middle classes.

For the rich, there were subtler gradations. A vehicle shipped from Europe trumped a Japanese import, but such were the advances in Indian automotive engineering that both could be overtaken by the top-of-the-range Tata Safari, with walnut panelling, smoke-tinted windows, a back-seat snack tray and an 'Aroma Ganesh Frame', a fragrant neck cushion fashioned in the shape of the elephantine Hindu god that ensured the vehicle was both 'fresh and blessed'. At the flash-cash end of the market, the super-rich could afford Lamborghinis and Maseratis, though it is hard to imagine cars more unsuitable for roads strewn with people, rickshaws and cows. The ridiculously super-rich could go one better. Whenever venturing out onto the roads, a millionaire in Pune ordered his chauffeur to drive behind him in one of his lesser European models, say his Porsche or BMW, so that no one would run into the back of his Ferrari.

Being able to afford air travel was another social indicator, and, naturally, whether you turned left or right on boarding the plane. Often, as I nibbled my way through the samosas, oblong pizza slices and stale cheese-and-tomato sandwiches in a departure lounge lined with glass-fronted fridges, I would wonder whether the upper tiers of the caste system would ultimately be replaced by two broad categories: business and economy.

Your destination was also germane. Having the economic wherewithal to leave the country was a sure sign that you had truly arrived in India. New money brought new bundles of contradictions and paradoxes. Consumerism had become so rampant, for instance, that in many quarters it actually came to be expressed with less ostentation. Fridges had become so commonplace that status-conscious families no longer felt the need to show them off in their lounge rooms and relegated them to their rightful place in the kitchen.

Always, there was the temptation to report that the love of money was making India less sacred, but we did not succumb. Long before US television evangelists started preaching the gospel of prosperity, Indian holy men emphasised the compatibility of spirituality and commercialism. A BBC colleague offered a deft summation. 'Contrary to the belief of many Westerners, India is not a profoundly spiritual country but a proudly materialistic one,' he wrote. 'The object of most religious practice is to ensure material success.' A strong piece of analysis, and penned, it is worth pointing out, in the 1950s. Then, as now, religiosity was often regarded as transactional, an insurance policy against failure and a down payment on success.

In any case, modernity usually came with traditional religious trappings. On the opening day of the new financial year, the first investment made by a stockbroking house in Mumbai's financial quarter was to pay a few hundred rupees to a Hindu priest, who brought work to a halt by performing pujas on the floor in the middle of the office. Similar rituals played out on the forecourts of car showrooms across the country, as families had their new Marutis consecrated with marigold chains and the engine daubed with the Hindu swastika.

Now, it was possible to download the Nokia mobile-phone jingle in a holy ringtone, although places of worship still tried to prohibit their use. 'Please switch off Mobile Phone' read a newly minted sign at the entrance of the gold-domed Sikh temple, or gurdwara, in Old Delhi. Yet few pilgrims took any notice. Modern-day Indians were still prepared to put up with countless indignities, from water shortages to regular power outages, but they baulked at being denied the use of their mobile phones.

Much of our time was spent chronicling the changes that were overtaking India, and occasionally we witnessed them unfold dramatically before our eyes. Back in the shanties that flanked the runway at Mumbai Airport, we had heard it was demolition day – part of a slum-clearance programme that provided a useful illustration of how far India was prepared to go in its unswerving march towards the future. Mumbai was determined to become Shanghai, and for an image-conscious city the slums surrounding the airport were not only an ugly eyesore but also a sorry advertisement. As a result, they were the next on the list in a slum-clearance programme that had already razed some 70,000 shanties to the ground.

With the yellow bulldozers already rumbling through the nearby streets, the Jadhav family had been given ten minutes to gather up their lifelong possessions and leave. Bharati Jadhav, the matriarch of the family, was dressed immaculately in a copper-coloured sari with a ruby-coloured tikka on her forehead, while her bespectacled husband wore pressed slacks and an ironed shirt. By Indian standards, they could hardly be described as impoverished, but, like hundreds of thousands of upwardly mobile working families in Mumbai, the only place they could afford to live was a tiny shanty, which they shared with their three children.

Eavesdropping as ever on misery, we filmed as Bharati hurriedly fastened a bag containing some pots and pans, the bare essentials, and listened as she spoke in a voice of rising panic: 'If they demolish now, where do we go? They are going to smash down our shelter, and we will have nowhere to live.' Minutes away from being made homeless, they had no idea where they would sleep that evening, since the government had not offered them any alternative accommodation.

On the scrubland outside, as the planes continued to land over her shoulder, one of Bharati's more feisty neighbours tried to raise a mob. 'We'll stop the bulldozers,' she cried, with her sinewy arm thrust into the sky and her head contorting from side to side, 'even if we have to die.' Given her fervour, it was tempting to describe her as a sari-clad revolutionary. But all she was trying to do was preserve the status quo.

When the bulldozers rolled around the corner, she stood in the way of the demolition crew for a few futile moments, while men from the shanties hurled bricks and rocks at the advancing machines. Yet a squad of policemen wielding lathis, the thin antiquated bamboo batons that for generations had kept agitators in their place, quickly brushed them aside. Within minutes of arriving, the bulldozers' mechanical arms reached into the corrugated iron huts and wrenched them savagely apart.

Now, without even tilting or readjusting the frame, the camera captured the new destroying the old: the shot showed a bulldozer entering from the side of the screen, while Bharati watched helpless and mute as its iron claws ransacked her long-time home. Here was the flipside of India's grand new boast that nothing could stand in the way of progress.

Successive Indian governments had an appalling record of managing change in a way that balanced the needs of corporations and foreign investors with the interests of the poor. There was no greater monument to their failure than the skeletal remains of the Union Carbide chemical factory in Bhopal, where a poisonous gas leak in 1984 killed at least 3000 people at the time, claimed 8000 more lives in the years afterwards and left over 500,000 people nursing injuries. Returning there to mark the 20th anniversary of the world's worst ever industrial disaster, we saw for ourselves the broken sacks of pesticide still littering the site and the piles of toxic waste that had not yet been cleared away.

In the shanty opposite the factory were the victims themselves, many of whom still awaited proper compensation. Cows continued to amble around the site, from which the nearby slum-dwellers drew their milk. The wells that locals relied upon for their water remained poisoned. A helpful security guard, who patrolled the site with a double-barrelled shotgun slung over his shoulder, told us of his failed attempts to prevent local children from playing among the ruins. Then, as the fumes seeped into his nostrils, his knees buckled beneath him, and he started to faint. No wonder Bhopal had become a byword for corporate and official negligence.

In covering the anniversary, we listened to the testimony of survivors, highlighted the ongoing litigation aimed at bringing justice for the victims of the disaster and visited the local hospital to film the room where foetuses cut from the bellies of pregnant women killed by the gas cloud were stored in over-sized glass jars – a real chamber of horrors.

To our lasting regret, however, the BBC unwittingly added to Bhopal's misery. We did so by falling prey to the most terrible hoax, which for a time that day made us the focus of the story. It started the week before when a producer in London was duped by a fake website purporting to be the corporate home of The Dow Chemical Company, which now owned the plant. She rang the telephone number that appeared on the phoney website and arranged for a company spokesman to come to our Paris bureau on the morning of the anniversary. Live on air, in an interview with a presenter in London, the spokesman made the most startling announcement: that Dow would not only clean up the factory site but also hand out vast sums in compensation. It would be financed, he said, out of the liquidation of Union Carbide. As if to prove how fast a lie can travel, the news reached Bhopal in an instant, where it was met with near riotous joy from the hardened activists who had fought Dow Chemical for years. The markets also delivered their verdict, wiping over four per cent of the value of Dow Chemical's share price in the space of 23 minutes.

It is still shocking, and enraging, to recall how easily London was duped. Alarm bells should have started ringing even before the 'Dow Chemical Company spokesman' was allowed on air, for he turned up at our Paris bureau in an ill-fitting suit, accompanied by his own camera crew, which was not the normal corporate look. His unusual name, Jude Finisterra, might have raised suspicions. Subsequent Google searches revealed that Finisterra means the end of the world, while Jude, of course, is the patron saint of lost causes. Then there was his startling announcement: the liquidation of a multi-billion-dollar company, Union Carbide.

By now, the alarm bells should have been deafening. Here was an American corporate titan announcing the liquidation of a giant subsidiary live on BBC World News from a remote studio in Paris, with a boggle-eyed spokesman with a weird name wearing a ragged suit that looked like it had been borrowed from a mime artist on the Champs Élysées. Please.

Soon, a real Dow Chemical Company spokesperson, desperate to halt the slide in its share price, was interviewed from London and given the easiest of rides by a presenter who now had to apologise for our mistake rather than tackling her on theirs. Then, the hoaxer himself was allowed back onto our airwaves to revel in his mischief. Later, a group calling itself the Yes Men made a film claiming that the people of Bhopal were deeply appreciative of their brilliant trickery, because it had highlighted the Dow Chemical Company's hard-heartedness. But I witnessed the elation of these people when they learnt of their windfall and saw their despair when it was cruelly snatched away. Other than to marvel at their own cleverness, the main thing the Yes Men did that day was to further victimise the victims.

Back in Delhi – a city where argumentative debate was often the highest form of entertainment – much of the dinner-party discussion at the time centred on whether India's rapid advance was a wholly good thing. Perhaps the memory of Bhopal, an early American encroachment into the Indian market, offered something of a cautionary tale, given the new-found reliance on foreign investment. Not only was the gap widening between rich and poor, bringing about even more ghastly disparities, but also there was a danger that India was losing itself in the rush for globalisation.

Old South Asian hands bemoaned the intrusion into their favourite local markets of fast-food chains such as McDonald's, Subway and Pizza Hut. (Are not pizza-delivery boys always the storm troopers of globalisation?) High-end jewellers and opticians selling titanium frames and sunglasses by Chanel and Dior were crowding out booksellers. Edge-of-town supermarkets – a new innovation in India – threatened to kill off the trusted corner shop, while air-conditioned malls endangered bustling, traditional markets.

Preferring denim and tight-fitting T-shirts, women now wore saris less commonly. Young men sported the latest Nike, Adidas or Reebok leisurewear. Much of India's rapid new-millennial growth had been propelled by Western paranoia over the Y2K bug and the skill of Indian outsourcing firms to deliver cheap fixes. Now, it was India itself that was at risk of contamination from the twenty-first century.

Whenever the debate was limited to the narrower question of whether economic growth was benefiting Indian society as a whole, I found it hard to side with the naysayers. The statistics, even without being tortured, spoke for themselves. In the early 1980s, before the evisceration of the Licence Raj and the opening up of the economy to outside investment, 60 per cent of Indians lived below the international poverty line. In 2005, when I was there, the figure had dropped to 41 per cent, with the sharpest falls in poverty coinciding with the fastest spurts of growth.

For all that, I was glad to have experienced so much of the old India before it was totally eclipsed by the new. One morning in Delhi, I found myself discussing this question with a high-ranking public servant who moonlighted as a public intellectual, who had written a series of quite brilliant books on the rise and character of the Indian middle class. Clearly, he was a strong believer in a more egalitarian society, and confidently predicted that a rising tide would eventually lift all the boats, to use the voguish economic analogy of the times.

He spoke with eloquent conviction, and it was moving to hear him talk so hopefully of a less iniquitous country. Yet the moment we finished the interview, he nonchalantly pushed a buzzer concealed in the arm of his chair, at which point a waiter came scurrying in from the pantry next door to serve us tea. It was hilariously incongruous, but he performed this ritual with a complete lack of embarrassment or self-consciousness. Like many Indians, I suspect, he was a well-intentioned macro-economist, but more self-serving as a micro-economist. Much as he believed that the poor should get a far better deal, he rather enjoyed the luxuries that the inequality of Indian society brought to his daily life. I recognised this train of thought, not least because, like most foreign correspondents stationed in Delhi, I had fallen prey to it myself.

Certainly, prosperity was no guarantor of progress. Consider what unfolded in Gujarat, one of India's richest states, where communal rioting erupted in 2002 that led to the slaughter of almost 800 Muslims and over 250 Hindus. With homicidal fury, Hindu mobs, wearing saffron bandanas and brandishing swords, iron bars and trishuls, tore through the streets of Ahmedabad, the state capital, and a string of towns destroying mosques and setting alight Muslim-owned businesses.

Then they murdered their owners and gang-raped the women and children, 20 men at a time. One Muslim man who tried to protect his sister-in-law and young child had his skull cracked open with a sword and his eyes doused with diesel oil. Then he was set alight. His sister-in-law was stripped and raped, then drenched in kerosene and burnt alive. Then, the three-month-old baby that she had cradled in her lap was dumped into the flames. Afterwards, the local gravedigger told of finding the bodies of three pregnant women by the side of the road, with their stomachs slashed open and the foetuses hanging out. From survivors also came testimony of how young Muslim girls cast themselves onto the fire rather than being held down and raped.

To their shame, the police and state authorities did nothing to prevent the violence. Indeed, the accusation has always been that they were accomplices to the slaughter and allowed the mass murders in revenge for an arson attack on a train returning Hindu pilgrims from the holy town of Ayodhya in which at least 58 people were killed. The chief minister of Gujarat, the Hindu extremist Narendra Modi, was also accused of taking no action to prevent the riots.

In India, the burning of a train was always likely to provoke an especially grotesque response, for it recalled the horrors of partition. Some of the worst violence took place within metres of police stations, where unmanned switchboards echoed to the noise of the violence outside and the sound of ringing phones. The first pogrom of the incredible India age, what was especially alarming was how technology had been co-opted by the murderers. They used computer printouts of voter-registration lists to identify the homes and businesses owned by Muslims, along with mobile phones and texts to better coordinate their attacks.

If wealth and prosperity had failed to eradicate the savagery of communalism, it had actually aggravated another Indian problem that had been handed down through the ages: female foeticide, the abortion each year of 500,000 female foetuses. Not wanting to be saddled with expensive dowries or run the risk of losing their landholdings when their daughters got married, parents who discovered they were expecting a baby daughter regularly opted to pay 500 rupees ($10) for a quick abortion.

Here, increased prosperity brought increased access to prenatal ultrasounds and sonograms, which, in turn, brought increased rates of female foeticide. Already, there was a welter of statistics to show that sex selection was worst in the most affluent parts of the country: Punjab, Haryana, Gujarat and South Delhi, the middle-class haven that was the home to most foreign correspondents. While the Indian Government had enacted laws to prevent expectant parents finding out the sex of their child, doctors were rarely prosecuted for revealing the results of ultrasound tests. Instead, the same spirit of consumerism that was driving the Indian economy was also depressing the female birth rate. Moderately well-off Indians could choose the sex of their babies just as easily as they could select the colour of their new Marutis.

In a Punjabi village just a couple of hours' drive from Chandigarh, the state capital, it was easy to find evidence of female foeticide. The village birth register from the past 12 months showed that 34 boys had been born compared with just 19 girls. Since January, just one female name had been added to the ledger, and now it was almost November. Cars equipped with mobile ultrasound machines drove from village to village, so women did not even have to leave home to find out the sex of their foetus.

Local women spoke openly about having abortions, with little sense of shame and no fear of prosecution. At the local maternity hospital, we were allowed to film a mother giving birth, and we arrived in the operating theatre just as the young mother, Neelam, was being administered a trickle of anaesthetic to numb the pain from her Caesarean section. Neelam had already given birth to a daughter and desperately wanted to give her husband a son. So there was a heightened sense of tension in the operating theatre as the surgeon slid his scalpel across her stomach and pulled from her womb the tiny infant. With the Caesarean section a complete success, the safe arrival of such a beautiful ball of life should have been greeted with delight. Sadly, it was a joyless birth. Neelam had produced a second baby girl.

Handed the little girl, not yet ten minutes old, the women of the family were disapproving and edgy, fretful perhaps of how they would break the news to the menfolk, who had not even come to the hospital. On the maternity ward a few minutes later, as Neelam slowly came round from her anaesthetic, one of the ladies – her sister, I think – approached us and thrust the newborn towards us. 'Would you like to name the baby?' she asked. We laughed off the suggestion and prepared to leave. But just as we were saying our goodbyes, the same woman came towards us and thrust the baby at us more determinedly. 'Could you take the child?' In another time, the family might have thrown the unwanted baby down a well. A visiting film crew offered a tidier means of disposal. That very week, a dear Australian friend had suffered the unspeakable agony, after several rounds of IVF, of giving birth to a stillborn child; and here was a family blithely trying to give away their newborn.

A couple of years later, in 2007, India marked the 60th anniversary of its independence. By then, Pratibha Patil, India's first female president, was the country's ceremonial figurehead, while Sonia Gandhi stood at the head of Congress, India's once-more-dominant political party. Women proliferated in the upper ranks of Indian society and even ran a couple of its most thrusting companies. But what of that little baby girl in Punjab? All that we could hope for was that she had just celebrated a birthday of her own.

—

The legendary BBC correspondent Mark Tully had by far the best answer for anyone who made the mistake of asking him how he coped with the poverty or suffering in India. He merely reported on the plight of slum-dwellers, he would pointedly reply, and its true victims were those who lived with it every day.

If anything, the subcontinent had long been one of the more aristocratic of foreign postings, and even though news organisations had applied razors to their foreign budgets, we continued to enjoy lives of luxury compared with the correspondents who had gone before. When one of the BBC's former India men arrived in Delhi to report on the British handover in 1947, he was instructed always to wear a cholera belt – 'a swaddling band of flannel worn around the waist' – and a sturdy pith helmet whenever he stepped into the sun. Despite these precautions, he still came out in a rash of angry boils and became so frustrated that he cast his 'inflaming corselet' aside.

Back then, light relief for the international press corps occasionally came from a poker-playing American reporter, a former colonel who worked for the Associated Press, who enlivened card schools by sporadically yelling 'Guess I'll sweeten the freakpot' and 'Red threes are wild!' With martial proficiency, he also took the lead in organising field trips outside of the capital. 'Equipment to include portable typewriter, bedding roll, two bottles Scotch (NOT Indian), light reading and cash for poker (minimum stake Re 1),' he instructed his colleagues on the eve of a railway journey to Bombay. 'NB: DO NOT forget Scotch, Bombay is PROHIBITION TERRITORY.'

By contrast, we hardly had to suffer for our art. I lived in a gated community directly opposite Lodi Gardens, a gorgeous parkland dotted with palm trees, Mogul tombs, green parakeets, young lovers reclining furtively against its trees and corpulent 50-something fitness fanatics who marched around its perimeter with the exaggerated arm and leg movements of the honour guards at the Wagah border crossing.

Though the BBC no longer footed the bill for a full complement of domestic staff, it was easy enough to afford out of your own pocket a cook and cleaner. My 'Man Friday' was a diminutive Punjabi called Satay Singh, who made a mean paratha for breakfast and put such razor-sharp creases into my regulation foreign-correspondent khaki chinos that I had to be careful when walking near parked cars.

I did not bother with a driver, much preferring to take my

chances with the Michael Schumacher wannabes from the taxi rank on Lodi Road. In a city lacking in excitement, screeching around the roundabouts and tree-lined boulevards of Lutyens' Delhi in their black, green and yellow Ambassadors was sure to get the blood pumping at the start of the day.

My only other member of staff was an elderly security guard who insisted on saluting whenever I entered my apartment, even though I almost begged him not to. Some salute it was too: ramrod straight, as if clenching a 500 rupee note between his buttocks, with his quivering palm angled, Benny Hill-style, into his right temple. His primary role was to be the first line of defence against Kashmiri insurgents or, perhaps, disgruntled Naxalites. After arriving home late at night, however, I was usually half-undressed and about to get into bed by the time he stirred from his slumbers in his sentry box at the gate.

When it came to recreation, I had arrived in Delhi on the cusp of change. Reporters in search of a cooling libation no longer had to rely solely on the bar at the Imperial Hotel, with its barmen dressed in black turbans and scarlet tunics set off with shimmering gold epaulettes. Nor the Foreign Correspondents' Club, a dingy hangout memorable only for a wonderful black-and-white photograph that hung in its hallway showing Rajiv Gandhi and his beautiful young bride, Sonia, sharing ice-cream cones at India Gate – a snapshot of innocence from the days when all he wanted out of life was to fly jetliners and all she hoped for was to live in suburban obscurity.

Now, fashionable new bars and restaurants were opening all over town, many of which would not have looked out of place in SoHo, Brooklyn or TriBeCa. I also became a fairly regular, if reluctant, participant on the Delhi cocktail circuit, which was educational from both an anthropological and an anatomical viewpoint. Indian women, I soon learnt, were usually about ten times as interesting as their husbands, while a serving tray piled high with steaming basmati rice was something best avoided. Not being entirely au fait with the Delhi scene, I also found myself on occasions chitchatting away to highly placed VIPs without ever knowing it. One night, it was a ludicrously pompous elderly gentleman, with a toxic wit, skin like it had already been embalmed and an ear for his own voice. Just before I went for the humdrum conversational ice-breaker 'So what do you do?', I suddenly realised: I was speaking to the Nobel laureate V. S. Naipaul, who offered proof that you should never judge an author by his cover photo.

With my journeys through India often taking on the feel of a gastronomic safari, I soon came to realise that curries neither had to blister the walls of your mouth nor be coloured shocking red, and also that they were best enjoyed before consuming ten pints of lager, rather than vice versa. If it was Punjab, then it was *dal makhani* for supper. If it was Calcutta, then it was fish curry, a Bengali *macher jhol*. Though Lucknow would argue, Hyderabad served up the finest *biryanis*, while Chennai opened up a whole new world of *dosas*, *hoppers* and the other delights of Tamil cuisine. What de Gaulle said of cheese in France was even truer of India's local delicacies: how could anyone hope to govern a country with over 246 varieties of curry? Trying to sample as many of them as possible became a mission and hobby.

An enthusiastic cricketer, I also joined the Foreign Correspondents' Club XI, but I proved an abject failure with both bat and ball. Instead, I owed my continued selection to a small but salient technicality: in a team packed with local journalists,

I *was* the only foreign correspondent. In younger days, I was a belligerent, if somewhat agricultural, middle-order batsman, who peppered the famed 'cow corner' with one inelegant boundary after another. But on subcontinental pitches against subcontinental spin bowlers, I found it impossible to locate that presumably sacred section of the ground.

It did not help that, because of the high demand for manicured pitches, games often started before breakfast on a Sunday morning. It meant that while I was chasing balls that pitched way outside off-stump, the effects of the previous night's Kingfishers were still chasing me.

Though rarely able to last more than a couple of overs in the middle, at least I got to spend time with my favourite teammate, a business reporter who chatted away in the manner in which many Indian journalists continued to write. Chronically dependent on British idioms, storms for him usually came in teapots, mountains rose up out of molehills, leopards never changed their spots and stable doors were always closed long after the horses had bolted. On the field, he could also be relied upon to turn in a performance noticeably more hapless than mine. Indeed, he always seemed to play the game on the stickiest of wickets.

Much of my cricket came to be viewed from the boundary, and on occasions even counted as work. For a time, cricketing ties between India and Pakistan were not just part of the Indo-Pak peace process, they pretty much *were* the Indo-Pak peace process. But perhaps the most exacting test of this cricketing détente came later in Ahmedabad, the state capital of Gujarat. It was not only the city that had witnessed the worst atrocities during the 2002 genocide but also the ground where Imran Khan had led his Pakistan team onto the pitch wearing batting helmets to protect them from missiles hurled from the stands.

Gathering material for a radio news report, I stepped into the commentary box hoping to record some atmospheric sound effects. Alas, my arrival came around the time that a real-life BBC cricket reporter was scheduled to offer a brief spell of expert summary. Seeing the letters BBC on the laminated credentials dangling from my neck, the commentator naturally assumed I was the said reporter, so he beckoned me over to the vacant chair alongside him and handed me an open microphone.

Here, I should pause briefly to emphasise the coveted seat that I now occupied. On Indian television at that time, one of the most popular reality shows was a cricketing version of *Pop Idol*, where thousands of youngsters competed for the chance to become a full time cricket commentator. One of the most frequently aired commercials featured a young woman who had longed all her life for the chance to climb into the commentary gantry, a dream that came miraculously true when she applied a coat of *Fair and Lovely* skin whitener. The climactic scene showed the young woman seated in the Test-match commentary box, with microphone in hand and with skin unblemished, as her mother looked on proudly from the sofa at home, wiping a tear from the corner of her eye.

As for my own commentary career, it started with the gentlest of full tosses: I was asked to pass judgement on the blossoming innings of the great Sachin Tendulkar, a subject I was more than happy to rhapsodise on for the time it took the bowler to walk back to his mark and to start his run-up. Unfortunately, tougher questions followed that I should probably have let go through to the wicketkeeper without offering a shot. What did I make of the state of the pitch? What was a realistic target for the Indians? How about the inconsistent batting form of the then Indian captain Sourav Ganguly? 'Form is temporary, class is permanent' was all I could summon up, as I started to tread the dark path of sporting cliché.

What I lacked in expertise, I made up for in praise for the Indians, knowing that kind of material would go down well with the listeners at home. But all it seemed to do was irritate my fellow commentator, who I now noticed was rationing my airtime. Realising I had perhaps overstayed my welcome, I made my excuses and left, and noticed on the way what might have been the source of annoyance. I had been absolutely convinced that I was broadcasting on All India Radio. Regrettably, I had actually stepped into the commentary booth of Radio Pakistan.

—

'Do not drink from a bottle labelled "Strong Indian Beer" and never predict the outcome of an Indian election.'

Soon after arriving in Delhi, a kindly fellow correspondent passed on these two pieces of irreproachable advice. Needless to say, I disregarded both. I cannot remember the consequences of my Strong Indian Beer lapse, which I suppose rather neatly made his point, but when it came to Indian politics at least I had a defence. The 2004 election could easily be foretold, for near universal was the view that the governing party, the Hindu nationalist Bharatiya Janata Party, or BJP, would romp home to victory. The BJP was ideally placed to profit not only from the booming economy but also from its happy slogan, 'India Shining', which encapsulated the optimistic spirit of the times.

A 79-year-old prime minister, with two artificial knees and a penchant for fried trout, the party's leader, Atal Bihari Vajpayee, could hardly be said to personify its thrusting message. Yet by the standards of India's political gerontocracy – his deputy, Lal Krishna Advani, was also in his late 70s, a group of 50-somethings were dubbed the party's Young Turks and one of the country's former leaders, Morarji Desai, did not become prime minister until the age of 81 – he had not yet reached the crest of the hill, and was still a half-decade or so away from being considered over it.

The BJP's image-makers also did their best to make him look as sprightly as possible, even going so far as to bully camera crews at his rare press conferences into not shooting his wobbly knees. From walking ten minutes each day on the treadmill to going cold turkey on the fried trout, Vajpayee himself tried to appear as vigorous as his faltering body would allow.

Neither was he prepared to let technology leave him floundering in its wake. In the early weeks of the campaign, I recall being woken early one Saturday morning by a telephone call from the prime minister only to realise a few words in that it was a recorded message sent to virtually every mobile-phone subscriber in the capital. The septuagenarian was trying to harness the zeitgeist, even if his wheezy voice brought unintended meaning to the phrase 'breathless change'.

My first sight of his opponent, Sonia Gandhi, came through a billowing cloud of fluttering rose and marigold petals, on a road choked with exultant banner-waving supporters. Her caravan of Tata Safaris nudged its way into Amethi, a hardscrabble town in Uttar Pradesh and the Gandhi family's long-time political fiefdom. Joylessly playing out her role as the matriarch of the clan, Sonia protruded from the first four-wheel drive, her arm projected almost robotically into the air. The recipient of the kind of adulation that would rouse even the most lifeless of politicians, she struggled even to manufacture a smile. Sonia gave the appearance of hating politics and detesting campaigning, all of which was entirely understandable given the tragedy that had befallen her beloved husband, Rajiv.

During the 1991 election, he had been assassinated at a late-night rally near Chennai, when a female assassin from the Tamil Tigers knelt deferentially at his feet and then detonated a belt packed with high explosives. All that was left of him were his head and his feet, the latter of which were still enclosed within an expensive pair of training shoes that he wore to help ease the pain of punishing days on the hustings.

After the murder, Congress pleaded with Rajiv's Italian-born widow to become the standard-bearer of the Gandhi clan, and eventually, some six years later, she relented. But her halting Hindi and awkwardness among crowds made her an uninspiring campaigner. 'A personality cult without a personality' was how one Delhi commentator witheringly described her. 'Illiterate in three languages,' scoffed another. Others simply regarded her as an Italian interloper, usually neglecting the unsettling question of why the Congress Party had failed to identify a plausible, home-grown alternative.

That ongoing search partly explained why we had travelled through the Uttar Pradesh countryside to Amethi, where Sonia's son, Rahul, was about to make his political debut. For years, he had lived in London, where he was caught in the telephoto glare of the Indian paparazzi wearing pinstripe suits and Jermyn Street shirts, and occasionally with his Colombian girlfriend on his arm.

Now that he was making his prodigal return to India, these Western accoutrements were banished from view, and instead he wore the uniform of the Indian politician: a long white kurta with his vest visible underneath. Gone was the bouncing gait of the Mayfair playboy, and instead he moved in slow motion, his face solemn, bowed and covered in flop sweat.

In this shrunken form, Rahul Gandhi was being propelled into a world that he appeared to find thoroughly alien. Tellingly, when he emerged from the rundown municipal office where he had gone to file his papers as a parliamentary candidate and was confronted by the usual flying wedge of Indian reporters, he made a beeline for me, the only white face in the crowd. I asked him if he could personally revive the Gandhi brand, but he smiled benignly and turned away.

Later on, I put the same question to his mother, after following her from village to village, having been promised a proper interview by her advisers: 'There are many people who say that the dynastic appeal of the Gandhis isn't as strong as it used to be. What do you say to that?'

'I don't know,' she replied. 'You might have seen today. You might have been with us. You might have noticed whether that is true or not.'

She had a point. Earlier on, she had to change vehicles because rose petals had clogged the engine, and Rahul had a signet ring torn from his finger by clamorous supporters. 'You think the Gandhi name is as strong as ever?' I continued. But she turned her back on me and jumped into her car, leaving unanswered a question that most commentators thought could be dealt with in a single word: no. For all their attempts to revive the brand, the Gandhis were thought to be finished.

As a correspondent used to the control-freakery of American elections, where a candidate's every outing was tightly scripted and intricately choreographed, the chaos and feast of colour that came with Indian elections was a wonder and joy. Both countries put on impressive shows, but it was like comparing the meticulous staging of a Broadway production to the outlandishness of Bollywood.

The path to the White House seemed somewhat two-dimensional and prosaic compared to the journey it took to get to the prime minister's residence on Golf Club Road. Whereas America could only boast the elephant and the donkey, India had as symbols for its political parties the lotus (BJP), the open hand (Congress), a hurricane lamp, an alarm clock, a car, an aeroplane, various models of bicycles, a bow and arrow, a pair of spectacles, the hammer and sickle, an inkpot and pen, a ladder, an electric light bulb, a conch, a mango, an umbrella and even a lady farmer carrying paddy on her head.

For new parties keen to enter the fray, the Election Commission of India had only three symbols left unclaimed: the balloon, the wardrobe and, more understandably, the banana. Whereas America had the Democrats and Republicans, India could boast an alphabet spaghetti of parties that made election tally boards look like the screens at the NASDAQ stock exchange.

A Pythonesque splitism, recalling the People's Front of Judea and the Judean People's Front, was also in evidence. There was an Indian Congress Party, a Nationalist Congress Party and even an All India Trinamool Congress Party. On the extreme left, the Communist Party of India vied with the Communist Party of India (Marxist). The world's biggest democracy had also produced what was surely the world's longest list of candidates for a single seat: 1033 in a constituency in Tamil Nadu. It turned the ballot paper into a booklet the size of a railway timetable.

Instead of red, white and blue balloons and bunting, there was a technicolour blaze of flags, banners, bandanas and posters with hand-painted portraits that made even the most physically unattractive of candidates look like screen idols. Giant-sized likenesses of the main party leaders were fastened to multi-storey scaffolds at the site of election rallies. To boost attendance at these gatherings, women were offered free saris. To boost turnout at the polls, men were offered free beer the night before – although a strict prohibition on alcohol was always in place on election days themselves.

The plural, of course, is deliberate, because so gigantic was this exercise in democracy that it had to be staggered into four separate rounds, with different parts of the country voting on different days. With a breathing space between each round, the security forces could be bussed and trained around the country so as to maintain order.

As well as being afflicted occasionally by electoral violence, the system was plagued by corruption, cronyism, intimidation and widespread bribery. Hundreds of candidates were also convicted criminals, some of whom orchestrated their campaigns on mobile phones from their prison cells. But lest Indian democracy sound like some kind of feudal throwback, it is worth remembering that its brand-new hi-tech electronic-voting machines were more advanced than those used in many polling stations in America, even if they had to be lugged into remote mountain villages on the backs of elephants. As local commentators never tired of pointing out in the wake of the Florida debacle, Indian elections also upheld the quaint idea that elections should be decided at the polling booth rather than in the courts.

In making television out of all this, the elephant shots were always received gladly, but in 2004 we also thought we had come up with the superlative film sequence to illustrate the feeling that Indians had never had it so good. Filmed in the soft early-morning light of the Hyderabad spring, first it showed a line of portly, sari-clad women hopping on the spot, laughing uncontrollably. Then we cut to a tight huddle of middle-aged men in complete hysterics wagging their fingers semi-accusingly at their cohorts, as if they had all awoken from a dream and realised they were completely naked. Next came another group of balding men wafting their arms gently in the air, like drowsy seagulls slowly swooping in to land. Finally, we showed a bespectacled Sikh gentleman with his turban fastened tightly around his chin, who looked like he had just been told the most hilarious joke known to man. After putting the report to air, we never did think to ask what the members of this Yogic Laughing Club, one of thousands that meet every morning in parks across India, thought of our report. Even though it made them look certifiable, one hoped they would have seen the funny side.

After filming the laughing club, we drove seven hours into the countryside of Andhra Pradesh, where the parched terrain of cropless farmland provided a wholly different electoral landscape. On a water-starved field, which had not absorbed a drop of monsoon rain for the past four years, a farmer told us the story of his brother, Hana Manteredi, a 45-year-old who could no longer repay his loans because he could no longer harvest a crop. At the tiny family home, his wife, Lakme, and two teenage daughters peered up at a portrait of Hana that was garlanded with flowers – a common household memorial. A proud man who believed he had failed his family, he had taken his life by swallowing pesticide. Across Andhra Pradesh, some 2000 farmers had done the same, and in this part of rural India the country only shined through the spirit of the hard-pressed people left behind.

Our report from the countryside gave us much-needed balance. Up until then, much of our coverage reflected the metropolitan bias of the metropolitan elites, who were the prime beneficiaries of the country's new abundance. It was almost as if we had been partially blinded by the 'India Shining' slogan.

Our tunnel vision was particularly unforgivable given the evidence of a twin-track election on our doorstep in the Indian capital. Early one morning at Delhi golf club, where Mogul tombs flanked the lush fairways and where the annual membership fees cost more than most Indians earned in a lifetime, we interviewed my landlord, Amit, a successful entrepreneur who perfectly framed the poll. 'India may be shining for me,' he said, as he strode towards the green in a monogrammed polo shirt, 'but not for my caddy. Ask him if India is shining. I don't know whether he'll agree. Does he have clean water? A place to stay? Food? Education? That's what he's looking for. The rising stock market doesn't concern him.'

Another journey well worth making during the campaign was to Ayodhya, the sacred town in Uttar Pradesh that doubled as a political fault line. It was there in 1992 that a mob of Hindu nationalists ransacked and demolished the Babri mosque, which had been constructed in the sixteenth century by the first Mogul emperor of India. Nowhere in the history of modern India had there been such a flagrant act of religious vandalism, and it unleashed communal rioting across the country in which more than 2000 people were killed, most of them Muslims.

Hindu nationalists believed fervently that the Mogul invaders had deliberately built the mosque on the birthplace of the Hindu god Ram, in order to subjugate India's Hindu masses. Now, 400 years on, they believed it was time to balance the historical ledger, even though there was no historical evidence to suggest that the mythical Ram had ever walked the earth, nor incontrovertible archaeological proof that a Hindu temple had once occupied the site. However, for diehard Hindu fundamentalists, to use a phrase that many religious scholars consider theologically nonsensical, there was no more ringing issue.

In a stonemason's yard nearby, the components of a new temple were being chiselled out, block by block, pillar by pillar, with bearded sadhus consecrating the craftsmanship with tridents in hands. Names of wealthy donors, many from overseas, were etched onto the bricks, and huge prefabricated pillars and slabs of finished sandstone panelling were piled high, with each individually numbered to aid in the eventual construction. A flat-pack temple awaited assembly.

Back in the early 1990s, when it was little more than a fringe party, the BJP had organised the great *yatra*, or procession, which had not only led to the destruction of the mosque but also laid the foundation stone for its speedy rise to power. In 2004, however, party modernisers believed it could run on the twin themes of peace and prosperity. This meant downplaying the more medieval aspects of its platform, namely the Hindu nationalism, or Hindutva, which promised to end the supposed privileges Muslims had come to enjoy, such as their constitutional entitlement to be polygamous.

Vajpayee, who was often called 'the acceptable face of the BJP', attempted to fudge the Ayodhya question by suggesting it should be a matter for negotiation and the courts. Yet, if the BJP won the election, many feared that onsite construction work on the new temple would soon commence. That was most certainly the intention of the BJP activist we interviewed, who proudly told us he had taken part in the destruction of the mosque. Now, he spent his days touring the streets of Ayodhya, in the shadow of the disputed site, in a jeep mounted with four megaphones and draped with the saffron and lotus flower of the BJP. He gripped a small microphone as if he were about to crush it and yelled with a primal scream, 'We'll tear down more mosques and build more temples.' Indians who cherished the country's secular ideal – the founding belief that all faiths could live in peaceful co-existence without government interference – feared this was the true intention of the Hindu nationalists and the BJP.

His might have been a lonely BJP voice during the 2004 campaign had it not been for mounting evidence, after the first two rounds of voting, that the 'India Shining' slogan was not cutting through. Now, the inevitability of a BJP victory had been brought into serious question, as the party's internal polling showed that two very different elections were unfolding: one in the cities and the other in the countryside. Even the ever-popular Vajpayee was struggling to draw big crowds to his rallies, however many free saris were handed out. To bolster its fortunes, party chieftains therefore decided to call on a figure they knew could mobilise the Hindu masses, even at the risk of some reputational damage: Narendra Modi, the chief minister of Gujarat, who up until then had been kept largely hidden from view. As if illuminating some great Hindutva sign in the skies above Ahmedabad, they called on him to finally join the national campaign.

Again, the action unfolded in Uttar Pradesh, the Florida and Ohio combined of Indian politics, which harboured the most people, over 190 million, and thus the most parliamentary seats. Here, Modi descended from the skies for his first campaign appearance in a saffron-coloured helicopter, as if engaged in some great aerial rescue mission. Then he took up his place on the dais, in a sumptuous claret-upholstered throne.

Scornful of the international press in general and the BBC in particular, Modi had walked out of an interview with a colleague just a few months previously. So, when he spotted us positioned below the podium, he decided to get his retaliation in first. The BBC was here to abuse him, he shouted to the crowd. It would say, 'Modi is a Hitler.' Rather usefully, now we did not have to.

His speech over, Modi exited the stage with his hands clasped in a namaste as a guard against our questions. Then he climbed back into the belly of his helicopter, which left behind a cloud of dirt and a swirl of controversy. The BJP had returned to its Hindu nationalist roots, and now Sonia Gandhi had a rallying cry, if only she could come up with the right words to voice it.

When Delhi went to the polls in the final round of voting, the BJP was expected still to triumph, even if talk of a landslide had now receded. As the votes started being tallied, however, a great and unexpected drama began to play out: Congress and its allies appeared to be nudging ahead. The first tallies, like the exit polls from the initial rounds of polling, were treated with extreme caution. Hours later, though, the trend was unmistakable. In an election thought to heavily favour the incumbent government, a mood of anti-incumbency was sweeping across the country. Inside our rickety rooftop studio, with its commanding view across to the Lok Sabha, a string of seasoned commentators expressed near disbelief that Congress seemed on the verge of victory. And no one was more surprised by this unexpected turn than Sonia Gandhi herself, who reportedly came close on a number of occasions that morning to vomiting.

By now, hundreds of jubilant Congress supporters, with bandanas tied tight around their heads, had rushed to her Lutyens bungalow at 10 Janpath in New Delhi, where they let off long strings of firecrackers, banged and clattered their drums and screamed 'Sonia Jindabad! Sonia Jindabad!'. For this yelling throng, the politically miraculous had just become real.

This frenzied setting seemed perfect for a quick piece to camera delivered, at deafening volume, over the cries and exploding pyrotechnics. What made it even more atmospheric was the close-up sight of firecrackers spewing flames and sparks as the camera panned from Sonia's supporters to me. However, the very thing that made the piece to camera look so dramatic also made it mildly hazardous, for these small fountains of fire were spewing sparks into my hair.

Viewers who watched our report later that night might have wondered why I chose such a climactic moment to coif my hair, at that time a rather extravagant bouffant that cost me the princely sum of 30 rupees from a barber in Khan Market. What they could not quite make out was that a stray spark had embedded itself in my scalp, briefly causing my hair to catch alight. To this day, my scalp bears the scar.

Still, there was no time to nurse my wounds, since the press pack had been granted rare access inside 10 Janpath for a photo opportunity with the victor. Not for the first time, it helped to have Nik, a multi-storey cameraman, at my side, who got a fabulous series of semi-aerial shots showing the Indian media pressing in on the new prime minister-in-waiting. With Sonia Gandhi standing before them, her thick mascara even darker than ever, the scene seemed almost Fellini-like. Inspired by the moment, I got a little expansive in my scripting. 'So the paparazzi treatment for the Italian-born leader,' I shouted. 'Written off as a lightweight when the campaign began, today she was living *la dolce vita*.' It was a textbook case of letting a script-line strangle the real story. Sonia was not revelling in her triumph. Rather, she was completely traumatised, her *vita* far from *dolce*.

For much of the following week, Sonia remained a prisoner in her own bungalow, from which rumours emerged that she was about to turn down India's top job. First, they were whispers. Delhi tittle-tattle, little more. Then, as Sonia used some weirdly ambiguous language to describe her intentions, the whispers turned into frenzied conjecture. Now, thousands of worried Congress supporters converged on 10 Janpath from all over the country, many carrying mattresses to sleep on as they mounted round-the-clock vigils. Others threatened to go on hunger strike if she refused to become prime minister.

Even senior Congress figures became gibbering wrecks. As a BBC colleague interviewed one party elder live on air, the elder broke down in gushing tears, completely inconsolable. When finally he regained his composure, and retrieved his head from my colleague's now drenched shoulder, a producer from CNN who had seen his on-screen meltdown pulled him to one side. Would he mind reproducing precisely the same emotional pyrotechnics for a live cross with Atlanta in ten minutes' time?

By far the most bravura performance that week came from a former Congress MP, who stood before the crowds outside 10 Janpath on the roof of his chauffeur-driven jeep, manically waving a pistol at his head, as if his arm were made of rubber, and threatening to pull the trigger. So madcap was the scene that this pratfalling performance looked like Bollywood's take on Mel Brooks's *Blazing Saddles*, with the suicidal former MP cast in the role of Bart, the black sheriff.

While the madness of Queen Sonia played out on the street outside 10 Janpath, the BJP started to mobilise a blatantly xenophobic campaign. Effigies were burnt. One of the party's chief ministers resigned her post and took to wearing a white sari in mourning. An activist from the RSS, the quasi-paramilitary wing of the BJP, even committed suicide in an act of martyrdom.

By now, the markets had also been spooked, with investors not only troubled by the sense of uncertainty but also fearful that Congress was about to jump into bed with the communists to secure a working majority in parliament. In a single day, the Bombay Stock Exchange shed 17 per cent of its value, the most dramatic slump in its 129-year history.

Hoping to soothe the nerves of international investors, the incoming treasurer, Dr Manmohan Singh, granted the BBC an interview in which he argued that there was no need for panic. Mid-sentence, however, as the camera continued to roll, an agitated aide thrust a live mobile phone towards him. It was the outgoing treasurer on the line, warning that the economy was indeed disappearing down the toilet. For a broadcast journalist, there are few worse irritations than a ringing telephone in the middle of an interview. This, then, was a rarity: an interview where an errant mobile provided its highpoint.

Sonia Gandhi also sought to calm her party, by inviting its new parliamentarians to a garden party on the lawns of 10 Janpath. However, she failed to put in an appearance herself, and kept them waiting for five hours. In her loaded absence, all they had to feed on were rumour and speculation. As dusk faded into night, and waiters wearing small Nehru hats ferried cold water to keep the MPs from fainting in the still-boiling heat, it was left to the ever-reliable Dr Singh to speak on her behalf.

Once again, he stepped before the cameras, this time without interruption, to assure his party, and a watching nation, that there was no reason for concern. But no one believed him. Sure enough, soon the summons came to gather in the Central Hall of Parliament, where Sonia intended finally to make clear her intentions. In the wood-panelled chamber, where life-size portraits of Indira and Rajiv Gandhi peered down on her like baffled ghosts, their reluctant heiress revealed that her 'inner voice' had spoken and told her she should not become the prime minister.

Immediately, there was uproar, as MPs raced to the lectern to plead with her to reconsider. From the press gallery high above, the scene looked so feverish that it felt like watching an actor's workshop where the students had been told to improvise on the theme 'the world will end in 60 seconds'. Amidst this pandemonium, Sonia remained unmoved, like the anti-diva she always was. Her mind was made up. Though she had struggled under the burden of the Gandhis' dynastic legacy, she could not shoulder the burden of office.

With Sonia Gandhi turning her back on a job that would have granted her inordinate power, an election that was supposed to turn on economic growth, consumption and greed had ended with an act of selflessness. It also meant that Dr Manmohan Singh, her soft-spoken confidant and counsellor, became prime minister. Thus, the largest job in Indian politics had gone to the politician with the smallest ego.

There was a certain poetic justice in all this. A man with

a DPhil in economics from Oxford, who had served both as the governor of the Reserve Bank of India and then as finance minister in the early 1990s, no Indian had done more to prepare the ground for the country's rapid spurt of economic growth. So it was entirely fitting that he ended up the ultimate victor in the 'India Shining' election, although he himself was far too self-effacing ever to make so bold a claim. Just as importantly, he also became India's first Sikh prime minister. To requisition the BJP's failed slogan, perhaps India was now truly shining: the country's economy was in the safest of hands, and so, too, was its secular ideal.

Chapter 9

Battlefields in Paradise

Automatic gunfire is accompanied by such deafening acoustics that when it erupted in the Kashmir Valley late that afternoon we feared gunmen had stormed the hotel lobby three floors down, when, in actual fact, they were a good half-mile away. Ever since the insurgency against Indian rule began in 1989, visits to Srinagar were regularly interrupted by bursts of shooting that bounced off the mountains encircling the city with a numb echo. Never before, however, had we been so close at the start of a gun battle between Islamist militants and the Indian Army.

Our first, uneasy instinct was to haul from their black carry bags our sky-blue bullet-proof vests stamped with the word 'PRESS', which were always on hand during visits to Kashmir, the only Indian region with a Muslim majority. Next, we ran downstairs to place the source of the gunfire.

It was April 2005, and days before we had flown into Srinagar to cover the opening of a historic new bus service linking Indian-administered Kashmir and Pakistani-administered Kashmir, the first time locals had been able to make legal crossings between the two since the first Kashmir war in the late 1940s. Islamic militants, who feared this goodwill gesture might serve to quell the revolt, had vowed to turn the buses heading in either direction into 'coffins on wheels'. Now, on the eve of the inaugural journeys, they mounted a pre-emptive strike. The passengers about to make the crossing had been billeted overnight in a tourism centre in the heart of Srinagar, which temporarily became the most heavily protected building in Kashmir. To our astonishment, the bursts of gunfire appeared to be coming from that very complex.

In the three minutes or so it took to rush there, the battle subsided, which was usually an indication that Indian commandos had either killed the militants or surrounded them. So we used this lull in the fighting to edge as near as we could get, since it was rare to get the chance to film a stand-off at such close range. A narrow passageway led to a courtyard in the centre of the building, where the fighting had sounded the fiercest. But, at the very moment we entered, the gunfire opened up again. With the passageway acting like an echo chamber, the noise was so thunderous that it sounded as if a militant was standing at the other end, spraying bullets in our direction.

In panicked unison, we all turned on our heels and scrambled for whatever cover we could get. On the street side of the passageway was a military checkpoint stacked with sandbags, so I dived inside for cover and found myself pressed up against an Indian soldier. But immediately I realised that I should have kept on running.

Along with this lone soldier, I was stranded in the middle of what instantly had become a no-man's-land – a 30-metre gap between the Indian military's positions and the militants running rampant inside. To make a dash for it now was to risk being fired upon by the Indian soldiers crouched behind their armoured jeeps with their guns trained on the building. To stay put risked being picked off by the militants. In the mad tumble, we had taken shelter directly below a row of first-floor windows, and a gunman could have hit us with a grenade with the most effortless of lobs. No wonder the Indian soldier raised his finger slowly to his mouth, almost maternally, like a mother putting down a newborn, so that we would not make a noise.

At this moment of frozen indecision, with so much flying lead in the air, I feel almost honour bound to say something along the lines of 'This was when my training kicked in', or 'These kinds of situations went with the territory'. As a foreign correspondent, are these not the adrenalin-saturated moments that we live for? When life seems real? When the surge of epinephrine released by the fight or flight response feels like a narcotic?

Alas, my neurotransmitters often let me down in such situations, and my body and mind succumbed to something nearing numbness. I was not hugely invigorated, but neither was I hugely fearful. The events did not unfold before me in complete slow motion, but neither did it feel like real-time speed. It was not quite the sensation of being a spectator, but neither did I consider myself fully to be a participant, because the events before me seemed oddly distant. Indeed, always in these life or death situations I experienced a strange feeling of apartness. At once real and unreal, it was akin to having an out-of-body experience without going the whole hog. A feeling, as you can no doubt tell from this tortuous circuitousness, that I struggled to make sense of.

Psychologists have a clearer take. What I am describing is a state of emotional detachment that comes not from a lack of emotion but from an excess of it; a defence mechanism that kicks in during extremely traumatic circumstances. In this most vivid, noisy and hazardous of situations, where the events could hardly have been more threatening or real, I was going through a process of derealisation.

As the stand-off continued, fire quickly engulfed the building where the militants were holed up, and with choking black smoke spewing from the upstairs windows we judged it was now time to make a dash for it. Our hope was that the Indian soldiers crouched behind their armoured vehicles would have had sufficient time to compose themselves, so they would identify me as a journalist rather than a gunman trying to escape.

Equally, the bursts of gunfire coming from the building were more intermittent and distant, suggesting the jihadists were either cornered or in retreat. At a lull in the fighting, we leapt up from the sandbagged bunker and performed a kind of crouched sprint, as if we were dashing from a crashed helicopter about to explode. Weighed down by the heavy flak jackets, it was not a particularly flattering sight, and it was expunged from our later news stories. Yet local cameramen providing material for the main news agencies, Reuters and APTN, thought the footage of our scrambled escape was sufficiently dramatic that it was soon all over CNN, which unleashed a spew of mocking emails from former colleagues in Washington. Rarely have I run 50 metres so quickly, but rarely have I looked so pathetic doing so. Though my pride was injured, at least my flak jacket survived unblemished, for the Indian soldiers could make out that I was a portly journalist making a mad dash for safety rather than a homicidal gunman hell-bent on destruction.

Even after we had crossed the Indian lines and found ourselves using their armoured vehicles as shields, we were not entirely out of harm's way. The next sustained rattle of gunfire came from a soldier a few yards away, whose knee and upper leg was now drenched in blood. Often in Srinagar, militants disguise themselves in military fatigues, so for a brief slice of time we thought a jihadist might be in our midst. But the soldier had mistakenly let off his weapon, badly wounding himself, and was now being reprimanded by his commanding officer. Despite his writhing pain, the soldier was apologising profusely, a sure sign he was a bona-fide Indian infantryman. We had lived to file another day.

—

For all its occasional dangers, the consolation of reporting from trouble spots in South Asia was that most of them were impossibly beautiful. Srinagar was not only ringed by saw-edged Himalayan mountains but also nestled on the banks of Dal Lake, whose antique houseboats, shikara water taxis, lotus flowers and giant water lilies were once again luring tourists prepared to brave the insurgency.

In Sri Lanka, the most fiercely fought-over isthmus in the civil war went by the dreamy name of Elephant Pass. In the mountain kingdom of Nepal, Maoist insurgents fought an ugly war with the Royal Nepalese Army amidst the most breathtaking scenery anywhere on the subcontinent, if not the world. Its frontlines were the most glorious of vistas. Pakistan and India also fought over Himalayan highlands. More than 20,000 feet above sea level, the Siachen Glacier had become the world's most altitudinous battlefield as well as its most pointless. In temperatures of minus 60 degrees, a greater number of soldiers were lost to the elements than to enemy action, and by 2003, when a ceasefire was declared, India and Pakistan had lost some 2000 personnel between them, mainly from hypothermia, frostbite and avalanches. Much closer to sea level, the Maldives was fighting a battle of sorts, and an existential one at that. Its low-lying atolls were being inundated by rising seawater, and to visit the country was to witness its watery eradication from the map.

At a time when the post-9/11 world was commonly framed as a clash of civilisations between the secular and Islamic worlds, South Asia's battlefields were also a timely reminder that other forces were at play, whatever the thinking in Washington.

Take Nepal. In the aftermath of 9/11, the Bush administration feared that the rooftop of the world might one day become a safe haven for groups such as al-Qaeda if the Maoists won the civil war. It had therefore decided to shore up the country's authoritarian monarch, King Gyanendra, by providing his troops with night-vision equipment and some 20,000 M16 rifles. But Maoist leaders thought this reasoning was laughable.

On one occasion, we drove deep into the countryside to one of the deprived villages that had become a nursery of the Maoist rebellion, where we waited for a small group of revolutionaries dressed in combat fatigues and carrying weapons stolen from the Royal Nepalese Army to emerge from the forestland. The local Maoist leader, a hawk-featured young man who arrived wearing a Nike baseball cap, considered hilarious the suggestion that this Hindu kingdom would ever provide a bolt-hole for jihadists. The Maoist fight, he said, was against the monarch rather than against President Bush, and he mocked the notion that they had become appendages to the axis of evil. 'Osama bin Laden and Saddam Hussein were creations of America,' he laughed. 'They're of no concern to us.'

Harder to characterise than a simple case of good versus evil, Nepal was in the throes of an ideological and feudal power struggle, the central figure in which was the king. Always the best time to observe him was on Army Day in Kathmandu, when the huge military parade ground in the heart of the city reverberated to the sound of bagpipes, billed in the programme as 'soothing military music' – a phrase that seemed doubly oxymoronic. Dressed in his green ceremonial uniform, his left breast pocket a blaze of medals, and a crimson-banded cap taking the place of his usual plumed emerald crown, King Gyanendra watched from a ceremonial stand as his troops performed parachute drops, a *feu de joie*, bomb-disposal exercises and quicksilver drills with the famed Gurkha kukri knives swirling extravagantly around their heads. Then, after dusk, he would appear before his subjects from the ramparts of Durbar Square, the old royal palace.

It was here in June 2001 that the king had been crowned, following an extraordinarily bloody royal massacre in which his nephew, Crown Prince Dipendra, unleashed his M16 and MP5K guns on the king, the queen, seven other family members and then himself – a shooting rampage memorably described by a foreign-aid official as a combination of Shakespeare, Ruth Rendell and Quentin Tarantino.

Gyanendra's ascension to the throne made him not only the monarch and commander-in-chief of the Royal Nepalese Army but also a living Hindu god. So, on Army Day, thousands of his more worshipful subjects gathered beneath the ramparts with heads bowed, carrying tea lights and burning incense. Fragrant though the air was, it was impossible to ignore the stench of democratic decay. Fearful of a popular uprising, the king had recently declared a state of emergency and placed many of the kingdom's politicians under house arrest. He had become a ruthless despot, known as much for his iron fist as for his emerald crown.

Just as the conflict in Nepal did not fit the post-9/11 template, the root causes of the Sri Lankan civil war were found in ethnic identity and nationalism – or ethno-nationalism, to use the inelegant phraseology favoured by academics who had studied the decades-old fight.

In a country whose name literally meant the 'Blessed Land', many Tamils whose ancestors had been brought from India by the British to work on the coffee and tea plantations yearned for their own homeland. When the country achieved independence in 1948, however, the Buddhist-Sinhala majority, who believed the British had discriminated against them, was determined to assert its dominance and relegated the Tamils to being second-class citizens.

Fiercely nationalistic then and now, successive Sinhala-dominated governments refused to countenance the division of their teardrop-shaped island. So, in the early 1980s, long-simmering ethnic tensions erupted into full-blown civil war between the army and the Tamil Tiger rebels – what turned out to be a 26-year conflict that claimed between 80,000 and 100,000 lives.

With the help of Norwegian negotiators, a ceasefire agreement had been hammered out in 2002 granting the Tamils a measure of self-rule over a large swathe of land in the north. But more recently the truce had fallen into disrepute.

To visit the rebel capital Kilinochchi was to see a state in embryo form. Though many of its buildings were half-ruined, derelict and pockmarked with bullets, post-war reconstruction was well underway. The town was dotted still with statues of Tamil war heroes, one of the biggest of which was a memorial celebrating the first female suicide bomber, but it could also boast a newly established police force whose smartly dressed officers were former rebels. They patrolled the streets in brand-new Toyota Land Cruisers with paint jobs that juxtaposed the word 'POLICE' with the paramilitary's fearsome insignia, a sharp-fanged tiger roaring ferociously.

On the main road through the town, known as the Highway of Death, because it had seen so many battles between the rebels and the army, the police had even set up speed traps for errant motorists. They were manned by former paramilitaries who now wielded nothing more sinister than radar guns. There was a small courthouse with a gabled red-tiled roof, where proceedings began each morning with the singing of the Tamil anthem and the raising of their flag. Just down the road was a modern secretariat administrative building with pretty landscaping, where the Tigers hosted Norwegian diplomats and other visiting dignitaries.

By far the most impressive landmark in the town was a martyrs' cemetery, the entrance of which was marked with a giant AK-47 driven insolently into the ground. Almost 2000 concrete tombs were laid out in regimented rows, and the only way to be granted a burial plot was to have laid down one's life for the Tamil cause. The Tigers had pioneered the use of suicide-bomb attacks – and through them killed two world leaders, the Sri Lankan president Ranasinghe Premadasa and, more audaciously, the Indian prime minister Rajiv Gandhi. A special section of the cemetery was hence reserved for the Black Tigers, volunteers who had made what was considered the utmost sacrifice.

For this reason, the Tigers did not like to use the word 'suicide'. They spoke instead of volunteers donating themselves to the cause and believed that suicide bombers died always with smiles of satisfaction on their faces. Nor did they look upon this sacred plot as a cemetery. Instead, they called it a sleeping arena and held that the dead bodies were seeds that would grow into trees once an independent Tamil nation had become a reality.

What they were demanding was a large, spear-tip-shaped area of land encompassing all of the disputed north and much of the western and eastern seaboards. So many people had died to achieve it that they were prepared to settle for nothing short. Sinhalese hardliners, who were always distrustful of the rebels, suspected the Tigers had entered into a ceasefire agreement so they could rebuild and regroup in preparation for a final military push for genuine statehood.

There was no shortage of volunteers determined to carry on fighting. On one visit to the cemetery, we met two young female volunteers, 24-year-old Suganthini and 25-year-old Iyali, who were dressed in their off-duty garb of grey skirts and grey checked shirts, and carrying bouquets of dark-pink rose petals. They had come to decorate the grave of their former comrade, Senthamilini, who had been killed during a face-to-face battle with the Sri Lankan Army in Jaffna, the largest and most strategically important city in the north.

As they stood at the graveside, the two young women thought of their friend's sacrifice and explained the reasons why they were prepared to pay a blood price themselves. 'The Sri Lanka Army killed my father in front of my eyes,' said Iyali, who had been inducted into the Tigers at the age of 16. 'And then they raped my sister. If my leader tells me to fight, I am prepared to die for the Tamil homeland.' At once dignified and hate-filled, hers was the authentic voice of Tamil separatism.

Only occasionally would you catch sight of rebels in their combat fatigues – a distinctive tiger-stripe uniform with horizontal flashes of green and dark brown – and they did not take kindly to being filmed. Always, we would look for the vials hanging from a thin black string around their necks, which resembled New Age pendants but contained enough cyanide for a fatal dose. With suicide always preferable to capture, the Tigers were trained to bite into the glass vial so as to cut the skin on their inner mouth. That way, the deadly white powder would be absorbed much faster into the bloodstream.

Just as the rebels were notoriously camera-shy, so, too, was their shadowy leader, Velupillai Prabhakaran. A corpulent man with an extravagant moustache – out of his combat fatigues, he could easily have been mistaken for a Venetian ice-cream vendor – Prabhakaran had launched the violent separatist struggle in 1975, when he assassinated the then mayor of Jaffna by shooting him at point-blank range.

Since then, he had built arguably one of the world's most pitiless and sophisticated militant organisations; one that could boast not only an army of committed fighters but also a navy and an air force capable of carrying out raids on Sri Lanka's main city, Colombo. Each battle was filmed so the video footage could be scrutinised afterwards to identify rebels who had displayed cowardice.

Always, we went to Kilinochchi in the hope of landing the scoop of an interview with Prabhakaran, and always we came away disappointed. Only once since the start of the civil war had he made himself available for a press conference. Held in 2002, two months after the ceasefire, the conference's security was so multi-layered that the 200 journalists who had ventured into the jungle to cross-examine him were put through a ten-hour vetting process. It was all part of his allure. Indeed, the secrecy that surrounded his movements, and the fact that he made only one public appearance each year, during the commemorations marking Black Tiger Day, added both to his mystique and to the psychosis of fear surrounding his name.

Instead of being granted an audience with Prabhakaran, we made do with his deputies. Usually, we would meet at a guest house overlooking a lagoon on the edge of Kilinochchi, where the Tigers put up visiting members of the Tamil diaspora from Canada and Britain – well-heeled donors who bankrolled the insurgency. On my first visit, they laid on a sumptuous seafood lunch, since the local fishermen always made sure to hold back the best lobster for Tiger leaders.

These kinds of encounters always presented something of a moral test. It was not so much the issue of whether we should meet rebels or militants. That was axiomatic. Whatever the conflict, we needed to hear from both sides. Far more ethically taxing was the question of whether to accept the hospitality of paramilitaries whose hands were splattered with so much blood, civilian as well as military.

As another slab of swordfish steak was brought from the kitchen, I definitely had serious qualms. All I would say is that we were aware that our hosts were guilty of the most heinous atrocities and human-rights abuses – from no-warning attacks on Colombo, in which civilians as well as Sri Lankan troops were regularly slain, to the forced conscription of child soldiers, which was a war crime – and we made sure to bring it up in dinnertime conversation. We may have been recipients of a free lunch, but we always went in determined that they should not be as well.

Just as we spent time with the Tigers, we also made sure to

meet their victims. Before that first trip to Kilinochchi, we visited a small house in the back streets of Colombo festooned with white ribbons that looked like carnival trappings. In Sinhalese communities, however, white was the colour of mourning, and the thin strips of fabric had been put up in honour of a policeman killed a few days earlier by a female suicide bomber. Launching the first rebel attack in the capital for almost three years, she had set out to assassinate a pro-government Tamil politician – the ninth time the Tigers had tried unsuccessfully to kill him.

The bomber had been intercepted at a security checkpoint outside the politician's office and dragged into a police station next door. At that point, she detonated her suicide belt. The policeman had borne the full brunt of the explosion, and in the living room of his home his dead body was laid out under a ceremonial arch made out of two elephant tusks, with the shrapnel wounds plainly visible despite all the cosmetic reconstruction work carried out on his face.

Here, again, I should add that we also met grieving Tamil families, who claimed their children had been the victims of extra-judicial killings carried out by the Sri Lankan Army. In some instances, the army shot dead young Tamils with little or no evidence that they were paramilitaries. Then, they forced their parents to sign forms declaring their sons to be rebels as a condition of handing over the dead bodies. On both sides, this was the dirtiest of wars.

Occasionally, we found ourselves in its very midst. Once, it happened on a trip to Trincomalee, a city populated both by Tamils and by the Sinhalese community on the eastern seaboard, which was configured around one of the world's most stunning natural harbours. It was January 2006, and with the talks process having broken down completely the Tigers had taken to expressing themselves almost exclusively through violence.

Five days before our visit, the Sea Tigers killed 13 sailors in a suicide attack on a Sri Lankan Navy vessel patrolling the coast. Just before we entered the city, the rebels launched a follow-up attack on the police checkpoint at the entrance to Trincomalee, spraying it with automatic gunfire and hurling grenades. As we drove in, with the acrid smell of explosives still putrefying the air, two military motorbikes flashed by with gun-toting soldiers perched on the back, who were setting off in search of the rebels. Another army unit waded into the jungle by the side of the road to flush them out.

Blocked from going any further, we waited in the darkness for over an hour, fully expecting a gun battle to erupt any moment – even half-hoping that it would, since it was rare to witness contact between the Tigers and the army. Eventually, however, when it was thought the danger had passed, we were allowed through the damaged checkpoint to our beachside hotel, where a pan-pipe version of 'Bridge Over Troubled Water' was playing in the lobby.

We had travelled to Trincomalee because the extreme Sinhalese nationalist party, the Janatha Vimukthi Peramuna party, or JVP, planned a three-day strike that would completely shut down the entire city in protest at the recent upsurge in rebel action. On the first morning of the strike, the Sri Lankan Army had agreed to let us film its street patrols. Alas, we never made it to our rendezvous. As we ventured from our hotel and drove through the shuttered streets, a spotter for the JVP appeared alongside our minivan on his motorbike, saw that we were a camera crew and then accelerated ahead to inform his superiors. None of us were particularly alarmed by this, but further down the road a crowd of rowdy JVP supporters formed a human blockade and brought our vehicle to an abrupt halt.

Many of the strikers had covered their faces with scarves, while one of the ringleaders gripped a hacksaw threateningly in his right hand. Having been drinking heavily throughout the morning, almost all of them were drunk. One of the more thickset men reached through the driver's window and yanked the keys from the ignition. Fellow strikers sprinted towards us from adjoining streets, having been alerted on their mobiles, and what started out as a knot of men quickly became a mob. Some of the strikers started kicking and punching our van, and became more threatening towards our driver and local producer, whom they had identified immediately as Tamils.

In less than a minute, the situation escalated to the point of death threats. Then came a brief lull, as the strikers seemed unsure how far they could push things. Perhaps sensing this hesitancy, a leader of sorts stepped forward: a short, wiry man older and less drunk than the others. He started shouting demands, the main one of which was for us to hand over our film.

Relinquishing footage is something we are always loath to do, and by now my cameraman, Phil – an old South Asia hand and one of the BBC's bravest shooters – was virtually sitting on his camera. (Rarely anything other than unflappable, the only time I saw Phil lose his cool was after we had gone through the fifth or sixth layer of security to get into that *loya jirga* in Kabul and he realised he had left his cigarettes outside.) Still, our bargaining position could hardly be described as promising. Determined not to lose all our shots, but with grave concerns for the safety of our driver and local fixer, we suggested a compromise. We would delete the offending shots and then return immediately to our hotel.

This seemed not only to pacify the short, wiry man but also to greatly excite two of his young charges, who were ordered to clamber into the back of our vehicle so they could act as censors. Both peered into Phil's viewfinder while he erased the footage, but they were too inebriated to realise that he had wiped only a few shots and was showing them a blank portion of tape as proof that he had done more. Had they asked him to fast-forward or rewind, he would have been rumbled immediately, but the sight of an empty viewfinder was enough to get not only a few thumbs-up but even a couple of appreciative slaps on the back. Finally, we shared common ground, like foreigners who had found it all but impossible to communicate until realising that they had both heard of David Beckham. Now, the mob seemed delighted, and they claimed a victory.

At these moments of intense danger, I was always amazed, and mostly amused, how the banalities of normal life could intrude. Occasionally, it would be my British credit-card company telephoning to say that they had put a bar on my card because it was being used, fraudulently, they presumed, in Sri Lanka, Kashmir or Afghanistan. Sometimes, it would be my dear mum reminding me that it was Father's Day at the weekend. On this occasion, it was my then girlfriend and now wife, who had just spent a restless night at my apartment in Delhi and called to tell me that I could do with a new set of pillows. Home furnishings would become a high priority, I promised, if ever we made it home.

Our keys returned, we headed back to the hotel. Within the hour, however, a Sri Lankan Army unit rumbled into the driveway to tell us we had to leave immediately, since the mob was threatening again to do us serious harm. They would take us in convoy out of Trincomalee and drive us about a hundred miles west, which was beyond the reach of the strikers.

This was problematic. Though the army would offer protection from the thugs of the JVP as we drove through the empty streets of Trincomalee, we now ran the risk of becoming targets of the Tamil Tigers as soon as we left the city limits. Even on a normal day, we would have pulled to the side of the road rather than travel in convoy with the army. Now, it was much more dangerous, because the rebels knew the only traffic leaving the shutdown city for the next 72 hours would be military vehicles. It meant they could spring one of their trademark ambushes: Claymore anti-personnel mines at the side of the road – a directional weapon detonated remotely by a rebel hiding in the paddy fields or jungle that fired metal balls into a kill zone some hundred metres long.

The very soldiers underwriting our security inside Trincomalee instantly made us targets as soon as we drove outside – a classic 'out of the frying pan into the firing line' scenario. What made it all the more worrying was that the Tigers would never be as hapless as the JVP. As in Afghanistan, driving through the countryside was a total crapshoot, but without the benefits of American armour-plating.

Fortunately on this occasion, our luck held, and by nightfall we had made it back to the safety of Mahogany Ridge: that place beloved of foreign correspondents, more commonly known as the bar.

—

Heartless though it is to say of a country threatened with extinction, the Maldives always offered light relief from the battlefields of South Asia. Certainly, there was a 'winning the lottery' feel to the call from an editor in London suggesting I head down there at my earliest convenience to cover its slow inundation.

It was the period, pre-Copenhagen, when global-warming stories were the easiest of sells. Still, even we thought a trip to this exotic paradise was pushing things a little far. We arrived in the capital, Malé, an island city protected from the rising seawaters by a three-metre-high wall, just in time for the celebrations marking Maldivean independence from Britain in the mid-1960s.

Part commemoration, part carnival, it was a peculiarly disjointed event that featured the Maldivean army marching in ceremonial dress, hundreds of schoolchildren dressed in bumble-bee outfits, and music from Barry Manilow. One minute, it was 'Gaumii Salaam', the Maldivean national anthem, played to a thumping martial beat; the next, inexplicably, it was 'Copacabana'.

The country's then president was Maumoon Abdul Gayoom, a bespectacled autocrat who had become Asia's longest serving head of government by crushing internal dissent and imprisoning his political opponents on distant atolls. Unknown to most honeymooners and tourists, the Maldives was pretty much a police state back then, and everywhere we went government spies followed obtrusively behind, despite all the palm trees offering cover.

That night, however, the president looked more like a maracas player given the night off from a visiting cruise ship, dressed as he was in slacks and a Hawaiian shirt. Due to interview him in his presidential palace the following morning, I made the mistake of interpreting his outfit as a sartorial cue. I therefore turned up looking 'beach casual', in sandals and a polo shirt. Regrettably, he walked through the door turned out in a grey business suit and woven silk tie: 'head of state formal'.

The president faced one of the most wretched policy challenges of any leader in the world. As much as 80 per cent of the Maldives' 1200 islands and atolls were no more than a metre above the waves, and government scientists predicted sea-level rises of some 90 centimetres by the end of the century. Within a hundred years, most of the Maldives was set to become uninhabitable, and plans were already in place to evacuate its entire population of 360,000 people.

The government was encouraging forestation to prevent beach erosion and pushing ahead with a plan to clean litter and debris from the country's coral reefs, a natural barrier against tidal surges. In the country's schools, lessons in environmental science were given the same priority as writing and arithmetic. However, as the president was all too aware, the fate of his country rested in the hands of leaders in Washington, Beijing, Delhi and the capitals of the other major polluters.

However authoritarian at home, it was a measure of the president's powerlessness abroad that he had written to George W. Bush urging the US president to ratify the Kyoto Protocol and not even received a reply. 'What happens here today will happen somewhere else tomorrow,' the president told us pleadingly. 'So it is not just the Maldives and three-hundred thousand people. It is the global population which is being affected.'

In Kandholhudhoo, a densely populated atoll in the north of the Maldives, we witnessed the helplessness of residents in the face of the inundation of their homes and businesses. Every fortnight, they were flooded by tidal surges, and the force of the waves had recently punctured a three-metre hole in the atoll's concrete defences.

Climate change had made obsolete a centuries-old weather

guide called the Nakiy used by local fishermen, and two-thirds of the local residents had volunteered to evacuate the island over the coming decade. It made sense to leave now and rebuild elsewhere, because the islanders were certain to face mandatory evacuations in the years to come.

All this produced strong material for our 'world in environmental peril' day – these kinds of theme days were becoming very popular in television news – even if the power of our reports was dented a little by the fact that I appeared live from a low-lying atoll in Bermuda shorts looking as if I were presenting a holiday programme or trying to flog Maldivean time-share. Still, though heavily outnumbered by the torrent of abusive emails sent by envious colleagues in London, there was praise from the president's office. He was delighted that we had shone a spotlight, however briefly, on his stricken land.

So appreciative was he of our efforts, in fact, that, as we waited in the departure lounge at Malé Airport to board our flight the next morning, one of his minions rushed up to us with three exquisitely crafted mahogany boxes embossed with the gold presidential seal. All of us immediately thought it was diamond-encrusted Rolex time, and we started to wonder how we could explain away these gifts both to the suits in London and customs at Delhi Airport. Then, our BBC consciences kicked in – that sense of incorruptibility enshrined in the rule that correspondents should never accept gifts. Here, though, I hope you will forgive me for breaching this diktat, for in that felt inlay box I saw another trophy for my office back in Delhi. It was irresistible bounty: six cans of tuna marinaded in tomato sauce.

—

The bus was ready now to leave – or the 'caravan of peace', as the Indians preferred to call it. Miraculously, all 24 of its passengers were prepared to risk the journey, despite being the targets of the attack on the tourism centre the previous afternoon. At Srinagar's cricket oval, where in the early 1980s local crowds cheered the visiting West Indians rather than the Indian national team – an act of disloyalty that foreshadowed the insurgency against Delhi – hundreds gathered to see them off.

In celebration, chefs prepared a traditional Kashmiri feast. The Indian Army deployed a bagpipe band, wearing Highland berets and tartan. Prime Minister Manmohan Singh appeared with a Formula One-style chequered flag to wave the bus on its way. In Muzaffarabad, the administrative capital of Azad Kashmir – Free Kashmir, as the Pakistanis called it – the departure was less formal but more boisterous.

To mark 'the day of the bus', crowds clogged the streets, men clambered onto the rooftops, and garlands and rose petals were showered on the passengers as they stepped onto an air-conditioned coach painted with a special green and yellow livery. 'Today is the day that another Berlin Wall will come down,' shouted Waqar Amer, who now worked as a tour operator after serving for decades as a colonel in the Pakistani Army. All along the 62-kilometre route between Muzaffarabad and the Line of Control, well-wishers came out to cheer, whistle, clap and sing. 'Long live peace!' they shouted. 'Long live friendship. Kashmir is one!'

The Muzaffarabad bus was the first to reach Kaman Post, the steel bridge that marked the crossing between Indian- and Pakistan-administered Kashmir – the Peace Bridge, as it was called. That week, Indian soldiers had painted its steel girders in the saffron, white and green of the Indian tricolour but then had been forced by the Pakistanis to redecorate in a more neutral white. The Indians had also constructed a grand ceremonial arch on their side of the bridge that was far more imposing than the Pakistanis' more modest gateway.

This was much more than the usual South Asian one-upmanship. Primarily, it was intended to show that the Line of Control should now be seen as a border, fixed and immutable, and that Indian-administered Kashmir would never be part of Pakistan.

To drive home the point, the Indians had built a reception control with a manicured lawn, ornamental garden furniture, antique Victorian style lamp posts that looked like they had come from the set of a Sherlock Holmes film and what were being touted as the best public toilets in the entire subcontinent. As the status-quo power, the opening up of the bus route unquestionably favoured the Indians. It explained why the Indian official delegation in Srinagar included not only Dr Singh but also Sonia Gandhi, and why not a single Pakistani official had travelled to Muzaffarabad to wave off the bus.

Whatever the diplomatic ramifications, the prime beneficiaries were the Kashmiris, who walked slowly across the bridge. People who had not seen their relatives for 35 years. Brothers and sisters who had been separated at birth. Grandparents who had never cast eyes on their grandchildren, or even heard them speak or laugh. Now, as they reboarded their coach on the other side of the Peace Bridge, they were within 160 kilometres of meeting them. Ever since the first Kashmir war in 1947 – the year of partition – the road to Srinagar had been laid with anti-tank mines to repel a Pakistani incursion. Now, the mines had been cleared away, and the Indian Army stood at the side of road, in 50-metre intervals, to protect the coach from being turned into a coffin on wheels. Panicky rumours of a jihadist ambush proved to be just that, and while the militants did manage to explode a grenade, it went off without causing any injuries.

Srinagar was in near darkness when the bus finally arrived, since shops and businesses had shut down for the day because of a strike called by Kashmiri separatists in protest at the restoration of the bus link, which they had interpreted as a sign that Kashmir would remain forever divided. Yet there was still a mood of jubilation at the convention centre on the edge of Dal Lake, where the bus disgorged its passengers and the family reunions unfolded. In the embrace of his brother for the first time since the late 1960s, Shah Ahmed could not contain his emotions. 'I have waited so long for this moment,' he cried, as he held a bouquet of flowers with one hand and hugged his brother with the other. 'Thank you, Pervez Musharraf. Thank you, Manmohan Singh. You have united a family today.'

A definite watershed moment, the bus trip fuelled hopes of a less violent future in Kashmir, but other corners of South Asia were aflame. In Sri Lanka, where the ceasefire survived in name only, the Tamil Tigers had effectively resumed their armed struggle. In August 2005, they had even been audacious enough to assassinate the country's foreign minister, Lakshman Kadirgamar. An ethnic Tamil who had always been a hate-figure for the rebels, he was killed at his private residence – shot four times in the head and chest at the side of his pool after finishing his Friday-evening swim. So expert was the sniper attack that it had the feel of the opening of a Robert Ludlum thriller. More ominously for Sri Lanka, it also had the feel of the resumption of all-out war.

Nepal, meanwhile, was in the throes of revolution. More than a year after King Gyanendra had declared a state of emergency, he was confronted not only by the Maoist insurgency in the countryside but also by tens of thousands of demonstrators on the streets of Kathmandu burning effigies and shouting 'Hang the king'. Still able to command the loyalty of his army, Gyanendra had adopted the tactics of embattled autocratic monarchs down the ages, which was to order his troops to fire live ammunition on his subjects.

Conversely, the mob had also learnt the lesson of successful revolutionaries: to march towards the gunfire. Gyanendra was holed up in his royal palace – a modern pale-pink building in the centre of Kathmandu with architectural echoes of a southern Californian mega-church – fending off appeals from one-time allies, such as America, for the restoration of democracy.

His son, Crown Prince Paras, was rumoured to be touring the capital in a helicopter, issuing shoot-to-kill orders to the troops down below. As the civil unrest escalated, the king turned his palace into a bunker and imposed a strict shoot-on-sight curfew in the capital. If anyone stepped onto the streets in the centre of the city, they risked being killed by his troops. Instead, the protesters amassed outside the curfew zone on the carriageway encircling the capital in what had the makings of a Ring Road Revolution.

Because the rules of the curfew also applied to the media, covering the demonstrations was fraught. The security forces had started blockading hotels used by international journalists, to prevent us from filming the army slaughtering its own people. To outwit them, we had to switch hotels continuously, sometimes in the middle of the night.

We also refused to abide by the rules of the curfew, thinking, hoping and occasionally praying that the army would not risk the diplomatic fallout of turning their guns on us. This was a tricky call, for neither the Royal Nepalese Army nor the Kathmandu Police were known for their media savvy or self-restraint. On the first morning of the shoot-to-kill curfew, our tactic was to venture out from the hotel into the empty streets a few metres at a time, a so-far-so-good strategy that initially worked well. But its first real test came when we edged towards our first group of soldiers, who were dressed in full combat gear.

In these situations, boldness is the only option – readers who have marched brazenly into the reception of a luxury hotel to make use of the toilet facilities with a feigned sense of belonging might recognise the feeling – and we neither deviated nor slowed down. The soldiers looked at us, and we at them. We kept on edging forward. More glances. A few more steps. No response. Then we walked past the soldiers, with their guns remaining at their sides.

Emboldened, we returned to our hotel, jumped into our four-wheel drive and drove through the abandoned streets in search of a demonstration. At a crossroads close to the city centre, there was a stand-off between security forces and protesters. As soon as we got out to film, the police started manhandling us. In situations like this, Paul, our bureau editor, would come into his own. A black-belt when it came to wrestling with pig-headed South Asian public officials, he spent ten minutes sparring over the semantics of the curfew. A clever ruse. It provided just enough time and commotion for my cameraman and I to slip away to film the protesters through the police lines, and to get a sense of how many Nepalis had bravely defied the curfew.

Clearly, it was thousands. Once Paul saw we had gathered

the shots we needed – the sequence ended with a policeman smothering our camera lens with his riot shied, which was pretty much what we had hoped for – he brought the argument with the commanding officer to a speedy and surprisingly cordial end. Then we were ordered off the streets. At this point, the police expected us to drive away, but a kindly resident beckoned us over and offered us refuge in his house. Even better, he had a rooftop with an aerial view of the disputed intersection and a patio from which to angle our laptop-sized satellite dishes into the sky and start broadcasting to London.

The police commander was temporarily flummoxed. No longer on the streets, we were adhering to the strict letter of the curfew. But although he could do little to punish us, his officers started threatening our hosts. Not wishing our hosts harm, we decided to leave. As we went down the narrow stairway and out onto the streets, a riot policeman tried to arrest one of our Nepali fixers and started dragging him towards a police van, where he no doubt would have received a beating, or even worse. Fortunately, in the tug of war that followed, your correspondent came out on top. With the team still intact, we beat a slow retreat, furtively filming tracking shots out of the windows as we crawled back to the hotel. By piercing the media blackout, we had achieved a smallish victory, but to us it felt much larger.

After that first morning of the shoot-to-kill curfew, the police and army could not control journalists any more than they could contain the demonstrators. With the protests swelling in size, and with well-dressed, middle-class Nepalis taking part, we had free rein. There were even times when the army was spooked by our presence. On one afternoon, when a wall of protesters pushed its way around the ring road, a truckload of troops took up position, with rifles cocked like a firing squad. With their commanding officer barking out orders, it looked as if we were about to witness a horrible massacre. They had the firepower to mow down dozens of protesters, and this had the feel of a make or break moment. How ruthless were the military prepared to be? What sort of sacrifices were the protesters prepared to make?

When we jumped out of our vehicle to start filming, however, the troops immediately became camera-shy. With the demonstrators now within brick- and bottle-throwing range, the commanding officer first ordered his men to lower their weapons. Then, he shouted instructions for them to leave. On these kinds of moments, revolutions can turn, and the way was now clear for the demonstrators to surge even closer to the royal palace.

The following afternoon, at another main intersection along the ring road, the riot police were helpless again as the protesters ran amok. Now, they trashed an apartment belonging to a police officer, hurling its entire contents from the balcony onto the streets and then dousing them in petrol. Next, they ransacked a government tax office on the other side of the road, tossing its files into the air and again setting them aflame.

Just two days earlier, we would have thought twice before following the protesters into the courtyard of the government buildings, fearing the army would corner us all and then open fire. By this stage, the army and police had killed 15 protesters. But now the protesters were rampant. Amidst the bedlam of that courtyard, there was even just enough time to record a piece to camera, and, at the very moment we started filming, a protester hurtled into frame wielding an iron bar and started smashing up the tax office. He displayed such demented fury and exquisite timing that it looked as if we had primed him to do so. Those 15 seconds of footage also neatly encased the havoc of Kathmandu. The king remained on his throne, but the mob was in the chair.

Once his staunchest backers, the Americans started distancing themselves from Gyanendra. The US ambassador even raised the spectre of a Saigon-style escape, with the king suffering the humiliation of being airlifted from the ramparts of his palace. Faced with so much hostility on the streets and now more reluctant to fire indiscriminately into the crowds, army chiefs also called for the restoration of democracy. With the demonstrations entering their third week and a massive rally planned for the next day, the king became so alarmed by the tumble of events that he appeared on television close to midnight to finally back down. Following a script virtually dictated by the army, an ashen-faced Gyanendra agreed to restore democracy. It was an extraordinary sight. A king and living Hindu god was begging the forgiveness of his people.

The following morning, shops reopened, the streets were full again of rush-hour traffic and the police turned their attention to scolding errant drivers rather than beating protesters with their bamboo batons. In a central park, not far away from the royal palace, a rave-like victory party erupted, while elsewhere in the city, as the lilac blossom started sprouting on the trees, the residents of the capital could once again enjoy the blooming of the Kathmandu spring.

Then, as we all looked forward to a respite after two weeks of dodging rubber bullets and worse, a call came through on Paul's mobile from Colombo. A female suicide bomber had carried out an attack on the army headquarters in the heart of the city, badly wounding one of the country's most senior military chiefs. Straight away, we were checking the flight connections from Kathmandu to Colombo, for another corner of South Asia would doubtless soon be aflame.

Chapter 10

Year of Disasters

On a coastline made ghostly by the drifting palls from funeral pyres and the attendance of so much death, the Suryakumar family huddled together on the brick-strewn ground where their beachside house had stood. When the Asian tsunami had hit Velankanni – a pilgrimage town close to India's southernmost tip – on Boxing Day 2004, they had lost four children in as many seconds. One had survived and been taken to the local hospital. Now, the family had just received word that she, too, had died.

Sarita, the young mother, thumped her forehead with her open palm, out of misery and in self-reproach. When the waves had hit, she'd raced into her home and grabbed hold of her two youngest children. But she had not had the physical strength to hold on. 'I remember the look on their faces as the waves swept them away,' she told us. 'No mother should ever have to go through this.' With that, her fragile body gave in to a violent spasm of grief, and she buried her head in the lap of her elderly auntie, whose sari muffled her wails.

The old lady wept, too, her head jolting from side to side. Then she admonished her niece. 'You gave birth to them,' she cried. 'You should never have let them go.'

This was a community where the waves had taken an entire generation. Along a stretch of coastline just a few miles long, 1500 children had been killed.

Now, bodies decomposing in the airless humidity littered the shores. Crows picked on the remains. Smoke from the bonfires covered wrecked houses in a grey film of ash. Fishermen stared blankly at their broken boats, many of which had been tossed hundreds of metres inland. Others tried to salvage and repair their nets, which were entangled in the concrete slabs and jagged bricks strewn throughout their communities. Some just peered vacantly out to sea, traumatised by the idea of ever venturing out again. Of the 15,000 fishing boats in the town of Nagapattinam – one of southern India's worst-affected communities – just three were seaworthy.

Having lost his two sons, his house and his fishing boat, Gopal knew he would be the last in a long line of fishermen from his family. All he had left was his daughter, a cheery little girl who tried constantly to rally her father even though both her eyes had been injured by the waves and were now wholly bloodshot. 'Unless I get government aid, I might as well kill myself and what's left of my family,' Gopal cried.

Further inland, at one of Nagapattinam's many makeshift orphanages, two young sisters, Shivaranjini and Divya, told us that their mother had been killed and their father, another fisherman, had lost his livelihood. He no longer had the means to raise them and had had to give them up. 'We came here hoping to get an education,' said ten-year-old Shivaranjini, an angel-faced young thing with neatly tied pigtails. 'Then we can look after him.'

Every so often, parents came to the door of the orphanage in the hope of finding their lost children. They might have heard there was a girl who looked like their daughter, or a boy who met the description of their son. Not once, however, did we witness a successful reunion.

If anything, in this trans-national disaster, Sri Lanka had been hit harder. Normally so enchanting, the road to Galle was lined with wreckage and misery. The destruction started just south of Colombo, first with some scattered debris and then with a few half-demolished seafront houses. Thereafter, it got steadily worse. In some places, all that remained of once-sturdy houses was their concrete foundations, laid out on the ground like life-sized architectural plans. Small fishing boats had been hurled hundreds of metres inland. The beaches were scattered with rubble, splintered timber and uprooted palm trees.

Just over halfway to Galle was the small town of Peraliya, where hundreds of panicked locals had tried to escape the walls of water by clambering aboard a train that traced the line of the coast – a service known as the 'Queen of the Sea'. Yet the force of the five-metre waves lifted the train from the tracks and overturned its packed carriages. Within seconds, they filled with water, drowning hundreds of passengers, while hundreds more were wrenched out to sea in the undertow.

Some 800 bodies were recovered from the wreckage of the train's rust-coloured carriages. The remains of another 700 or 800 victims were never found. So buckled and contorted was the railway track that it looked like a corkscrew ride at a fairground. Well over 1500 people were killed aboard the 'Queen of the Sea', instantly making it the world's worst ever railway disaster – an astounding fact relegated to footnote status because of the scale of the catastrophe elsewhere. What made this disaster all the more remarkable was that Peraliya was a west-coast town, when it was the east coast of Sri Lanka that should have borne the brunt of the tsunami. Such was the refractive effect of the advancing waves that the tsunami wrapped itself around the lower half of the island and devastated a coastline that one would have thought sheltered.

The fortress town of Galle on Sri Lanka's most south-westerly corner had produced some of the most disturbing television footage from the Boxing Day Tsunami, which is why we headed there first. We saw how the waves had upturned buses and swept them through the centre of town like broken twigs. Entire families had tried to climb through their windows and clamber onto their roofs, as they were buffeted in the swirling currents. Below the ramparts of the old city, the Test cricket ground was covered in muddy water and scattered with the carcasses of buses, cars and tuk-tuks. Most troubling of all was the number of dead bodies laid out at the sides of the roads. Nik, my cameraman, was among the first foreign journalists to arrive, and he saw piles of dead children. Death has an awful, sulphuric stench, and the air that night was full of it.

Remote and difficult to get to at the best of times, the north-east of the island had taken much longer to reach. Here, in the fiefdom of the Tamil Tigers, entire towns had been obliterated, almost wiped from the map. The Tiger stronghold of Mullaitivu, which had always shown the scars of civil war, had been virtually flattened. The tsunami had done in seconds what the Sri Lankan Army had failed to achieve in nearly 20 years.

On the waterfront, the shattered shell of a church, its concrete altar now exposed to the skies, and the private residence of the head of the Sea Tigers, which had undergone a speedy repair job, were pretty much all that remained. The landscape was empty of humans, since everyone had relocated to tented camps further inland.

Among them were the surviving children from an orphanage, Tender Sprouts, that cared for the sons and daughters of victims of the civil war. Of the 175 children housed in its seafront dormitories, only 30 had survived. For weeks afterwards, some of these poor young souls were so traumatised that they could not even utter a single word. Others had learnt a new one: 'tsunami' – a term that I myself had never used and that I'd found myself repeating over and over as I flew into Sri Lanka so as to lock it in my mind to get the pronunciation right.

It was far too soon to reach for consolation, and to ponder what good might spring from an undiscriminating disaster that had shown no regard for ethnicity, wealth, military rank or religion. In those early days, however, came the pregnant hope that the tsunami might break the impasse in the peace process between the government and the Tamil Tigers. It was not uncommon, after all, for natural disasters to produce a kind of peace dividend.

I had seen this for myself during the Bam earthquake in Iran, which by unfortunate coincidence had struck on Boxing Day the previous year and killed more than 26,000 people. Amidst the wreckage of the medieval town, we witnessed the improbable sight of an American emergency medical team from the Federal Emergency Management Agency, or FEMA, being protected by the Iranian Revolutionary Guard – not that the doctors, nurses and spinal-injury specialists needed any security. In a land where 'Death to America' was still the fuming cry, Iranians queued up to have their photographs taken with Americans whose bulky ski jackets were embroidered with the Stars and Stripes. It had been the first official US delegation of any kind to travel to Iran in over a decade, and its presence was all the more remarkable given that Tehran had been declared a founding member of the 'axis of evil' by George W. Bush.

Hoping to achieve an almost immediate breakthrough in Sri Lanka, a negotiating team from Norway – the original brokers of the ceasefire agreement – flew to Colombo to revive talks. Encouragement also came from a speech at the national mourning service from the country's president, Chandrika Kumaratunga, whose husband had been killed by the Tamil Tigers and who herself had come close to being assassinated when a suicide bomber attacked her in 1999 at an election rally on the steps of Colombo Town Hall.

'Nature has treated us equally,' said Kumaratunga, who had been left partially blinded by the assassination attempt. 'Can't we treat each other likewise?'

But the Tigers were unimpressed. Blatant propaganda, they scoffed, intended primarily for international consumption. Shortly afterwards, Kofi Annan, the then UN secretary-general, was barred by the government from visiting Tamil-held areas during a tour of the tsunami zone.

Alas, disputes over the distribution of aid threatened to drive the two sides even further apart. Calculating that Tamils had borne two-thirds of the casualties and the damage, the Tigers argued they should receive a corresponding proportion of international aid. Fearing the Tigers would use the money to rebuild its navy, which had been badly hit in the tsunami, the government maintained that aid should not be distributed by a 'terrorist organisation'.

Eventually, six months after the disaster, the Tigers and the government arrived at an agreement, but it broke down within weeks. The hardline Buddhist party, the JVP, whose thugs had surrounded us in Trincomalee that time, petitioned the Supreme Court, which ruled that the Tigers were terrorists and thus should not receive aid.

Across the Bay of Bengal in Indonesia – the first country to feel the force of the Boxing Day Tsunami – talks in Aceh province between separatist rebels and Jakarta led to a landmark agreement ending almost 29 years of conflict. It was a triumph of disaster diplomacy. By contrast, the childish quarrel over aid in Sri Lanka led to a fast deterioration. Those Norwegian officials who returned hoping to revive their peace plan instead found themselves documenting a steep escalation in violence. Six months afterwards, there were five killings a day.

The chance of a more permanent peace had gone, and both sides prepared once again for all-out war. By year's end, when we visited tsunami-hit communities in Tamil-held areas, mothers told us they lay awake at night listening out for the wallop of crashing waves and the crack of gunfire as rebels once more took on the army.

—

Covering the tsunami entangled us in the usual ethical thicket of eavesdropping on the misfortune of others. Awful as it sounds, the most terrible days for the victims of natural disasters or conflicts often provided the most professionally rewarding moments for reporters retelling their stories. Rarely was the competition between rival news organisations more intense than in the aftermath of natural disasters.

Often, this was equally true of correspondents working on

the same side. Prized was the boast of being the first reporter on the scene, or the first to broadcast live, in high-definition quality, from the rubble. The aim was to own the story, to become the face and voice of it.

Grotesque as this sounds, for some there was an element of sport. This was partly because disasters came with the allure of awards, the pursuit of which could breed a certain callousness and insensitivity. A BBC film crew in the Congo had set the gold standard in the 1960s, after the evacuation of a planeload of Europeans. 'Anyone here been raped and speaks English?' a reporter bellowed – a pitiless line of enquiry that the legendary foreign correspondent Edward Behr appropriated as the title for his memoirs.

Nowadays, the vast majority of correspondents are far more emotionally intelligent, and they approach disaster coverage with great humanity and sensitivity. From the Asian tsunami to Haiti, the best coverage is usually the most tender-hearted. But our trade abounds with tales of journalistic tactlessness. One particularly sorry example, which sounds too bad to be true, involved a reporter in Bosnia who was told he could film young children who had sustained terrible injuries from shelling. When shown a child who had the top of his finger ripped off, he was completely unmoved. 'Is that it?' he reportedly asked, with a look bordering on disgust.

War and disaster zones could make decent-minded reporters completely take leave of their senses. Perhaps the most extreme recent example came from an Australian reporter in Iraq who had seen a group of young children playing on some unexploded missiles. She instructed her translator to ask them to do it again for the camera, and then repeated the charade for a second time so the cameraman could shoot it from a different angle. What made this lapse even more inexplicable was that the very story she had set out to cover was on the dangers to children of the hundred or so decaying surface-to-air missiles littering Baghdad. I ran into her a few years later, and she seemed charming and thoroughly right-thinking, but in the pressure of that moment her judgement had gone terribly awry.

Few of us have plumbed those depths, nor even come close. Still, I confess on occasions to having listened to the wrenching testimony of a survivor or a victim and then inadvertently responded with the words 'That's great' at the end of a particularly strong soundbite – a terrible professional tic. My charge sheet would also list what for correspondents is, I am afraid, a routine misdemeanour: of prolonging an interview up until the point where the interviewee succumbs to his or her emotions. As a young reporter, I always thought myself fortunate, charmed even, to have bypassed local newspapers, even though they have always offered the best of journalistic apprenticeships – the 'University of a Thousand Frozen Doorsteps', a colleague calls them. It meant I never had to force 'an entry into many a stricken home', to borrow from Evelyn Waugh, when, say, a child was killed in a road accident. As a foreign correspondent, however, I have done more than enough of it in disaster zones.

Often the corollary of the 'Anyone here been raped and speaks English?' technique is overly sentimental prose drawn from the Heart on the Sleeve school of reportage. Christopher Hitchens offered the most unpitying parody of this overwrought style: 'As I stand here half-canned and weeping in the burning hell hole called . . . the body of a child lay like a broken doll in the street.' I dare say most of us have lapsed into this patois of disaster. I know I have. Perhaps readers will identify shades of it above. The temptation on radio and television is also to deliver this kind of commentary with an overly dramatic voice, as if we were acting the script rather than merely reading it. 'Ham and cheese', we sometimes call it, or 'the full Ploughman's' in the most extreme cases.

With reporter involvement – or RI, as it is called for short – much more fashionable now than it was in the past, plaudits often go to those who have successfully inserted themselves into the story in as heroic a manner as possible. Often, their actions genuinely are heroic, and life-saving. But the best correspondents, I would suggest, show self-restraint in how much of this reaches the screen, downplaying their involvement and making sure that the victim remains the focus of the story.

Here, CNN has crossed a threshold, dispatching its on-screen doctor, the neurosurgeon Sanjay Gupta, to war zones and disasters, where he regularly performs surgery. It always makes for gripping television. It usually saves lives. Dr Gupta is clearly a fine doctor and a decent human being. But it is not the primary function of news crews, and it takes reportage into an entirely different genre.

Natural disasters can also produce a lot of grandstanding and silliness. A staple of hurricane coverage, especially in America, is to be blown off one's feet, ideally in a live cross back to the studio or, if not, during a piece to camera. Again, theatre rather than journalism.

Likewise, disaster coverage normally follows a standard timeline. The focus in the early days is the devastation, the bereavement and the first arrival of aid, which is usually filmed from atop a heavily laden truck or peering down from the winch door of a helicopter to show the hands of its recipients, outstretched, clambering and desperate. On day five or six of an earthquake, there is generally a miraculous rescue. By then, an argument will have erupted over the sluggish arrival of government aid. In Islamic countries, the natural follow-up is to show how radical extremist groups, with links to terrorist organisations, are filling the void. Wherever the disaster, always there will be stories about looting, however small the outbreak, falsely implying a mood of savagery that frankly rarely exists (commonly, crime rates drop after major disasters).

In the aftermath of the Haiti earthquake, Steve Coll of the *New Yorker* – one of the finest foreign correspondents working today – neatly summed up these subgenres of disaster reportage. He spoke of the Last Miracle, that miraculous rescue; the Interpretation of Meaning, where correspondents would ponder the jolting impact of a major catastrophe on victims' faiths or belief systems; and, finally, the Heading to the Exits stories, in which the 'laundry-less reporter forecasts a slow recovery complicated by political fall-out and imperfect relief efforts'.

The lack of a decent laundry service hints at the logistical problems correspondents commonly face: the need for food, water, shelter, power and a place to answer the call of nature. Arriving in Iran to cover the Bam earthquake, our first priority, once we had picked up visas from a friendly consular official in Dubai and cleared the noticeably less friendly immigration officials in Tehran, was to find a hardware shop where we could purchase a generator. Without electricity, we might as well not have been there.

Next, we stocked up on food and water, though we always came weighed down with military-issue MREs – meals ready to eat, or 'meals rarely edible', as they were sometimes known. Then we put up our tents for a week of extreme camping. Transportation is always problematic, since roads are often completely impassable and the only way to reach some of the more remote areas is by military helicopter. So, even if it meant burning up valuable daylight filming time, it was always worthwhile to spend five or six hours waiting, shot-less, on the ground at a military airfield miles from the disaster zone, because of the pictorial riches that lay in store at the end of the flight.

Admittedly, two-dimensional imagery often fails to convey the magnitude of a disaster, but aerial shots provide our best hope of hinting at the scale. Occasionally, flights over a disaster zone can also throw up the kind of telling detail usually only available at ground level. One of the more memorable examples came during the tsunami, when the Indian coastguard flew a photographer over the seldom-seen Indigenous communities in the southern archipelago of the Andaman and Nicobar Islands. Hovering overhead, he captured the most astonishing snapshot of an almost totally naked tribesman aiming his bow and arrow into the sky. Rarely did these military facilities, as they are called, disappoint.

My only letdown came on the longest and most logistically intricate military relief mission that I had ever reported on: an attempt by the US military to provide assistance to the victims of Cyclone Nargis in Burma – a tropical storm that killed more than 130,000 people in May 2008. From Singapore, a small group of journalists was taken onboard a US supply ship up through the Strait of Malacca to rendezvous with the USS *Essex*, a massive amphibious assault ship that had taken up position, along with its carrier group, just over the horizon from the Burmese coast.

For days, we were flown from ship to ship, watching the

marines and sailors make preparations for a huge delivery of aid. With dozens of helicopters, hovercrafts and landing craft primed to go, the US military could have delivered tonnes of aid within the hour. However, the Burmese military junta refused American assistance, and the carrier fleet waited off the coast for a further three weeks before finally being defeated by the generals' heartless intransigence.

Finding shelter in disaster zones was occasionally problematic, though usually easier than one might have imagined. Covering the tsunami in Galle, we took up residence in five-star luxury at the Lighthouse Hotel, a dreamy resort designed by Geoffrey Bawa, Sri Lanka's most celebrated architect. Reporting on the destruction in some of the more isolated villages on the east coast of the island, however, we ended up sleeping in a wave-wrecked house swarming with mosquitoes and that still reeked of death.

In Bam, after spending the first few nights in a tent village and sharing a toilet block with the Iranian Revolutionary Guard, we risked staying in a hotel on the fringes of the quake zone that had such wide cracks in the walls that you could almost peer into the next room. In southern India, we started off at a decent-enough hotel about a mile inland, and by the end of the week we were actually running it. Fearful of another tsunami, the manager simply did a runner, leaving Vivek, our producer, in temporary charge. Not only did he organise the kitchen and housekeeping staff but he also started taking bookings from the other foreign journalists arriving in town. For an impromptu party on New Year's Eve, he managed to rig up a sound system in the garden at the rear and procured a few crates of south-Indian beer and a stock of Old Monk rum.

Unforgivable as it no doubt sounds, I have rarely been at a

New Year's party where the revellers drank so quickly and so hard, and as the sun appeared over the palm trees along the devastated shoreline there was still a small group of stragglers supping the last drops of Old Monk. All I can say in our rather feeble defence was that after almost a week of being surrounded by such awfulness, we needed to disappear for a few hours into drunkenness. Early the next morning, we returned to the relief camps and orphanages nursing hangovers that seemed a reasonable price for escape.

Like many of my colleagues, I have tried to expiate any feelings of guilt about prying into the misery of others with consoling thoughts about opening up viewers' wallets and increasing the pressure on foreign governments to donate more aid. Often, we sponsored survivors ourselves, and gave them food and rebuilding money. In Sri Lanka, I would even like to think we played a minor role in saving international aid agencies a small fortune by hectoring the finance minister so much on air and off that he finally decided to drop an import levy on the four-wheel-drive vehicles and trucks shipped in to help the relief effort that were waiting still on the quayside.

There were times, too, when survivors appeared to draw a measure of therapeutic comfort from having their stories retold on camera, and they perhaps even experienced something of a catharsis. Still, the pressure and temptation of professional competition meant that our motivations were not always as pure as they should have been, and I often came away from disaster zones with even stronger feelings of existential anguish than usual.

—

Confronted by a looming book deadline in October 2005, now less than 48 hours away, I was seated at my desk long before dawn that Saturday morning in the hope of having it ready for the printers by the end of the weekend. When the screen on my laptop appeared to be quivering slightly, my first thought was that it must be time for a screen-break. When it started visibly vibrating and rattling, along with my desk and the pictures hanging on the wall above, it was clear that a gigantic earthquake had hit the region. In the short time it took for the walls of my bedroom in my Delhi apartment to stop shaking, which I suppose must have been 15 seconds or so, over 75,000 people had been killed.

To begin with, we could only guess at where the quake might have hit. Gujarat, where an earthquake had killed 20,000 on Republic Day in 2001, was one possibility. Another, more optimistic, scenario was that the epicentre would be traced to a remote mountain range in the Himalayas, where the death toll would be nowhere near as high.

Within a few minutes, the first wire reports started to appear, as one-line flashes on my computer screen. An earthquake had hit Kashmir. Early estimates of its magnitude varied from 6.8 on the Richter scale to 7.8 – eventually, we would settle on 7.6. According to seismologists, it was a shallow quake, some six to ten miles underground, which meant that it would cause much more damage at the surface. Its epicentre was on the Pakistan side of the Line of Control, and there were early reports, so far unconfirmed, of damage as far away as Islamabad. From the Pakistan capital came eyewitness accounts of an apartment building collapsing in on itself, burying hundreds under the rubble. Thought to be a luxury block of flats, it was almost sure to house foreign diplomats or businessmen. Perhaps someone we knew.

Exact information, as ever in the immediate wake of a major disaster, was hard to come by. Phone lines were down. The mobile network was out. Landslides blocked the roads that snaked from Islamabad into the mountains, where the devastation was sure to be worst. From the Delhi bureau, one team set off for Srinagar, while we dashed to the airport to catch the only flight of the day to Lahore.

By now, a team from our Islamabad bureau was outside the Margalla Towers, the high-end residential complex, where one tower had been flattened and another partially demolished. It was feared that some 150 people were buried under the collapsed concrete, a high proportion of them women and children. From the airport, we headed there too, for on that first night the Margalla Towers served as 'ground zero' for everyone's quake coverage, a dramatic floodlit backdrop where rescue workers dug into the rubble in the hope of pulling people alive from the wreckage, stopping occasionally during aftershocks. There were 20 that day.

Later on, we learnt that more than 250 people had perished in the Margalla Towers, yet it hardly merited a mention in the days after. That number simply paled in comparison with the mounting death toll elsewhere. In the cruel way that news assigns a hierarchy to such things, Saturday night's lead story had become almost incidental by early Sunday morning. As roads started opening up into the worst-affected areas and military helicopters launched relief flights, everyone headed for the mountains.

To begin with, we lingered, for early the next morning Ali, our Islamabad-based cameraman, and I managed to finagle our way aboard one of the Pakistani Army Puma helicopters conducting an early sortie over the disaster zone. First, we headed to Muzaffarabad, the alpine capital of Azad Kashmir, where it looked like a hundred Margalla Towers had collapsed.

Following the line of the Neelum River into the city, we looked down on half-demolished hotel buildings that resembled toppled dominos, and suspension bridges that looked to be dangling from frayed strings. Already, it was estimated that over half of the buildings in the city had suffered some kind of structural damage.

After circling the city, we swooped in to land on a cricket field, which was now a tent-strewn field hospital. Doctors and nurses tended to young children with the most hideous head and facial injuries, wrapping bandages around their heads to staunch the bleeding and to contain the swelling. So swollen were their bruises, so reddened their wounds, that it looked like they had been clubbed over and over again with iron bars. Broken limbs were being encased in plaster casts. Emergency amputations were being performed. Saturday had been a school day in Pakistan, and the carelessly constructed classrooms had been among the first to fail.

Close to the field hospital was one of the schools that had been half-destroyed, where the piercing stench that always accompanies death was already overwhelming. Nobody knew how many dead children were buried beneath the rubble. Inside one of the wrecked classrooms, we saw the lifeless body of a young girl – she could not have been more than eight or nine – hanging from one of the collapsed rafters. Incomprehensibly, freakishly even, she had been strangled in the wreckage, with her headscarf acting like a noose. Because of the time it takes to reach the scene of natural disasters, usually the dead bodies have been covered up or stretchered to some kind of makeshift morgue. But here the little girl's body just hung there motionless, as if frozen in time, with relief workers too afraid to touch it lest they bring down the entire building. Of all the sights I have experienced in conflict and disaster zones, this remains the most vivid and haunting. Much as I would prefer to delete it from my mind, to drag it into some mental trash basket, I fear it has become part of my permanent memory, fixed and immutable.

From Muzaffarabad, we flew further up the Neelum Valley, edging closer all the time to the epicentre. We were actually crossing over some of the most staggering scenery that Pakistan has to offer – lush mountains, flowered meadows, tumbling escarpments, grand canyons – but it was impossible to appreciate the beauty of the setting, for the landscape was strewn with destroyed farm buildings. Each twist in the river valley brought more destruction.

Then we caught our first glimpse of Balakot. A once-pretty tourist town, now it was unrecognisable as a place where people had lived, worked, worshipped, studied and slept little more than 24 hours before. The landscape was strangely colourless. A grey clutter. Close to the river, there was a mound of rubble where the town's mosque had once stood, its fractured minarets pointing up at odd angles into the sky. The bazaar, normally so bustling, was a heap of shattered bricks and knotted metal. The roads were blocked with overturned lorries; those lavishly decorated Pakistani trucks that looked more like mobile shrines, whose gaudy colours were now darkened by dust. So complete was the devastation that the chopper pilot could not make out a clearing where the helicopter could safely land. The Kashmir quake had a new ground zero.

Before dawn the next morning, we set off in convoy to reach Balakot by road – a journey not without risk given the continual danger of landslides and rockfalls. Our biggest obstacle, however, was a badly damaged suspension bridge that looked like it might collapse at any minute into the river valley 20 metres below. Somehow, it remained open, but only to light vehicles and pedestrians. The question for us was whether it could withstand our heavier four-wheel drives.

Determined to become the first journalists to reach Balakot, and fortified by the usual 'luck favours the brave' sense of invincibility, we thought initially we should risk it, despite the fact that our vehicles were laden with broadcasting equipment. In these situations, it also takes a courageous person to confess to cowardice. Helpfully, however, our Pakistani drivers pointed out that Balakot was now within walking distance. So we trekked into town following the line of the river and witnessed from the ground in more detail what we had seen the previous afternoon from the air.

To our left as we entered the town were the remains of a boys' school. Of its 700 pupils, 500 were feared dead. Its basketball court was laid out with white plastic body bags containing dead children. Next to it, a team of men had started digging up the playground. A mass grave. Above the school was a steep escarpment with sweeping views of the Kunhar River, which had clearly been Balakot's most sought-after place to live. The earthquake had made it the most treacherous.

Clambering up through the wreckage, we caught sight of a group of men peering hopefully into the flattened floors of a hillside house. From metres down, they had heard the cries of an 18-month-old boy. Minutes later, young Ibrahim was dragged from the rubble, given his first nourishment in 48 hours and handed to his overjoyed father. 'Thanks to God!' shouted the old man, and then he started sprinting down the hill, presumably to reunite Ibrahim with his mother.

Away to our right, another rescue was underway. Shaukat, a

man in his 20s, was trapped under some collapsed masonry, and his family members did not have the combined strength to drag him out. Standing just 20 metres away was a unit of Pakistani Army soldiers, the usual bunch of ball-scratchers, who refused to help. Often, a camera crew can shame the indolent into action, and we stormed over to the unit and started remonstrating. Not having received orders from their superiors to pull people from the rubble, the commanding officer explained, they would be unable to offer assistance.

We shouted some more, brought the camera in accusingly close, and eventually he agreed to follow us up the hill. In a matter of seconds, Shaukat was free. Needing to head back towards Muzaffarabad, where a team following up behind us had established a tented base camp and set up a satellite so that we could file our report back to London, we left Balakot a short while afterwards. By the time we did so, the mass grave was full of bodies, and the workers had started digging a new one – the coda to our report.

Among the structures badly damaged by the earthquake was the Peace Bridge at Kaman Post, linking the two sides of Kashmir. The early signs were that this might become a helpful metaphor: an emblem of how both Pakistan and India had suffered losses. With more than 1500 people killed in Indian-administered territory, certainly there was renewed hope that this shared disaster would bring about a speedier rapprochement between Islamabad and Delhi.

The offer of help from India had been immediate, and Pakistan was just as quick to accept. Completing within days what they had been unable to achieve in decades, diplomats even agreed to open up five crossing points along the Line of Control so that aid convoys could deliver food, tents and medical supplies to some of the remote mountain communities more easily reached from the Indian side.

For all that, though, Pakistan's India fixation, its refusal to be portrayed as the lesser neighbour, prevented it from going further. When Delhi offered to send helicopters into Pakistani-administered territory to drop aid, Islamabad said it would only accept help if the choppers were piloted by Pakistanis – a ludicrous demand, which Delhi, or any other government, would never countenance. (They did, though, agree not to shoot each other's helicopters out of the sky.) Instead, the aid remained undelivered. Always, the Kashmiris had paid the heaviest price for the stubbornness of Pakistan's and India's leaders, and that remained the case in the aftermath of the earthquake.

By now, help was coming from all over. Washington had diverted hulking great Chinooks en route from Kansas to Kabul, which vastly bolstered the airlift capability. Black Hawk helicopters, stripped of their machine guns, were also flown over the border from Afghanistan. Yet this created an altogether different problem. The quake zone was a hotbed of militant Islam, and one of the Chinook pilots claimed his helicopter had narrowly avoided being hit by a rocket-propelled grenade fired from the valley down below (although a Pakistani military spokesman, faithfully parroting the usual script-lines downplaying the jihadi threat, said the pilot had confused road dynamiting with enemy fire).

In the hours following the earthquake, jihadists had also proved themselves to be adept first-responders, because they were so intimate with the terrain and could also perform battlefield first aid. By contrast, the reflexes of the Pakistani military had been much slower, which was partly because over 400 soldiers had been killed in the quake and a further 700 injured. Though the military top brass had always claimed that the army was the one Pakistani institution that could guarantee stability, it was not meeting the requirements of the moment. Jihadists were filling the void. Certainly, the relief camps lining the valleys were crowded with volunteers affiliated with militant groups, the most active of which was Jamaat-ud-Dawa (the Preaching Society), an offshoot of Lashkar-e-Taiba (Army of the Righteous).

As infidels, I suppose there was a slight risk that we, like the Americans, would be targeted, but the only time we harboured any concerns for our security was when we set off in an 11-boat aid flotilla up the Indus River into the remote tribal areas bordering Afghanistan. Our aim was to reach cut-off communities in the Black Mountains, an area that, since Kipling's day, had never looked kindly on expeditions involving the British. So called because of the dark forests of sycamore, oak and pine trees that rose up sharply from the river, the Black Mountains were stunning. But a *Time* correspondent who joined the aid armada was convinced they drew their name not from their topography but from the fate that befell Westerners foolish enough to venture up the valley. He likened the trip to the movie *Deliverance*, where a boat party of city boys led by Burt Reynolds were terrorised and sodomised by a bunch of back-woods hillbillies.

The Pakistani doctor leading the expedition did little to allay his fears. He had taken to calling the expedition Operation Congo, a voyage into the heart of darkness. Long before the creation of the state of Pakistan, the tribal leaders who ruled the mountains were suspicious of outside interference, and many regularly crossed the border into Afghanistan to fight alongside the Taliban against the

Americans. Word had come from the mountain villages, however, that help was desperately needed, even if it came in boxes stamped 'USA'.

As the arrow-shaped flotilla nudged up the Indus, local tribesmen scrambled down the steep banks to the water's edge. Many had guns slung over their shoulders, and we waited to see how we would be received. But the turban-clad tribesmen seemed much less concerned by the presence of outsiders than by what we had brought with us. Casting their eyes over our cargo, at first they seem aggrieved. 'We don't want flour and cooking oil,' shouted one of the villagers. 'We just need tents.' But then massive rolls of tarpaulin were hauled from another boat.

The tarpaulins were designed to shelter 60 people each, but with countless mountain people homeless there were not enough to go around, because we had to keep some back for other distressed communities further upstream. This raised the possibility that the armed tribesmen would prevent us leaving. But, in my experience of disasters, especially in poorer countries, the victims are often impressively selfless, and though the survival instinct is incredibly powerful, so, too, is the desire to help others. So, with the sun dipping behind the mountains, they eventually waved us on our way so we could make the next delivery by nightfall.

With winter fast closing in, the Pakistani Government and international aid agencies faced a much tougher race against time, as the rush to get aid into the mountains unavoidably came to be called. The earthquake had struck in early October, and there was just a three-week window before the first snowfalls arrived. Not only would many mountain villages have to contend with four metres of snow, sub-zero temperatures brought with them the danger of a second wave of deaths. Just as alarming, of the 450,000 tents needed to provide shelter through the winter, international donors had so far pledged a fifth of that number.

Still, somehow Pakistan managed to avoid a second catastrophe and the dire warnings never came to pass. Its people had survived another calamity and, as usual, soldiered on.

—

Even though stories are often sapped of their emotive power with each passing day, an unwritten convention of major-disaster coverage is to return to the scene a month on, then three months later, then six and finally on the first anniversary. So immense was the scale of suffering and destruction with the tsunami, however, that whenever we returned the plight of the victims and survivors always had the capacity to stir and sometimes shock.

In Sri Lanka, we boarded the train service that was running again between Colombo and Galle, so that we could sit in the guard's van alongside Wanigaratna Karunatillek. A gentle and dependable man who wore a thick black woollen tunic even in the baking heat, Wanigaratna had been in charge of the 'Queen of the Sea' on the morning of the tsunami, and now had to revisit his memories every working day.

Once, his job was one of the most envied posts on the railways. Now, it was among the most wretched. 'Every time I make this journey, I feel sorrowful agony,' he told us. As we travelled south, he described how the coastline had become a graveyard and place of death. Yet the most painful stretch of the journey came when we reached Peraliya and he looked out over the buckled carriages of the 'Queen of Sea', which had been left at the side of the rebuilt track. 'When I see the wreckage, my heart is in pain,' he told us. 'Tears come to my eyes.'

Further down the coast in Galle, the tent shanties that had gone up in the immediate aftermath of the tsunami had been replaced by rows of wooden huts that offered only temporary accommodation but were more substantial nonetheless. The bus depot was operational again, and the concrete stalls at the fish market were shimmering with freshly caught tuna now that the fishermen had rebuilt their boats and returned to the sea. Even the cricket pitch was playable again.

In the north-east, the seafront at Mullaitivu not only remained unoccupied but also had now been declared uninhabitable, with a strict prohibition on rebuilding homes close to the ocean. No longer trusting of the sea, many locals had not yet ventured back into the waters.

We happened to be in town the day that the surviving children from the Tender Sprouts orphanage returned to the seashore, a journey that involved crossing a massive physical and psychological threshold. Clutching tight the hands of their friends and teachers, they felt the sensation of sand under their feet for the first time in six months. Then, in motionless trepidation, they felt the waves splash around their ankles. To begin with, they stood in the ocean, waited for the wave to break and then sprinted back towards land. Then they started playing and gurgling with laughter, as they realised the sea no longer posed a threat.

On our return to southern India for the first anniversary of the tsunami, we met dozens of young mothers who, years earlier, had been encouraged by the authorities to have birth-control treatment, which usually involved tying their fallopian tubes. All of them had lost sons and daughters, and feared they might never be able to bear children again. In Nagapattinam, the corridors of the local hospital were busy with bereaved mothers waiting in line for consultations for procedures that would hopefully give them the chance of falling pregnant again. Still, out of the 50 reversal operations so far performed, just two had been successful.

Selvi, a middle-aged woman with a deep-red pottu, a Tamil version of the bindi, on her forehead, had lost all her five children. She had paid to have the treatment, and for eight months running she had thought she might be pregnant. Each time, however, her overdue period eventually arrived. 'What is the point of living,' she said, 'if you can't have a family?' More than 200 families in this town alone had lost all their children.

In a relief camp nearby, Gita and her husband, Vasu, performed regular pujas before a shrine decorated with candles, garlands and portraits of their two daughters, five-year-old Jyothika and her younger sister, Sofia. 'It would have been better if one of us had died,' said Vasu, as he stared blankly at the photographs with a tear racing down his face. Yet here, at least, there was hope. Gita had paid for the reversal treatment and now was four months pregnant. If the newborn turned out to be a girl, she planned to name the baby after her eldest daughter. 'Now we are looking forward to our daughters being reborn,' said her tearful husband.

Before leaving Nagapattinam, we heard from doctors at the local hospital that a woman who had lost her children in the tsunami and then had the reversal treatment was about to reach the final stage of labour. Matarasi had got pregnant two months after the tsunami hit and was more than happy to withstand the pain of labour after the agony of losing a child. To begin with, the labour was routine, but as the baby moved down into the birth canal there was a problem.

The female doctor on duty pressed her old-fashioned stethoscope to Matarasi's swollen belly and detected from the hurried heartbeat that the baby was in distress. Her diagnosis was instantaneous. The umbilical chord was wrapped around the baby's neck and threatening suffocation. Immediately, Matarasi was rushed into the operating theatre for a Caesarean section.

In the courtyard outside, her mother thrashed around on the concrete floor, beating her chest and throwing her head violently from side to side. She feared both her daughter and the unborn baby were about to die.

Both did survive, but there was a fear that the baby might be brain-damaged through lack of oxygen at birth. Our footage was so harrowing that when we filed our report back to London the editor of the evening news decided that viewers would not be able to bear to watch it and simply edited out Matarasi's tortured labour. The Asian tsunami and then the Pakistani earthquake. It was the end of our year of disasters, and neither we, London nor our viewers could bear much more. Alas, there was no respite for the victims we left behind.

Chapter 11

The Search for an Indian Bride

To be dispatched to the subcontinent as an unmarried correspondent was to embark upon a journey pregnant with romantic possibility. The BBC had long offered a nuptial variant of Nehru's tryst with destiny: the almost certain prospect of finding an Indian bride.

Folklore had it that every bachelor who crossed the threshold of the Delhi bureau had departed, three or so years later, with an Indian wife – a happy custom that stretched back to the founding days of the Indian Republic. And lest this sound like some matrimonial leftover from the British Raj, the women in question had been not only exceptionally beautiful but also especially feisty – character traits rendered in even sharper relief as city-based career women became full participants in India's economic revolution. Approaching Indira Gandhi International Airport late in 2003 on my first trip to the country, with the lights of Diwali flashing by underneath, I naturally wondered if my prospective wife was somewhere down below.

Alas, I had arrived in a country more engrossed with sex than with love. An Indian version of the British lads' mag *Maxim* was about to make its subcontinental debut, featuring in its inaugural issue a buxom Bollywood star with an hourglass figure pouting on its cover, two bikini-clad models helpfully demonstrating how to perform the Heimlich manoeuvre, and, more incongruously, the story of a police inspector from Uttar Pradesh who was convinced he was the modern-day reincarnation of the Hindu goddess Radha, who dressed during his off-duty hours in a sari.

Bollywood directors, who at moments of cinematic passion had traditionally cut away to shots of blooming flowers or gently swaying trees, now allowed the 12 million Indians who went each day to the movies to see couples not only kiss on the screen but also embrace each other with lustrous passion – perhaps even to shed a layer or two of clothing. The first lesbian-themed movie, Deepa Mehta's *Fire*, had already hit the screens, with an Indian version of *Brokeback Mountain* just a few years down the track. Cleavage jutted out from almost every other billboard, and just as the flesh-quotient of Indian advertising had hit new highs, so, too, had the scandal-quotient of Indian journalism.

Rarely a week would pass without some plump, 50-something politician being caught on hidden camera in a state of semi-undress and semi-arousal, with his trousers around his ankles and his off-white vest still struggling to withhold his cascading rolls of flab. It was one of those unwritten rules of Indian politics: not even the most libidinous parliamentarian would ever remove his vest.

Tempting though it was to insert these stories into the 'new India' file, it was not where they belonged. As anyone familiar with the *Kama Sutra*, the ecclesiastical eroticism of the sculptures carved into the temples at Khajuraho or the rampant promiscuity of the Indian gods and goddesses, who made their Greek cousins look like shrinking violets, the licentiousness of the Indians was anything but new. Had it not been for the intervention of those three great passion killers, the Mogul invaders in the tenth century, the Britishers in the nineteenth, and the puritans of the Indian freedom movement in the twentieth, this age-old debauchery would have gone on uninterrupted and uninhibited for the last thousand or so years. Now, it was back in full swing.

In releasing its first nationwide sex survey, *Outlook*, a respectable current-affairs magazine, spoke of 'a continent of unfulfilled desires that awaken disturbing lust and longing'. Its poll on 'forbidden sex' produced data to prove it. Over 92 per cent of the respondents in Ahmedabad admitted to having sex with their boss or the boss's spouse; 31 per cent of women in Bangalore revealed they would like to experiment with a threesome; and 46 per cent of women from Mumbai confessed they would like to attend male stripper shows. Some of the findings were staggering. In Delhi, 12 per cent of women admitted to watching a pornographic film with their boss. Others simply confirmed what everyone had long suspected: the inexorable horniness of Indian men, 80 per cent of whom said they would 'agree to have casual sex with anyone they find attractive'.

If the survey made for sparkling reading, the letters page in *Outlook* the following week was still more entertaining. 'The latest issue of *Outlook* is nothing short of pornography,' an enraged reader had emailed. 'We would like to unsubscribe if this is to go on, since we have children and working staff at home.'

Later, these sex surveys also came under fire from the *Financial Times*, not on moral grounds but for their statistical probity. Sticklers for the figures, the *FT* had crunched the numbers of another sex survey in a rival current-affairs magazine, *India Today*, and uncovered discrepancies. While 47 per cent of women claimed to have enjoyed multiple orgasms, only a third knew what was actually meant by the term. From an anthropological perspective, what was also illuminating about the sex surveys was the urge to quantify debauchery, because it combined two of India's great passions: sex and statistical measurement (this same fascination with numbers also helped explain some of cricket's popularity). For mathematically minded Indians, it did not get much better.

Alongside essays on the latest moves in the Indo–Pak peace process and the Naxalite–Maoist rebellion in central India, the current-affairs magazines also reported on a new breed of sexual entrepreneur, the Indian gigolos, or 'Aunty's Lovers', as they were sometimes dubbed. Their client base was the middle-aged 'desperate housewives' – one of an increasing number of phrases imported from America – who lived in the more well-to-do suburbs of Delhi and Mumbai.

'Their world is about desire and passion. Of frustrated and loveless women,' noted *Outlook*, which illustrated its exposé with a full-length picture showing a primed Indian gigolo standing on a double bed astride a single rose, wearing nothing more than a medallion, a skimpy pair of scarlet briefs and a look of wild abandon. To complete this seductive look, his head was thrust back, as if writhing with ecstasy, and the tips of his fingers had made a slight incursion into the top of his knicker elastic.

Gigolos could apparently make anything from 5000 to 20,000 rupees a night – good money – and the more accomplished among them were 'SMS and net-friendly' and could 'eat with a fork and knife or chopsticks'. Their online advertisements, which offered to cater to every craving and vice, were a delight. Take Roshan, who punched in his credentials in bold capital letters, presumably to offer proof of his virility. He wrote:

> I am well educated/well bred with good etiquette. I
> am looking for well bred/well educated ladies with
> real erotic/sexual drive. Complete satisfaction assured
> with specialised foreplay/after play techniques. Long
> enduring performance dotted with soft caress/kisses.
> Special emphasis on lower back and g-spot. Oral action,
> deep penetration, doggie position, table edge stroke . . .
> and much more.

Whether able to perform table-edge strokes or not, if these gigolos
were even half as entertaining in bed as they were online, it was
easy to see why so many aunties had become slaves to their sexual
desires.

Though reports of this burst of licentiousness were no doubt
exaggerated, sex had become one of India's fastest growing
industries. That made many Indians happy, but it was also
making many of them sick. With the rates of HIV infection
soaring, India ran the risk of surpassing South Africa as the global
hub of Aids. To drive along the new highway linking Delhi and
Jaipur in Rajasthan was to witness how quickly the disease could
spread. All along, temptation lined the route, and there were long
stretches where virtually every house was a brothel. In certain
villages, all but the most dowdy of girls grew up to be prostitutes.
Long-distance truckers looked upon these roadside hookers like
Western travellers would regard a motorway services station. Sex
was the easiest of sells and the cheapest of thrills – less than a
dollar a time.

Nagma possessed the kind of sultry beauty that could easily
have made her an actress or a model, but she had grown up in a
village alongside the highway and from a very early age had been

groomed for prostitution. We interviewed her at the end of a long working day, but still she was striking in her lilac sari with her chestnut hair gathered up in a neat ponytail. It was easy to see why she was both a truck driver's favourite and a public-health official's worst nightmare.

'It doesn't seem to matter if you use a condom or not,' she told us. 'I don't know anyone who's died of Aids.'

Whether Nagma was simply lying or in denial, it was hard to tell. But a quarter of the prostitutes in India were thought to be carriers of the HIV virus, and even if she did not personally know any victims yet she would do so soon.

Here was another instance, as with female foeticide, where India's rapid economic development had exacerbated the problem. Mile by mile, the government had embarked upon a massive highway-construction programme – its biggest infrastructure project since independence. Yet new roads acted like poisoned arteries and were spreading Aids around the country almost as quickly as the drivers could travel from one town to the next.

Harmeet Singh, a long-distance truck driver from South India, who usually spent three out of every four weeks on the road, was at high risk of becoming a carrier. A regular client of the sex workers of Rajasthan, he refused to wear a condom because he hated rubber-insulated sex. How we managed to persuade him to appear on camera I cannot quite recall, but Harmeet admitted to cheating on his wife, and he explained that he much preferred sex without safeguards, even though he understood the risks. 'When you're drunk and in a hurry,' said the father of two, 'it's easy to forget to use a condom.' Harmeet said he could not help himself, even though he was aware he might one day infect his wife with the HIV virus.

The grubbiest, most sordid side of India's thriving sex industry was found in the whorehouses of Falkland Road, or the cages of Mumbai, as they were aptly known. Here, girls as young as nine years old were forced into prostitution, since the younger the child the higher the price the brothel owners could charge. Locked up like hostages and rarely allowed to step outside their filth-ridden workplaces, they were forced to have sex as many as 30 times a day, seven days a week. Most were daubed with heavy make-up – crimson lipstick, thick mascara, false eyelashes – to make them more alluring.

Outside the barred windows, Mumbai police officers patrolled the street but did nothing to stop this underage sex or to help free the girls. Instead, the girls' only hope of liberation came from charity workers who monitored the brothels and occasionally mounted raids. Even then, the girls often hid under their mattresses and beds as the raids unfolded, because they were so frightened of the brothel owners and fearful of being set free.

Filming on Falkland Road always came with risks, because the brothel owners often dispatched henchmen armed with guns, knives and hot chilli peppers, which they rubbed in the eyes of prying cameramen and journalists. And again, the police offered no protection, since they were commonly in cahoots with the racketeers.

Given that Mumbai had become so protective of its international image, we managed once to persuade the local authorities to mount a raid on one of the brothels where spotters from the main rescue charity knew young girls were being held captive. Yet, for three consecutive nights, we waited for the go-ahead from police but were given excuses each time – a delay that gave corrupt officers more than enough time to tip-off the brothel owners and for the girls to be spirited away. Sure enough, by the third day our spotters from the rescue charity reported that the girls had been taken to another of Mumbai's cages, and shortly afterwards the police rang to tell us, with phoney apologies, that the raid had been cancelled. We left Mumbai with barely a picture in the can.

Determined not to be thwarted by corrupt policemen, we decided to come at the story from a different angle. By far the most popular girls on Falkland Road came from Nepal. Indian men preferred their light-coloured skin to the darker complexions of home-grown prostitutes and were prepared to pay a premium. Some 40 per cent of the prostitutes in Mumbai had been spirited over the border from the mountain kingdom as victims of human trafficking. So the next time we went to Kathmandu to cover the latest skirmishes in the Maoist rebellion, we tried to find out how easily the girls were trafficked.

Our starting point was a refuge in the Nepalese capital that took in girls rescued from sex slavery in India. Its dorms and classrooms were packed with teenagers, the majority of whom had become virtual orphans since returning to their homeland. Most families disowned them after discovering they had worked as prostitutes. Tragically, the refuge also doubled as a hospice, because more than 80 per cent of the girls and young women rescued from India returned infected with HIV. In one room, we were shown a beautiful 24-year-old woman, whose face was drained of colour, whose body was contorted in pain and whose frail hands quivered uncontrollably. With only a few weeks left to live, she could not even summon up the strength to utter a single word. Another victim of Falkland Road, she could hardly even blink.

On the border between Nepal and India – a crossing point marked with a magnificent ornamental arch – we joined a team of volunteers from the charity trying to intercept the young girls before they could be trafficked. At the side of the busy road, they maintained a small clapboard checkpoint that was decorated with photographs of young women they had managed to save – a collage of the most touching portraits of innocence.

Each year, they managed to save 2000 girls from sexual servitude, which sounded like an impressive rate of interception. But the traffickers still spirited 12,000 over the border. Congested with trucks, cars, noisy motorbikes and horse-drawn carts, and shrouded in heavy early-morning fog, it was difficult to make any sense of the chaos at the border, but the spotters were quite brilliant. Shortly after we started filming, they flagged down a cart loaded with a dozen people, after a 17-year-old girl with a pretty face and an empty stare caught their eye.

A woman claiming to be her auntie, who had promised to take her over into India so she could experience the novelty of riding on a railway locomotive, sat alongside. Questioned in the hut by the side of the road, however, she was quickly found out to have no familial connection with the perplexed young girl. She did not even know her name. Realising she had been rumbled by the spotters, the woman ran out of the hut and disappeared into the crowd.

Later on, the young girl was taken back to her village, still oblivious to the fact that she had been saved from becoming the latest victim in one of the world's fastest growing crimes. Other girls were much less fortunate. For them, that decorated arch on the border between India and Nepal became the gateway to a wretched life in the cages of Mumbai.

—

By now, two Diwalis on, I could report progress in my search for an Indian bride. Help on the matchmaking front had come from my best friend from college, a British-Indian whose father had survived the post-partition journey from Pakistani Punjab to Delhi, where he had trained as a doctor before falling in love with a British nurse and settling in the UK.

Over for his cousin's wedding, an extravagant four-day bash with the usual brass bands, thrones, turbans, white stallion and whisky, my friend introduced me to one of his relatives, a delightful woman called Madhu. Madhu ran a fabrics company and suggested I meet one of her clients, an attractive young woman who made regular visits to the capital on business – a lingerie designer, I was sure she said.

Our first introduction came at a trendy new restaurant that was a favourite haunt of the Bollywood glitterati and that could hardly have been more beautiful: a rustic former boarding house on the edge of the ancient city, with whitewashed walls and ornate ironwork, which was illuminated by what looked like a thousand tea lights and candles. At its heart was a stunning courtyard, with antique furniture configured around the twisted roots of a giant banyan tree.

In Hindu culture, the banyan tree is seen as wish fulfilling and divine. For Buddhists, its habit of supplanting host trees is viewed as a metaphor for the overpowering strength of human desire. Unfortunately, however, our evening followed more closely the words of the southern Indian proverb that nothing grows under the banyan tree.

Dispensing with routine conversational ice-breakers, we ended up arguing over the Iraq war, of all things, and the quality of the pre-war intelligence. Here, I trotted out my usual formulation that Saddam Hussein had duped everyone over the existence of weapons of mass destruction, not least his own commanders, who were led to believe that there was a stockpile of such weapons. She, however, would have none of it, and she immediately wrote me off as an apologist for the Bush administration and a callow, America-loving blowhard. Then she launched into a tirade against the media, and how reporters had given George W. Bush a ridiculously easy ride in the run-up to the war. It was at this point that I volunteered, tentatively, that I had been one of those self-same correspondents.

'Nice guy, shame about his politics,' she told her colleague, rather unfairly, as they left the restaurant that night. For my part, I went home that night thinking she was beautiful, feisty and smart as a tack, but woefully misguided.

Happily, other dinners followed, where the chat strayed beyond weapons of mass destruction and steered clear of other potential minefields. Eventually, she latched onto the fact that I was neither a neo-conservative nor even a recovering neo-conservative. We started to get on better. We found there were areas of common ground – a deep love of all things Indian, for a start. Perhaps there was even a flicker of mutual interest. Why, it might even have qualified as a spark. Still, the dear woman who introduced us was always in attendance, which meant our get-togethers were always heavily chaperoned affairs. We also tended to meet in that outdoor restaurant, where our table fell under the sprawling banyan tree. Under its shadow, there seemed little likelihood that our friendship would ever blossom into romance.

Then came our first unchaperoned dinner, which went better

than either of us had expected. We met again the following night, on what could only be described as a date. Later that weekend, there was even the old-fashioned *Brief Encounters*-style romance of a railway-platform farewell as she boarded an overnight train to Dharamsala in the Himalayas. As the guard blew the whistle, a hawker tried to pinch her bottom and I tried to steal a kiss – and hopefully I benefited from the comparison.

After the train disappeared into the Delhi night, we did not catch sight of each other again for another ten weeks, but there were texts, emails, long-distance phone calls and flowers. Lots of texts, emails, long-distance phone calls and flowers. We started to lay plans on how we could share holidays together; on how we could live together; on how we could make a life together. At the start, our chances of success seemed remote, but in a country where astrologers are often the ultimate arbiters of the viability of a relationship, the stars were falling into something at least nearing alignment. I was prepared to make my move.

Back in London, I told my then boss that my search for an Indian bride had taken a wholly unexpected turn. While I had upheld the tradition of finding love in India, my journey into matrimony had strayed much further afield. The object of my affections came not from Delhi, nor Mumbai or Chennai. In fact, she did not hail from anywhere in South Asia. Instead, I had fallen in love with an Australian: a beautiful blonde Sydneysider who regularly travelled to Delhi on business – 'the Aussie knicker lady', as she had become known to friends and colleagues, even though, as I had learnt by now, she was actually a full-blown fashion designer.

Sydney would be my next move, I boldly told him, even if it meant inflicting irreparable damage on my BBC career. My boss, however, could hardly have been more accommodating. For the first time in over a decade, the Sydney posting was about to become vacant. Better still, I managed to land the job.

The next time we returned to South Asia together was to get married 18 months later, although we chose Sri Lanka over India. No country in the world does nuptials with more colour or panache, but we feared that the digestive systems of our overseas guests might not be robust enough to withstand the traditional four-day curry-athon. Sri Lanka became our India-lite alternative. The Blessed Land came with its own problems, not least the resurgence of the Tamil Tigers, who, in the run-up to the 60th anniversary of Sri Lankan independence, carried out a string of attacks on Colombo. But the plan was to get married in Galle on the far south-western tip of the country, which, as we tried to assure nervous guests, was akin to attending a wedding in Penzance at the height of the Troubles in Northern Ireland. Fortunately, they were an adventurous crowd, and they were ready to disregard a plethora of official travel warnings that placed a blanket ban on the entire island. Not one of our guests pulled out.

Held in the faded Romanesque splendour of the Anglican church in Galle, which had been given a lick of fresh paint the day before, the wedding could hardly have been more perfect. True, the electric organ that we had hired arrived only a matter of minutes before the bride, but fortunately Nik was on hand to untangle the soundman trying to plug in the wires. Ideally, the elderly vicar would have stuck with the vows we had agreed on beforehand rather than improvising with the *Book of Common Prayer* – my beloved wife never expected to utter the words 'honour and obey' at her wedding, though there have been numerous occasions since on which I've reminded her that she did.

Likewise, we could have done without the threat of industrial action from the tuk-tuk drivers ranked outside our hotel, but once again Vivek's famed negotiation skills forestalled an escalation of the strike. The temperature also soared to over 45 degrees, which made it feel as though we were getting married in an exquisitely designed blast furnace.

Yet these small setbacks were immediately forgotten once the ceremony was over, and a cavalcade of decorated bullock carts, tuk-tuks and elephants set off in procession through the streets of old Galle. It marched to the brassy strains of a local wedding band led by a trumpeter who had seemingly modelled his technique on Dizzy Gillespie, right down to the near-exploding cheeks. Cocooned in this coastal citadel, the troubles of Sri Lanka seldom impinged. Just about the only time the Tamil Tigers entered the reckoning was ahead of the fireworks on our wedding night, in the strictly literal meaning of that phrase. The hotel had to warn the local army unit about the planned pyrotechnics, lest they be misconstrued as a seaborne attack from the Tamil Tigers.

Our honeymoon in the Maldives is worthy of mention if only because of the correspondent blagging that helped make it happen. Told that all the flights between Colombo and Malé had sold out, I suggested out of desperation that my travel agent mention to the booking clerks at Sri Lankan Airlines that I was a personal friend of the president's. This was a brazen lie, of course, but it helped make sense of the red-carpet VIP treatment lavished upon us at the airport after two premium seats miraculously opened up. Not only were we rushed through immigration and customs, which usually presented something of an obstacle course for departing journalists, but we were ferried everywhere in our very own golf buggy and treated in the executive lounge with near-regal deference.

On our return, however, it appeared that we had been rumbled when an officious-looking member of the ground crew boarded the special minivan that had arrived to take us from the tarmac to the terminal building and demanded that we identify ourselves. Trepidatiously, we raised our hands, fully expecting to be frogmarched off. Instead, the woman barked at the other business-class travellers to exit the bus immediately so we could complete the 30-metre journey in unencumbered luxury.

'South Asia always delivers' used to be our unofficial motto, as we went from country to country and from story to story. Never was that phrase more redolent with meaning than on the day that I married my wife, and the search for an Indian bride came to such happy fruition.

Chapter 12

Lie Back and Think of Australia

Never before had I arrived in a country with such a clear and resolute sense of how I planned to report on it. Determined to avoid ravenous sharks, randy koalas and rampant cane toads, I decided there would be no Antipodean animal stories. Nor would Crocodile Dundee-like characters force their way onto our airwaves, however many times they cried strewth, crikey or bonza. Rather than shoring up Australia's creaky stereotypes with more buttressing, I would attempt to target them with a wrecking ball.

Then, within days of touching down in Sydney in September 2006, a stingray lanced Steve Irwin in the heart, and his memorial service in Queensland became my baptism.

The setting was his beloved Crocoseum at Australia Zoo on the Sunshine Coast, where thousands had gathered to celebrate the adventurer's outsized personality and underdog success. Zoo hands lined the edge of the arena, cradling an assortment of Antipodean creatures in their arms – koalas, baby crocs and goannas. An elder from the local Gubbi Gubbi people, flanked by her two sons, whose bare chests were smeared with tribal decorations, delivered a eulogy in her native tongue and then led mourners in an ancient 'Coo-ee' wail.

John Williamson, the great outback balladeer, sang his most famous anthem, 'True Blue', with the back of a pick-up truck serving as his stage; while a member of children's music group The Wiggles, who was sombre by his own standards but frenetically upbeat nonetheless, sprang forward wearing his trademark sky-blue polo-neck to announce himself as the master of ceremonies. Thousands of mourners, bathed in brilliant white sunlight, watched from the terraces of the outdoor stadium, wearing mirror shades, zinc cream, open-neck shirts and safari fatigues. Khaki had temporarily become the new black.

Beamed in from New York – another hostile environment that held no fear for the Crocodile Hunter – the movie star Russell Crowe spoke first. 'You were headline news on CNN for a week,' said Crowe, conferring upon him that most treasured of Australian accolades: international recognition. 'There's not many zookeepers who could command that sort of attention, mate.'

Then, with their own video tributes, came other Hollywood celebrities. 'America just flipped for him,' opined the actress Cameron Diaz. The singer Justin Timberlake testified both to the warmth of Irwin's personality and the cold commercial calculation of the television executives who had put together the service. 'I may have only really spent a day with you guys,' he said, confessing to only the briefest of acquaintances, 'but it was a day I'll never forget.'

Stepping before the Crocoseum, Australian Prime Minister John Howard could boast a deeper friendship and spoke of a patriotic, hard-working, brave, family-orientated model citizen, a 'remarkable man' and a 'remarkable Australian'.

But the men who knew Steve Irwin best, from the days when he was a local oddball rather than a global sensation, were his mates – brave men now struggling to contain their emotions. His best friend, Wes Mannion, wept as he described the moment that sealed their mateship: the day when Irwin saved him from the gaping jaws of a monster croc in the swamplands of northern Queensland. 'I'll miss you, mate,' said Mannion, before breaking down.

Then came Steve's father, Bob, the founder of what was then called the Beerwah Reptile Park and the animal lover who imbued his son with such a fierce spirit of adventure. 'Please don't grieve for Steve,' he said, battling back tears. 'He's at peace now. But I'd like you to grieve for the animals. The animals have lost their best friend they ever had – and so have I.'

All this served as prelude for Steve Irwin's eight-year-old daughter, Bindi, who appeared with her hair tied in pigtails and a jagged crocodile tooth dangling on a chain around her neck. With her finger gently tracing the words printed on her script, and a Madonna-style microphone amplifying her already confident young voice, the pint-sized Bindi described a surely unique father–daughter relationship in which they 'filmed together, caught crocodiles together and loved being in the bush together'. Then came her pay-off: 'When I see a crocodile, I will always think of him.'

As the service came to its set-piece end, John Williamson reprised 'True Blue', while Irwin's mud-splattered pick-up truck was loaded up with his crocodile net, an olive-green sleeping mat and his surfboard. Then, the vehicle was driven at hearse-like pace out of the arena through an honour guard of zookeepers standing with their heads bowed. With that, other members of the Australia Zoo family converged on the arena, carrying wreaths of bright-yellow sunflowers, which they placed on the ground as

Williamson reached his coda. Finally, a boom-mounted camera swept from ground- to roof-level, like some woozy giraffe aroused from its sleep, enabling viewers to see what the sunflowers spelt out: the Crocodile Hunter's raucous catchcry, 'CRIKEY'.

As the mourners streamed out of the Crocoseum, past a tribute wall festooned with flowers, stuffed animals, national flags, rugby balls, inflatable crocodiles and a washing line full of khaki shirts daubed with felt-tip tributes, I asked them to share their thoughts. 'It's a bloody shame. We've lost a really good bloke,' said a local man bedecked in the national colours, with two flags in his grasp, one fastened on his black cowboy hat and three transferred onto his maudlin face. 'This has been the most emotionalist day of my life.'

Next to him was a pair of identical twins, who spoke with near-perfect synchronicity: 'The animals have lost a beautiful icon. We broke down when we saw his white truck being driven out.'

Finally, we interviewed a woman who had queued for 20 hours for her ticket, who had come wearing a safari hat decorated with the words 'Crocs Rule'. 'I'm hoping this will be closure,' she said, adopting the modern-day argot of collective grief, 'but I don't think so.'

If initially I had viewed Irwin's death as something of a personal affront, the three weeks between his death and his memorial could hardly have been more useful for such a tenderfoot correspondent. There was the character of the public mourning. Not being the type of people to dwell too long on bereavement, the reaction when the news first came through from northern Queensland, where Irwin had been filming the latest instalment of *The Ocean's Deadliest*, was measured and fairly muted. No

Diana-style overreaction here.

Over the next 48 hours, however, the public mood shifted discernibly, as news came through from abroad of a stronger reaction in America and Britain, where Irwin was arguably a much bigger star. As the Australian public watched foreign fans in an advanced state of sorrow, Irwin's death became a much more emotionally significant event in his homeland. Perhaps Australia's competitive instincts might even have been aroused.

Television channels changed their schedules to accommodate his death, the current-affairs shows mounted live broadcasts from Australia Zoo (one featured a presenter resplendent in a safari suit with a lizard perched on her shoulder) and the networks enjoyed a ratings bonanza. Indeed, the only programme that week to out-perform the fast-assembled Irwin tribute programmes was the fly-on-the-wall documentary *Border Security: Australia's Frontline*, which hinted at a quite different story altogether.

The main reason why Irwin's death became so engrossing, however, was that it fast became an intellectual event: part of that perennial debate, long-running and anguished, over Australia's national identity. Arguably an even more confronting figure in death than he was in life, the question of his contribution to Australian life became the subject of an ever more rancorous quarrel. It began as an argument between those who saw him as the living embodiment of some of Australia's most celebrated values – courage, resilience, humour, bawdy larrikinism and mateship – and those who bridled at how this caricature of a man had become Australia's most bankable global brand ambassador.

In the hours after his death, Russell Crowe had set the ball rolling by describing him as 'the Australian we all yearn to be'. But then came a counterblast from London from one of the country's cultural castaways, and a woman who could once have laid claim, like Irwin, to being the world's most famous Australian. In the pages of the *Guardian*, Germaine Greer launched a ferocious attack on Irwin for spawning 'a whole generation of kids in shorts seven sizes too small' who would 'shout in the ears of animals with hearing ten times more acute than them'. Deliciously, there was also a political edge to Greer's assault. Irwin had not only lauded John Howard as 'Australia's greatest ever prime minister', she complained, but only a few months before had also enjoyed a 'gala barbecue' with George W. Bush.

Now, posthumously, the wildfire warrior had become a cultural warrior, and his fellow Queenslander, the author John Birmingham, leapt, Irwin-like, to his defence. Birmingham started by savaging Greer – a 'feral hag' and a 'poorly sketched caricature of a harridan'. Then he skewered the 'inner urban elite', which had viewed Irwin as just a 'fucking moron' and, worse, a 'cashed-up bogan'.

Birmingham predicted that Irwin's death 'may become our very own Kennedy moment', and that he would take 'his place in the mass cultural afterlife next to JFK and Princess Di'.

The argument over Irwin had fast become a proxy battle between the urban elites and, seemingly, everyone else. Andrew Bolt, a columnist at Melbourne's *Herald Sun*, spoke witheringly of a 'cultural class that feels threatened by blokes in work boots who shout "crikey"'.

But the urban elites hit back. 'Irwin's death provided a trigger for a gratuitous outpouring of hatred directed at the "elites" who found his antics embarrassing, especially when they were represented as authentically Australian,' opined Clive Hamilton, the then head of the Australia Institute. 'It's the new face of the cultural cringe – we canonise anybody who makes it in the US or Britain no matter how lowbrow the performer.'

Perhaps this was precisely the kind of verbal punch-up that Steve would have wanted, and a fitting requiem. Unknown to most, three years before his death he had declared himself to be a conservationist not only of Australian wildlife but also of the country's colloquialisms. His grandfather and great-grandfather had fought and died for Australia, he had said back in 2003. He uttered each crikey, strewth and fair dinkum in their honour. 'They didn't fight on the frontline and get shot at by the enemy for us to forget who we are,' he declared. 'They weren't saying holy smokes or goddamn. They were saying crikey, strewth, fair dinkum, have a go ya mug. That's what they were saying, mate.' Evoking the Anzac spirit, forged in the trenches of Gallipolli, the most solid of sentimental buttresses, he concluded, 'I want to speak Australian, mate, because I believe that's what they fought for.'

What I was witnessing, then, was Australia's very own clash of civilisations: not so much the bush against the big cities but the battlers against the elites, and the lowbrow against the high. For a newly arrived foreign journalist, it was hard to think of a more instructive initiation. The stereotypes I had set out to avoid had become the subject of feisty debate. The stereotypes *were* the story.

Admittedly, not much of this dissonance came across in our coverage. The bosses in London, whose kids were traumatised by the death of their beloved Crocodile Hunter, saw Steve Irwin as a great Australian hero, and his memorial service as a fittingly Antipodean send-off. They especially liked the idea of Diana-lite mourning, and the sight and sound of hardbitten Australian blokes temporarily succumbing to their emotions. On television especially, we pretty much delivered the consoling certainties that were expected, from the elephants sauntering into the Crocoseum to the tribute wall of khaki shirts. Like the rest of the world, we loved this orgy of Australiana.

By the time we drove back to Brisbane along a road that would soon be renamed the Steve Irwin Way, even the memorial service had become a matter of contention. The debate centred on whether it could be described as authentically Australian at all. In its big box office staging, there was a showiness, even a brashness, that was at odds with the usual preference for understatement and muted ceremony. The pick-up truck and exotic animals became props in a production choreographed with an American audience in mind. Unlike the funeral, say, of the famed Australian cricketer Sir Donald Bradman, the service was not even televised in its entirety on free-to-air channels in Australia, since the global rights were held by the US behemoth Animal Planet.

Besides, this paean to the bush had been put together by Irwin's business partner, the Brisbane-based television impresario John Stainton, who admitted during his oration at the service to being a self-confessed 'city slicker'. Arguably, then, it owed more to Oprah than to the outback. Then came the counter-argument: the easy embrace of imported idioms, the idolatry of the bush from inhabitants of the cities, and the desire to impress audiences in America and Britain were the very things that made the memorial so faithfully Australian.

If nothing else, Irwin's death demonstrated that Australia was far more complicated than international news organisations, such as the BBC, liked to think. We preferred hearing about an assumed Australia, recalling the usual stereotypes, rather than anything more confounding or unfamiliar. No doubt, this is one of the reasons why big international news organisations have neglected the 'land down under', a phrase dripping with inconsequentiality. Generally, they have viewed it as a faraway backwater, where many of its stories, as F. Scott Fitzgerald might have put it, 'fell just short of being news'.

Long ago, Australia lost the legendary CBS news anchor Walter Cronkite – just as President Johnson lost him over Vietnam – who wryly observed that the country harboured too many reporters and not enough news. Australia's sheer irrelevance also provided the starting point for another American, Bill Bryson, whose book *Down Under* is probably the most widely read portrait of modern Australia. Before setting off for Sydney, Bryson sauntered the short distance to his local library and conducted a fruitless search of the *New York Times* index for 1997. Australia merited just 20 mentions, whereas Albania got 150. If anything, that year yielded an exceptionally rich harvest of Antipodean yarns. Over the following 12 months, just six stories were considered ripe for publication. Ending his adventures and travelogue, Bryson left readers with a departing thought, as melodramatic as it was melancholic: 'Life would go on in Australia,' he opined, 'and I would hear almost nothing of it.'

My hunch was that all this neglect was born of a false sense of understanding: the misplaced notion that because assumed Australia was so easily comprehensible there was no real need for any further enquiry. It was almost as if we allowed Australia's tourism advertisements to do our journalism for us. Every few years or so, another would pop up to reassure us that everything we supposed was true. The blokes still drank beer. The women were still blonde, bikini-clad and beautiful. The barbie was still aflame, like some Antipodean chariot of fire.

In my more evangelical moments, this was something I was determined to change, both out of national interest and self-interest. No longer should the tyranny of distance mean that Australia, and its resident correspondent, would suffer the felony of neglect. Any talk of 'relevance deficiency syndrome' would be confined to the past. And although coming to Australia still had the feel of a lifestyle sabbatical, part of my search for a balanced life, there was still enough of the egomaniacal foreign correspondent in me not to want to disappear entirely from public view.

So when I arrived in Australia, I planned to start with the internal contradictions and then work from there, in the hope of persuading London that this truly was a continent that defied neat encapsulation. Ahead of my BBC interview for the Sydney post, I even drew up a list of anomalies, which effectively became my pitch. How did the 'no worries, mate' nation come to enter the new century with the third-highest suicide rate among the world's rich club of nations and see the consumption of anti-depressants triple over the past decade? How was it that such a supposedly laid-back country had some of the longest working hours in the Western world? Why the sanctification of the bush and the outback in what was one of the most urbanised countries in the world? Why was the country regarded as so fiercely nationalistic when its competing states appeared surprisingly antagonistic? Why such a boozy reputation when its ranking had slipped in the world drinking league to a lowly 20th? Though the championing of the underdog and the trumpeting of the 'fair go' suggested that a spirit of egalitarianism still prevailed, why had those nostrums not always been extended to its original occupants or most recent arrivals, especially those conveyed by boat? Why did this fun- and larrikin-loving land have such a zealous and overbearing bureaucracy, a question of especial pertinence to Paul Hogan, its most celebrated comedian, who at that stage was being targeted by the tax authorities? Call that a stereotype? Even the word 'mate' had a dual meaning and could be deployed to indicate both genial camaraderie and snarling menace. My hunch was that we had got Australia wrong.

—

In coming to Sydney, I realised I had retreated from the frontline of news but found myself disorientated nonetheless by the speed at which I was flung centrifugally to its outermost margins. It was a case of Kabul one minute and Kylie the next. Literally. The Princess of Pop had recently announced that after a successful convalescence from breast-cancer treatment her global comeback tour would commence in Sydney. Naturally, London went ballistic.

Looking to infuse the story with greater depth and meaning, I was keen to report that Kylie had emerged from her brush with mortality a much more substantial figure, that the experience of going through a treatment she likened to being hit by a nuclear bomb had made her an advocate as well as a battler, a fully realised woman rather than the chirpy tomboy we had grown up with on *Neighbours*. What I was proposing, I suppose, was an Antipodean Angelina, a storyline that would work for both of us.

But the evidence supporting my thesis seemed a little weak. Take Kylie's first public appearance in her comeback week at a mansion overlooking Sydney Harbour, where the media assembled to watch her promote her new celebrity-branded fragrance, Couture. Consider the book she penned during her convalescence, *The Showgirl Princess*, a story she herself described as a true fairy tale, full of glitter, glamour and dreams. Finally, there was her long-awaited entry at the Sydney Entertainment Centre, through a trapdoor in the stage, enshrouded in a cloud of dry ice and enclosed in a stunning pink costume designed by John Galliano. In the age of the sermonising rock star, a beaming Kylie made do with the briefest of salutations: 'Good evening, Sydney! How are you feeling tonight?'

That same week, Israel had bombarded Gaza, Nancy Pelosi was about to become America's first-ever female house speaker, Aung San Suu Kyi had been allowed to leave her house for the first time in six months, Russia announced that the way was now clear for its entry into the World Trade Organisation, and the head of MI5 had warned that hundreds of young British Muslims had been radicalised to the point of jihad.

While all this was unfolding, the central question facing the BBC's new Australia correspondent was whether the diminutive Kylie would collapse under the weight of her feather tiara. For the news that night, I delivered my obligatory piece to camera with Kylie on stage and her fans ranged behind me. But for one of the first times in my television career, I rather hoped that the viewers would avert their gaze – or, even better, venture into the kitchen to boil the kettle. Those who were watching – alas, a few million – saw me resort to show-business cliché as I reassured the great British public that Kylie had tonight lived out her own fairy tale. With plumed pomp and musical majesty, the Princess of Pop was most definitely back.

Kylie hardly fitted into the new paradigm of Australian reporting that I had arrived determined to usher in. Nor did the only other entry in the news diary when I first landed in Sydney: the start of the Ashes – that ribald orgy of conditioned thinking. True to form, the Gabba – the Brisbane cricket ground – was boiling with Anglo–Australian hostility on the first morning of the series, as each set of supporters played out the role assigned to them by history.

Outside the Colosseum-style stadium, to the tune of the 'Battle Hymn of the Republic', a male-voice choir sang 'We shall beat them at the Gabba'. On a promotional stand next door, Ford motors sought to make further inroads into the Australian market by inviting fans to take part in 'Tonk a Pom'. Bringing to the game a carnival spirit that I have only since seen rivalled at Sydney's Gay and Lesbian Mardi Gras, fans streamed into the ground wearing wide-brimmed sombreros, green and gold singlets, and zinc cream smeared across their faces like warpaint. Many had inflatable kangaroos in their arms, the Southern Cross tattooed on their shoulders and tiny Australian flags transferred onto their faces that twinkled like stardust. Not to be outdone, the travelling English hordes arrived dressed in medieval chain mail, suits of armour and jester's hats. A couple of fans even turned up in drag, impersonating our queen and theirs.

'Good morning, everyone,' said Richie Benaud, the former Australian cricketer turned commentator, lending both his voice and imprimatur to the hype. 'In my lifetime, I've never known such anticipation for a sporting event.'

Then, England's lanky opening bowler, Steve Harmison, hurtled towards the popping crease, with the cherry-ripe new ball in his hands and the burden of an expectant nation on his shoulders. In a blur, he hurled down his delivery, which was caught at second slip by the England captain, Andrew Flintoff. Had the batsman, Justin Langer, played any part in altering the ball's trajectory, England could not have got off to a happier start. Alas, Harmison was solely responsible. His opening delivery had pitched so wide of the wicket that it had come close to landing in the outback.

Bodyline had been replaced by Shoddyline, according to the Aussie scribes, though it was Martin Johnson, that great sage of Lord's press box, who produced the superlative line of the day. 'Channel Nine chose the opening day to proudly unveil its new "infra-red hot spot camera" for detecting edges,' he noted, 'but it is still some way short of developing the technology required for Harmison's first ball, which could only have been tracked by a satellite device from Cape Canaveral.'

In the terraces, as well, an unexpected drama had started to unfold. Throughout the morning session, and well into the afternoon, the Barmy Army's travelling trumpeter had tried to rally the tourists with regular blasts on his bugle. A classically trained musician, Billy Cooper had taken his annual cricketing sabbatical away from the pit of the Royal Opera House in Covent Garden to belt out morale-boosting ditties such as *The Great Escape* theme tune, 'Rule Britannia' and 'Jerusalem'.

But it was his rendering of the theme tune from *Neighbours* that landed him in trouble. As the crowd joined together to espouse that perfect blend of good neighbourliness and understanding, a group of stewards and policemen moved in, wrenched the trumpet from his lips and ejected him from the ground. Bereft of Billy the Trumpet, the Barmy Army threatened to boycott the rest of the match, and when its members joined in the singing of 'You all live in a convict colony' to the tune of 'Yellow Submarine', it seemed especially redolent with meaning.

The Barmy Army interpreted the silencing of their bugler as a product of the Aussie win-at-all-costs mindset, and claimed to be the victims of some vast conspiracy hatched between Cricket

Australia and the police. What they failed to appreciate was that the Australian fans were also trampled by this crushing authoritarianism.

There was a backpack ban, food and drink had to be transferred into airport-style plastic bags, and pizza boxes were forbidden, since they could be used as projectiles. For the same reason, streamers, confetti and ticker tape also appeared on the contraband list. A beachball ban was also in place, and anyone who managed to smuggle an offending inflatable into the ground soon had it punctured if it landed within reach of a boiler-suited police officer or steward.

There was also a strict prohibition on the Mexican wave, with casino-style cameras equipped with super-slow-mo technology trained on every seat to pinpoint the miscreant who first flung his arms skyward.

Streakers tempted to sprint across the oval faced a lifetime ban, and a fine of 5000 Australian dollars. The Queensland Police Service's Elite Public Safety Response Team had even undergone anti-terrorist-training exercises in nearby Ipswich, although the only thing that was blown up, other than beachballs, was an inflatable sex doll that had to be ejected from the Vulture Street End.

On the eve of the Ashes, the Australian Human Rights and Equal Opportunities Commission even managed to elbow its way in, placing strictures on what fans could actually say. In describing the English team and their supporters, it ruled that the word 'Pom' was permissible but ran the risk of being racist if used in conjunction with stiffer forms of abuse, such as 'bastard' or even 'whingeing'. Hence, the phrase 'Pommy bastard' was banned, which seemed the colloquial equivalent of removing the red kangaroo from the Australian coat of arms and leaving behind a solitary emu.

Inevitably, this came to be described as political correctness gone mad, but it was actually Australian officialdom that was certifiable. For all the boos and catcalls directed at the police when a drunken idiot was hauled from his seat, still more unexpected was the meek acquiescence of the Australian fans in the face of this bossy authoritarianism. For me, of course, this was manna from heaven and the Australia I had yearned to cover: the land of punctured stereotypes.

Sadly, the cricket fitted the usual template. Australia thumped England five–nil, with the familiar tag-team of Glenn McGrath and Shane Warne showing that England's oak hearts had the fortitude of polystyrene. But if England expected Australia to rejoice in regaining the Ashes with Latin American-style horn honking, all-night benders, and an open-top bus tour through the canyons of Sydney's central business district, it would be sorely disappointed. Rather than celebrating the balancing of some imaginary historical ledger, or the righting of some terrible imperial wrong, Australian sports fans merely thought that Ricky Ponting and his men had restored the natural order. Accordingly, their celebrations were disappointingly restrained.

If anything, the main thing to report from the Sydney Cricket Ground during the final test was not the boisterousness of the after-match celebrations but the confected sentimentality of the farewell to three Aussie legends playing their final match: Shane Warne, Glenn McGrath and Justin Langer. They were serenaded by an English opera star, who belted out Francesco Sartori's 'Con te Partirò' as the trio fidgeted uncomfortably on the balcony of their dressing room.

More happily, it was also time to say goodbye to another Antipodean trope: that for Australians the Ashes were somehow defining – not so much a matter of life and death, as the great Bill Shankly would have put it, but far more important. That was another canard, however much us Poms preferred to think otherwise. Further evidence of this came after the 2009 Lord's Test match, when England managed finally to end a 65-year losing streak at headquarters. The programme editors back home desperately wanted me to brandish before the cameras the morning papers from Australia, presumably in the expectation that the front pages would be framed with black edging and funereal in tone, with special commemorative supplements chronicling the downfall of Antipodean cricket. Yet I was unable to report that the country had suffered any great national convulsion or breakdown. Instead, I suggested that in the Pavlovian pantomime that is the modern-day Ashes the audience participation in this corner of the planet has so far been fairly muted. Hordes of crestfallen Australians cussing the wretched British? That was quite definitely behind them.

If anything, in a curious historical inversion, I suspect that the Ashes have now become more important to modern-day Britain than to modern Australia. For a nostalgic nation that has spent the past six decades or so managing its post-imperial decline, the thought that Australia suffers enormous pain whenever it is beaten by the Old Country is deeply heartening. Likewise, it is soothing to think that the Aussies are motivated by a desire to balance an imaginary ledger, since it implies an outstanding deficit and a perpetual state of borrowing. What is more, it helps compensate for the neglect of other former dominions.

India, after all, is too busy becoming a superpower to dwell on the legacy of the Raj; America has for 200 years been defined by the revolution that ousted the British rather than its subjugation beforehand; and Canada's insecurities are a product of small-neighbour syndrome vis-à-vis the US rather than being the last North American outpost of the British Empire.

Australia is therefore unique, or so us Poms like to think: a country where the rivalry with Britain continues to arouse great passion, and we are flattered by the continued attention. Each morning of every Test match, the Barmy Army rose en masse to belt out the national anthem, with a slight, though wounding, alteration to the words: 'God Save *Your* Queen'. But perhaps it revealed more about the insecurities of the singers than the sung to.

Another British misconception about the Ashes is that the ritualistic eruption of Pom-bashing is a sign of Australians' hostility towards the British. The reverse, of course, is true. It is a sign of familial love. And just as there is no country in the world, with the sole exception of New Zealand, that offers an Englishman a warmer welcome, none feels more instantly recognisable.

Whether in politics, sport, law or public broadcasting, the British way retains its permeating influence, and an inordinate amount of cultural and civic space continues to be surrendered to the British-made or British-influenced. Australia Day celebrates the moment of British colonisation. British colours still adorn the Australian flag ('Britain at night', according to Jerry Seinfeld). Most of the country marks the monarch's birthday with a public holiday, a courtesy not even observed back home. There are still some 160,000 Britons eligible to vote in Australian federal elections, a fancy franchise shared with other residents from the British Commonwealth but with no other non-citizens. This is still a land of royal commissions, crown prosecutions, majestic coinage and of Her Majesty's warplanes, ships and prisons.

All of which brings us to the most conspicuous paradox that successive BBC Australia correspondents have been expected to explain: why such a strongly patriotic country still retains an English-born head of state. Leaving aside its nationalistic spirit, which has intensified over the past decade, should not Australia's laconic informality, irreverent larrikinism, lack of snobbery and egalitarianism have militated against the idea of hereditary privilege and an institution that sits at the apex of the British class system?

However, republicanism could never be described as an urgent national priority. Far from it. Constitutional inertia, of course, is partly to blame. The lack of consensus among republicans is obviously another reason. But perhaps the idea of having an English-born head of state does not seem especially incongruous because the British influence in Australia remains so pervasive.

The former Australian Prime Minister Sir Robert Menzies, for whom the term Anglophile seems wholly inadequate, had it sort of right in his much-lampooned speech in 1963 during a reception for the queen at Parliament House. Describing Her Majesty as 'the living and lovely centre of our enduring alliance', he sounded in parts like an elderly English professor with a crush on one of his students, not least the passage recalling the misty-eyed words of the seventeenth-century poet Thomas Ford: 'I did but see her passing by / And yet I love her till I die.' But that night in Canberra, Menzies also spoke of the joint allegiance between Britain and Australia that was 'an addition to our freedom, not a subtraction from it'. Almost 50 years on, that remains a resilient idea, and it might remain so even after Queen Elizabeth has gone and the influence of 'Elizabethans' – the small 'r' republicans who are intellectually in favour of an Australian head of state but do not want to offend Her Majesty by agitating for her removal – has waned.

Certainly, the republican movement has struggled to produce a counter-narrative. On the tenth anniversary of the failed 1999 referendum, a dozen or so republicans gathered on the grass avenue in front of Parliament House for a brief and slightly mournful ceremonial. The plan, as one of the organisers fussily explained it to his fellow republicans, was to converge slowly on the building's pillared facade from all sides of the great courtyard in front, as if to symbolise the groundswell of support from every corner of the land. Then wicker baskets of wattle would be placed at the doors, like flowers on a grave.

The organiser was thinking 'spectacle'. Alas, the policeman listening over his shoulder was thinking 'permit'. The poor chap from the republican movement had forgotten to apply for the necessary paperwork, and the police barred the protesters from stepping onto the courtyard. For Australia to become a republic, it requires still a great leap of national imagination. On that anniversary morning, its most ardent advocates were not even allowed to cross the road.

To emphasise Australia's Anglo-centrism is not to deny the transformational impact of other European and Asian influences, which have obviously grown in recent times as the proportion of UK immigrants has declined. Nor is it to ignore the cross-flow of cultural influences. After all, Britain has aped Australia in recent years, whether it is because so many middle-class toddlers are raised by Antipodean nannies or because we spent so many of our formative years in Ramsay Street.

When asked whether he preferred *Coronation Street* or *Eastenders*, Britain's new prime minister David Cameron unapologetically replied, '*Neighbours*.' Because of his breezy informality, the classless Tony Blair has been described as Britain's first Australian prime minister. Why, the *Sun* even launched a campaign to have Kylie Minogue's arse heritage-listed. For all that, the historic and sentimental link with Britain remains one of the single biggest keys to understanding modern-day Australia.

—

Away from work – a phrase that I had not much cause to use in the earlier phases of my career – life was good. Exceptionally so. Perhaps for the first time in over a decade, I could purchase tickets to the theatre or opera with near certainty that I would get to use them. I loved being so close to the ocean, and I made sure to walk our pet Labrador, Skip, along the coastal path that links Bondi with Bronte at least three or four times a week. I also became such an enthusiast of Australian food – that most luscious flowering of post-war multiculturalism – that I ran the risk of becoming a bingeing Pom. I had more time to catch up on the latest novels, which had always been a lacuna in my reading, and even became a founding member of a book club that met on the first Wednesday of every month. Again, I could usually guarantee my attendance, which would have been unthinkable in either Washington or Delhi, where news had a regular habit of completely obliterating extracurricular activities. After covering a declining superpower and an emergent superpower, I rather enjoyed the simple pleasures of living in the world's great lifestyle superpower.

Most importantly of all, I restored body and mind. Since

the earliest days of my career, I had suffered from a fairly mild, though occasionally debilitating, form of social anxiety. I hated venturing into a crowded room, a cocktail or supper party, or any confined space, and tended to break out in a Nixon-style flop sweat whenever I did. My great fear, especially in the heat of the Washington or South Asian summer, was that it would happen live on air, and that my shirts would start mopping up sweat in the same way that blotting paper absorbs ink.

To avoid this happening, I deployed various strategies. At cocktail parties, I would always station myself on the fringes of the room close to a door. I also tended to drink very quickly, using alcohol not so much as a social lubricant but as a coolant, which, given its dehydrating effects, was ludicrous, I know. During assignments on the subcontinent, I took to wearing black shirts – I had about eight of them. This drew criticism from London, where colleagues seemed to think I was trying to ape one of our legendary foreign correspondents, the great Martin Bell, who always wore white. But it was the only colour that would camouflage sweat.

As I have always been gregarious and fun-loving, colleagues, friends and even family members would be surprised with this admission. My powers of concealment were strong. And I would not want to falsely portray myself as a nervous wreck. If anything, I always prided myself on never missing deadlines, of having the confidence to alter scripts with just minutes to go before broadcast and of keeping my cool in the most inauspicious of circumstances. Nor had I ever shirked any assignment, whatever the dangers. Oddly, however, the thing that scared me most was to walk back into our overcrowded newsroom in London, which appeared before me like a cliff face.

Sydney brought a much healthier lifestyle and a wife who

plied me with vitamins, tonics and love. The results were pretty much instantaneous. After years venturing into trouble spots, I could muster the courage to walk into the middle of a crowded room.

Chapter 13

Rolling History

To appreciate more fully the historical magnitude of Barack Obama's victory in the 2008 presidential election, it is worth recalling what Washington looked and felt like in 1961, the year of his birth. For diplomats from Africa's newly decolonised nations, the American capital was viewed still as a hardship posting, where restrictive covenants written into leasing agreements barred them from renting houses or apartments in the more affluent areas of the city and where they were routinely denied service in high-end restaurants, hotels and barber shops.

At Union Station, black passengers, or Negroes as they were called then, stepped from integrated carriages onto segregated trains to continue their journey south. Even after President Dwight D. Eisenhower signed an executive order integrating the District of Columbia, the city's schools, churches and residential neighbourhoods remained segregated.

The US Congress could boast just four black lawmakers, all of them congressmen rather than senators, and the chances of enacting a meaningful civil-rights bill were hopeless given the intransigence of southern Democrat segregationists, and the unwillingness of the young new president, John F. Kennedy, born of inexperience and indifference, to confront them. The founding fathers had designed Congress so that a tightly organised minority could always thwart the will of the majority, and the Southern Caucus had accumulated so much power that the Senate became known as 'the only place in the country where the south did not lose the civil war'.

In Jack Kennedy's Camelot, the most senior Negro appointee was a genial newspaperman called Andrew Hatcher, who served as deputy press secretary and who sat proudly alongside the president at his first televised press conference. Quickly, however, Hatcher became a target of derision for a White House press corps that remained overwhelmingly white. The affairs of state were far too complex for the Negro mind, its members scoffed, and when Hatcher put his name to a press release containing a harmless typo – it misspelt Tufts University – there were calls for him to be sacked.

The most senior black New Frontiersman in the wider administration was Robert Weaver, a Harvard-trained economist, but his appointment came close to being scuttled by recalcitrant Southern Democrats who accused him of urinating in a New York housing project. Though the allegation was entirely specious, it played on the prevailing racial stereotypes of the time.

With neither Hatcher nor Weaver allotted much face-time with Kennedy, his most valued Negro employee was George Thomas. His task each morning was to lay out the president's clothes.

Just as the Kennedy era was beginning, E. Frederic Morrow, who had served under President Dwight D. Eisenhower as the country's first Negro presidential aide, provided a matchless insight into the mores of segregated Washington with the publication of his memoir, *Black Man in the White House*.

Morrow had to work under all manner of restrictions, not least the injunction that he should never be alone in the same room as a white woman. Looked upon as a 'big buck nigger', the fear was that he would inevitably try to sexually molest any female colleagues. Only one woman in the White House secretarial pool volunteered to work alongside him, typing up memoranda penned by Morrow on how to advance the black struggle, which Eisenhower ignored completely.

As I headed back to America in time for election day, 'Black Man in the White House' had taken on a much more favourable connotation. It was certain by now that Obama would defeat John McCain, and the best gig was to be in Chicago for his victory speech at Grant Park. As a late fly-in, I was assigned to Washington, which turned out to be an unexpectedly close runner-up. For, in a city unused to eruptions of happy emotion, the reaction bordered on the delirious. Thousands of exultant young people, a high proportion of them African-American, converged on Lafayette Park across from the floodlit White House, brandishing 'OBAMA/BIDEN' campaign signs, clutching red, white and blue balloons and whipping their American flags from side to side. Some chanted 'Olay, olay, olay, olay' in the manner of South American football fans. Others shouted 'Yes, we can. Yes, we can', the impudent mantra of the first-term senator.

The crowd swelled so quickly that I dare say it could have overrun the White House lawn. But now there was no need. According to their chants that night, these Obama supporters already had 'taken back the capital' and mentally evicted the incumbent, George W. Bush. With the party going until sunrise, it was almost impossible to sleep. From the blaring car horns to the joyous cries of the crowds, it was as if Brazil had won the World

Cup and relocated the victory party from Copacabana Beach to Pennsylvania Avenue.

As someone who had spent far too much time studying and writing about the civil-rights movement, I never thought I would live to report on a black Democrat becoming president, still less witness these kinds of scenes in Washington, which remained a predominantly African-American city. If it were to happen at all, I'd thought it would be an accident of history rather than a Whiggish progression, and that the first African-American president would hail from the Republican party – a right-wing Colin Powell-type, perhaps, or a mega-rich black business leader with evangelical leanings.

Obama's great success, of course, was to de-emphasise his blackness, to bleach his colour, and to refuse to locate his candidacy in the context of the tumultuous decade into which he was born. In the 1980s, Jesse Jackson had framed his candidacy as a natural extension of the civil-rights movement and boasted that 'hands that once picked cotton will now pick a president'. Echoing the great anthems of the struggle for black equality, his campaign slogan was 'Our time has come'.

In complete contrast, Obama eschewed the vocabulary of black resentment and black entitlement. He offered white voters the opportunity to feel good about themselves rather than feel guilty. Though he received the endorsement of veteran civil-rights leaders, such as the great John Lewis, he refused to portray himself as their natural heir.

When, through a quirk of scheduling and a quantum leap of history, he ended up giving his acceptance speech at the Democrat convention in Denver 45 years to the day after Martin Luther King delivered his 'I Have a Dream' speech from the pulpit of the

Lincoln Memorial, Obama referred to the 'young preacher from Georgia' rather than mention King by name. To become a history-defying candidate, he became something of a history-denying figure.

Fortunately for Obama, however, the 2008 election did not turn on the question of tolerance, or become a referendum on race. The global financial crisis, the ongoing problems in Iraq, plus the lapses and folksy incoherence of Sarah Palin helped shift the focus. Moreover, McCain, who himself had been the victim of racist smears, was too honourable to play the race card.

On that high, holy night in Washington, my editors instructed me to write two dispatches that could be broadcast around the world at the instant of a victory declaration: one for if McCain became president-elect and another for Obama. Needless to say, it was necessary only to compose one dispatch.

Most American journalists wanted to write this story – and to be part of it – which went a long way towards explaining his swooning press, especially during the elongated primary season and the months of trench warfare with Hillary Clinton. Some particularly dewy-eyed reporters even rhapsodised about the beauty of the mole on the left side of his nose.

Obama also came to enjoy the near-universal respect of the press pack, all of whom had devoured his autobiography *Dreams from My Father* and seen in it a quality of wordplay that they themselves would struggle to match. Doubts lingered about his cerebral air, and whether he had enough of the mongrel in him to slug it out in the Washington bear pit, but from the moment he addressed the Democratic convention in 2004 with his paean to post-partisanship, every political journalist who considered these things rationally knew they were watching a once-in-a-lifetime politician. An African-American was in the White House – one who would issue the orders and make the rules – and the Washington press pack looked forward to covering this black Camelot.

—

When first I was posted to Washington in the late 1990s, America was still the principal catalyst for global change and the sole superpower in a unipolar world. As it prepared to ring in the new millennium, US publishers rushed out a welter of self-congratulatory books on what had come to be known as the American Century. In the same spirit, the White House Millennium Council put together a time capsule that included a fragment of the dismantled Berlin Wall, Louis Armstrong's trumpet and footage of Neil Armstrong's moonwalk, relics that captured for posterity America's technological, military and cultural hegemony.

On New Year's Eve 1999, I was at the foot of the Lincoln Memorial for a concert featuring Aretha Franklin, Bono, Chuck Berry, Will Smith, Tom Jones and a film by Steven Spielberg with the expectant title *The Unfinished Journey*. The organisers, seemingly untroubled by the niggardly fact that the USA had not made much of an impact for 776 of the past 1000 years, called this celebration 'America's Millennium'. It ended with fireworks skipping across the Reflecting Pool, which ignited the base of the Washington Monument. When fully illuminated, the 555-foot obelisk stood like a giant national exclamation mark, or even a magnificent imperial erection.

More than a decade on, despite all the talk about Obama's election offering proof of the country's capacity for renewal and reinvigoration, there were unmistakable signs that America was in decline. A recession. The sub-prime-mortgage crisis. The near evisceration of Wall Street. The self-inflicted wounds of Iraq. The insurgency in Afghanistan. A diplomatic world in which America no longer had a clarion voice. A detention centre at Guantanamo that remained open despite President Obama's promise to shut it down, which undercut America's moral leadership abroad. A colossal national debt, much of it held by its ascendant rival, China. A much-quoted report from Goldman Sachs predicting that the Middle Kingdom would become the world's top economy by 2027. A *Fortune* magazine survey with only two US companies in the global top ten: Walmart, the number one, and Exxon Mobil.

The shelves in Washington bookstores, weighed down by so much national self-confidence at the start of the century, were heaving now with titles devoted to America's decline and the rise of the rest. Perhaps the satirical newspaper *The Onion* came up with the drollest take, greeting Obama's victory with the headline 'Black Man Given Nation's Worst Job'.

Though not a country usually associated with self-doubt, declinism had long been a theme in American commentary, whether it was post-Sputnik, post-Vietnam, post-Watergate or post-Tehran. Gore Vidal was even more precise when he identified 16 September 1985 as the date of the fall of the American empire. That was the day the Commerce Department announced it had become a debtor nation.

Each time, of course, America rebounded, but on this occasion a trifecta of morale-sapping convulsions had come within the space of a decade: 9/11, Iraq and the global financial crisis. More disconcertingly for the Americans, China posed a much more lasting threat than either the Soviet Union, which did not have the economic efficiency to ultimately challenge the US, or Japan, a potential rival in the 1980s and early 1990s that never had a big-enough population.

For all that, I suspect that Washington will long remain the most sought-after correspondent posting and by far the most consequential: the capital of the world's most dominant economic, military, diplomatic, technological and cultural power. An Anglo-centric world will continue to look to Silicon Valley for its hi-tech innovations; Wall Street for finance; Harvard, MIT and Yale for the gold standard in higher education and research; Hollywood for movies; Facebook, Twitter and Google for online smarts; HBO and AMC for the best in television; the *New York Times* and the *New Yorker* for the best in newspaper and magazine journalism; reruns of *Oprah* for daytime chitchat; southern California for fitness and lifestyle fads; New York for fashion; Houston and Cape Canaveral for galactic exploration; US research labs for the latest in biotechnology and nanotechnology; the great medical campuses in Boston, Chicago and Baltimore for disease breakthroughs; the San Fernando Valley for its silicone-implanted flesh; McDonald's, Subway and KFC for its fast foods; Microsoft for its operating systems; Apple for its gadgetry; and the US Armed Forces and its American suppliers for the most up-to-date weaponry.

Here, I run the risk of looking at America not so much through rose-tinted spectacles as ones coloured red, white and blue. We are talking, after all, of a country that produced not only Oprah but also Jerry Springer; of a City of Angels that fashioned not only *Mad Men* but also the O. J. Simpson trial.

Still, it is by no means coincidental that America's great laureate is Mark Twain, who warned of the perils of rashly composed obituaries. For so long as it remains the locus of the world's creative industries and the home of the greatest universities, it will be hard to write off.

America will continue to attract waves of hopeful new immigrants and some of the finest undergraduate and postgraduate brains. Three-quarters of the PhDs awarded in US universities now go to foreign students, a statistic cited as evidence of the country's decline. Yet America's singular success since the turn of the last century has been to usurp the world's best talent, in whatever field, and this remains the case.

Carrying on this brain gain, two-thirds of these foreign PhD students stay for at least five years after graduation. Tellingly, this is true for nine out of ten Chinese doctoral students, the highest proportion of any foreign nation. That would suggest that the American dream, however bruised, battered and hackneyed, retains its lure, promise and animating energy. George Orwell, who curiously never visited the country, made the uncharacteristically bland point that America always retained its founding spirit of revolution, which is doubtless true. But Don DeLillo made the more compelling observation that no country in the world is so unafraid of the future.

Just as America remains the land of the first chance, it is also the land of the second, which helps explain why it so regularly springs back. It is a country where, less than two years after impeachment, Bill Clinton ended his term in office with the highest approval ratings of any departing president; where Al Gore lost the presidency but achieved great celebrity and claimed an Oscar; where Captain Yee, the former Muslim chaplain from Guantanamo, went from a navy brig in South Carolina to being an Obama delegate on the floor of the Democratic convention in Denver.

Were I American, the things that would take some of the fizz and crackle out of my 4 July fireworks would be the state of the finances and politics. The gargantuan national debt has now surpassed $14 trillion, an all-time high that equates to over 95 per cent of GDP and some $90,000 for every working American. Ten years after 9/11, this Red Menace is now being spoken of as the gravest threat to national security, largely because foreign citizens and institutions hold almost half. A major upside, however, is that America simply cannot afford to send large armies into the Middle East or South Asia, and will not undertake the kind of Iraq-style open-ended military commitments that have sapped the country's morale and depleted its finances.

Now that the Iraq syndrome has come to loom as large in the minds of foreign policymakers as the Vietnam syndrome once did for their predecessors, traditional notions of hard power and soft power are being superseded at the Pentagon and State Department by talk of smart power, which is a snappier and more face-saving way of saying smaller budget, cost-effective power.

Washington politics is also impoverished. Since the end of the Cold War, which removed the patriotic imperative to present more of a united front to the Soviet Union, extreme partisanship has become the norm. Whereas once there was a clubby camaraderie on Capitol Hill, even among party rivals, something bordering on hatred now prevails. Politicians of all stripes rush to the television 'stake-out' positions outside the House and Senate chambers to denounce each other, using shrill and often hysterical language. In the Senate, the use of filibuster, a stalling tactic used to block legislation, has become routine. Once, it was deployed sparingly as a last resort, now it is everyday, making it all but impossible to tackle some of America's most pressing issues, such as the scale of the deficit and the impact of climate change. Indeed, the poor state of the politics and the perilous state of the finances are linked like conjoined twins.

With obstructionism the order of the day on both sides of the aisle, electoral mandates no longer have any currency, and the very legitimacy of the last three presidents – Clinton, Bush and Obama – has been contested. Winning the race to the bottom, some members of the Tea Party movement have questioned whether Barack Obama is a Christian or even a bona-fide American. Given how vituperative and deeply dysfunctional the country's politics has become, it was not particularly surprising that a gunman should attempt to assassinate Congresswoman Gabrielle Giffords, only that this kind of attack had not happened before. No wonder Rahm Emanuel, Obama's former chief of staff, took to calling Washington 'Fucknutsville' and then went home to Chicago, which now seemed positively genial in comparison. He had left behind a capital where politics had become conflict.

Were I to offer some other valedictory thoughts about the world beyond the Beltway, one would be that foreign correspondents could confirm the rumour, even if it requires regurgitating the banality, that the planet has indeed got smaller. What's more, globalisation runs the risk of making it drearily homogenous. A return trip to Delhi four years after my departure more than aptly made the point.

The Indian capital could now boast a newly constructed airport, an airy steel and glass hi-tech affair that would not have looked out of place in Dusseldorf or Stockholm, or, more pertinently to the Indians, Shanghai or Beijing. Inside, major Western chains had crowded out local shops: Costa Coffee, WH Smith, Reebok and the like. Flight crews from Kingfisher Airlines headed towards their gates dressed in high-heels, boob-hugging tunics and minimalist skirts rather than the saris traditionally favoured by Indian airlines. There was a Delhi Daredevils Bar, an American-style sports joint that took its name from the capital's Twenty20 cricket franchise and its merchandising cues from British Premier League football. No wonder. Many of its young Indian customers wore Manchester United and Chelsea shirts.

On the boating pond next to India Gate, the once-battered pedalos were now freshly painted in bright primary colours, their brand-new awnings emblazoned with the corporate logo of a foreign mobile-phone operator. In Khan Market – an enclave for literary Indians and expatriates – my two favourite bookshops had been closed down. One had been replaced by an interior-decor shop selling soft furnishings, while the other had been taken over by a high-end international jeweller. At the beautiful restaurant where I had first met my wife, the menu was now exclusively European, and its latest addition was a Tuscan kitchen. By now, the BBC had also succumbed to the Indian revolution by opening up a sparkling new bureau in a high-rise office block. Black leather armchairs that one might expect to find in the waiting room of a Los Angeles therapist adorned the reception. The newsroom was awash with plasma.

At least India was on the up. Much of the rest of South Asia was unravelling. Whether from massive flooding or the destabilising impact of attacks from al-Qaeda and the Pakistan Taliban, Pakistan was in a state of perpetual crisis. Benazir Bhutto had been assassinated, her widower, Asif Ali Zardari, had been elected president and now it was Pervez Musharraf who was living in self-imposed exile in London and plotting a political comeback. A massive truck-bomb attack had destroyed the Marriott in

Islamabad, and another of the region's marquee hotels, the Taj Palace in Mumbai, had also been the focus of a seaborne attack on India's commercial capital that had been planned in Pakistan and carried out by Lashkar-e-Taiba. Within the ranks of the ISI and the Pakistani Army, the belief still festered that militants remained useful proxies in thwarting the rise of India, even though they now posed a more serious threat to the state of Pakistan. On average, there was now one suicide bombing per week, and since 9/11 over 35,000 Pakistanis had been killed.

No attack more brutally encapsulated the deteriorating security situation in South Asia than the ambush of the convoy carrying the Sri Lankan cricket team in March 2009. Last-minute stand-ins for an Indian side dissuaded from touring Pakistan through fear of precisely this kind of attack, the players came under fire in the once-safe city of Lahore from militants trained to fight an insurgency in Kashmir and emboldened by the rise of the Taliban in Afghanistan. Cricket had long been considered beyond the reach of militants, so the strike on the region's shared and sacred game was presumably intended to signal that militants no longer felt constrained by any self-prescribed limits.

Perhaps the choice of location for the ambush was also intended as another nihilistic flourish: Lahore's Liberty Square. Hurriedly, the Sri Lankan team was flown afterwards by military helicopter from the fresh-cropped wicket of Lahore's Gaddafi Stadium and then on to Colombo. The players touched down at the capital's international airport, which just ten days before had been the target of an aerial attack from the Tamil Tigers. Militant attacks had been ever more audacious and ever more alarming. The already frail notion of jihadi self-restraint had become firmly oxymoronic, and such were the fears about the rise of violent Islam in a nuclear-armed country that foreign-policy experts started referring to the Pak–Af problem when talking about lawlessness in the region rather than using the usual Af–Pak shorthand.

In Sri Lanka, the aerial attack on Colombo proved to be the Tigers' last hurrah. The Sri Lankan Army launched an all-out assault, pursuing a strategy of total annihilation that forced the Tigers out of their strongholds and into the jungle. Barred initially from the battlefields, journalists were soon flown to what the government portrayed as a liberated Kilinochchi and Mullaitivu, which now looked even more ghostly than after the tsunami. With the Tigers surrounded in a three-square-mile strip of land, the army claimed the prized scalp of Prabhakaran himself, and the pictures of his bloated, bullet-ridden dead body were no less startling than those of Saddam Hussein with a hangman's noose around his neck. Soon, the martyrs' cemetery in Kilinochchi was flattened, and it became the site for a new divisional headquarters of the Sri Lankan Army.

The one-time mountain kingdom of Nepal was now a republic, and King Gyanendra had been banished from his Kathmandu palace. To complete his defenestration, a Maoist-led coalition came to power after the parliamentary elections, which followed the Ring Road Revolution. The Maldives had also ditched another autocrat, President Maumoon Abdul Gayoom – he of the exquisitely packaged canned-tuna fame – who had been replaced by the democracy campaigner Mohamed Nasheed. But its atolls were still being inundated by the waves.

In Afghanistan, the country's second presidential election held in 2009 had been even more farcical than the first five years earlier, and was marred by vote-rigging, ballot-box stuffing and intimidation from the supporters both of Hamid Karzai and of his main rival. As in 2004, the legitimacy of his victory was highly questionable. The security situation had also worsened. Almost 2500 Afghan civilians were killed in 2010, the highest civilian death toll since the US-led invasion. After a tortuously long review of US strategy, Obama ordered an Iraq-style surge but also signalled a withdrawal starting in mid-2011. It was a timetable that the Taliban would have interpreted as an unmistakable sign that America had lost its stomach for the fight. The police chief in Mazar-i-Sharif, who had been bullied by the warlords, was now dead, having been killed in a suicide-bomb attack by the Taliban. Even the heavily protected Kabul Intercontinental came under assault from militants, who killed a senior judge, a Spanish pilot, waiters and musicians performing in the hotel during a five-hour rampage. As for Kamila, the border region she lives in is still so dangerous that we have not yet managed to return.

Elsewhere in Asia, the rise of China had become the modish story of the times. When first I joined the BBC, Beijing – or Peking as it was still commonly called then – was regarded not so much as a posting as an academic sinecure. It was an ivory tower, where Oxbridge-trained sinologists were renowned more for the size of their brains than the volume of their output. It was almost as if they had been assigned for their own intellectual delectation, and that reporting was an extracurricular activity. The focus of a speedy expansion, Beijing has become one of our most important and busiest bureaux, with Shanghai another vital outpost.

Ten years earlier, our main bureau in Europe had received a Beijing-style boost in BBC investment, but, as the world's locus shifted from the Atlantic to the Pacific, Brussels was trying still to coalesce into a major power centre, and thus a major story. Pre-empting its emergence as a counterbalance to the US, the BBC had sent my happy band of trainees off to Brussels for a two-day fact-finding mission on the basis that the European parliament might one day rival Capitol Hill. But no one had yet managed to make an EU working-time directive sing on television, nor the endless summitry or treaty writing.

More recently, the European Union had appointed a kind of foreign secretary, so that any international leader could 'call Europe'. Yet Charlemagne, the *Economist* columnist and a fellow diarist from my high-society days at the *Evening Standard*, summed up the irrelevancy of the post when he relayed the gag doing the rounds in Brussels: if ever anyone dialled the European hotline, they would merely hear a recording, 'For French foreign policy, press 1. For British foreign policy, press 2 . . .' On the other side of what used to be the Iron Curtain, Moscow, which had always been seen as a stepping stone for Washington, was now viewed as something of a backwater and hardship posting.

In Iraq, as the US and British pulled out, the BBC also lightened its footprint. Correspondents looking for trouble in Mesopotamia started eyeing up Tehran instead. In Jerusalem, the peace process felt even more like a slogan lacking any credibility, as one British diplomat deftly put it, and Israel waited still for another Rabin. Instead, Benjamin Netanyahu, his old nemesis, was prime minister.

In Gaza, no longer was there any need for Hamas militants to slip furtively into the backs of cars to conduct interviews with visiting correspondents, as they had done on my first visit. Now, they ran the show. A terrorist organisation in the eyes of Israel, America and the EU, Hamas had risen to power in the 2006 Palestinian parliamentary elections, its landslide win in Gaza an inadvertent by-product of the Bush administration's push for democracy in the Middle East.

Across the Arab world, there was a new appetite for political reform. Its impetus came from the young, who demonstrated how a social network on the web could quickly take on the character of a revolutionary network on the streets. The Arab Spring, the most stunning popular uprising since the 1989 revolutions across Eastern Europe, brought down the Egyptian president Hosni Mubarak after 30 years, and then the Libyan autocrat Muammar Gaddafi, fatally, after 40. For all the panicked cries from embattled leaders that Islamic extremists were behind the demonstrations – here, they were essentially playing the 'war on terror' card as if it read 'get out of jail' – groups such as al-Qaeda were nowhere to be seen.

Elsewhere on the despot front, Kim Jong-il's bizarre reign was also in its final phase – the cover story of the *Economist* I had bought at JFK Airport to mug up for my BBC interview was on his ascent to power. In Cuba, a Castro, Raúl, was still in charge, which meant that while it was possible to enjoy a Happy Meal at Guantanamo, the same could not be said of Havana.

What of my homeland? Certainly, Britain remained conspicuously more post-Diana than pre-: less class orientated, vastly more celebrity obsessed, and regularly prone to exaggerated emotional responses, whether in celebration of long-awaited Ashes victory, the improbable success of Scottish songstresses on television talent competitions, the death of talentless reality stars or the premature exit of England from the World Cup.

In the hands of the mass media, and the tabloids especially, the British public seem especially malleable. Whenever I have returned during the dozen or so years I have been away, the country also seems to be in a state of crisis or in the midst of some tabloid feeding frenzy. Once, it was a fuel strike, when farmers and lorry drivers came close to bringing the country to a standstill by picketing a small handful of oil refineries. On another occasion, it was the tragic disappearance of the toddler Madeleine McCann.

Britain was also emphatically a post-Thatcherite country: deeply suspicious of Brussels and the rest of Europe, watchful of mass immigration, reliant for its prosperity on the financial sector rather than manufacturing, more meritocratic, and a nation in which both the unions and landed Establishment were still very much on the back foot. Tony Blair's success came from standing before the British people as Thatcher's true successor, while David Cameron owed his rise to being the heir of Blair. John Major and Gordon Brown struggled partly because they were less adept at handling Thatcher's legacy.

Once Britain's most polarising figure, the Iron Lady was now viewed widely, even by many of her one-time detractors, as the one person capable of delivering the electric-shock treatment that Britain had so desperately needed at the end of the '70s. However, even Thatcher could not completely arrest Britain's post-imperial decline, nor resolve the Acheson dilemma of finding a clear role after losing an empire.

Britain had also become a post-9/11 country. The attacks continued to define its politics and contributed to its mood of apprehension. Having aligned himself so successfully with Margaret Thatcher, Tony Blair ran into trouble when he walked in lockstep with George W. Bush. There had never been much public enthusiasm for Britain's involvement in Iraq, while there was also mounting concern about the blood price paid by British servicemen in Afghanistan. The radicalisation of young British Muslims meant the threat of home-grown attacks was ever present.

At least terrorism had largely been consigned to history in Northern Ireland. The Belfast terror tour that I made sure to embark on shortly before joining the BBC had now become a heritage trail. Sinn Féin has even set up a gift shop on the Falls Road selling mural mousepads, Republican resistance calendars and IRA fridge magnets.

Moreover, we could ponder the relative success of the peace process in fashionable, glass-fronted restaurants in city-centre streets once completely disfigured by the flying shrapnel of car bombs. In another unlikely twist, former Republican paramilitaries, such as Martin McGuinness, entered into a power-sharing arrangement with the Democratic Unionist Party, Sinn Féin's long-time enemies and Northern Ireland's most faithful practitioners of the politics of 'No'. Why, the queen could even visit Dublin, resplendent in emerald green.

In a country with a fixation with heritage and nostalgia, there were so many post-somethings. Outside of the arts and fashion, perhaps Britain had lost the knack of being pre-something. Yet winning the right to stage the Olympics in 2012 presented the chance to redefine itself with a forthcoming event rather than a landmark from history, such as the Blitz or the Somme. I happened to be in London on the night it edged out Paris, New York and Madrid, and there was a palpable sense of reorientation, especially among the young. Then, the following morning came the 7/7 bomb attacks that killed 52 people and made Britons less eager future seekers.

—

On the night of Obama's victory, CNN used what it described as hologram technology to teleport a correspondent,

Star Trek-style, from Grant Park in Chicago to its studio in New York so that she could be interviewed, face to virtual face, by the anchorman Wolf Blitzer. Though I am glad to report that the BBC continues to cling to the quaint notion that the point of having correspondents in the field is to leave them there, it showed the advances in technology that are continually speeding past our industry.

Young reporters no longer wield razor blades and chinagraph pencils nor suffer from Uher droop. Instead, they carry pocket-sized digital recorders that could easily be mistaken for a cigarette case. The BBC Washington bureau can now boast more than the two mobile phones that we used to share between correspondents, and that had to be signed out whenever taken from the office. Everyone has an iPhone or a BlackBerry, or often both. Editing equipment that used to fill an entire hotel room has been superseded by inexpensive laptops. The satellite technology required to broadcast from anywhere on the planet can also fit in carry-on luggage, while in many places satellites themselves are entirely superfluous because correspondents can broadcast over the internet via a glorified version of Skype.

The days are long past when we used to race miles, or sometimes even fly, to reach a satellite-uplink station so that we could bounce our stories, galactically, back to London. All we need now are our own portable satellite dishes, which are smaller in size than a breakfast tray. Transmitting a news report from the field back to base has become much like sending an email with a hefty attachment, so we just need a decent broadband connection.

Soon after joining the BBC, I remember an old hand in the newsroom who was something of a computer geek predicting that the future of journalism belonged to reporters who could master the logarithms of programming. How ludicrous, I remember thinking. But then came WikiLeaks.

More so than any other advance, the internet has revolutionised our modus operandi. News is just a click away, and it's incessantly updated with each blink of the eye. With the expectation that correspondents will file as soon as possible, deadlines have been drastically compressed and traditional news cycles have gone the way of the typewriter, the reel-to-reel tape machine and the newspaper copy-takers who used to sit at one end of a crackly phone line trying to decipher the dispatches of half-cut reporters in the field.

In harness with new satellite technology, the worldwide web has also brought about one of the greatest breakthroughs in global news-gathering: the ability to broadcast from anywhere at any time. Alas, it is also responsible for one of the greatest threats to global news-gathering: the ability to broadcast from anywhere at any time. Because of the preponderance of continuous-news channels – the BBC has four alone – and the round-the-clock demand for material, this has been particularly pernicious. The unrelenting demands of having to file every hour of every day means that not as much time is allotted any more for what correspondents need the most: patient observation to divine a country's underlying characteristics. On big, running stories, often journalists rarely get the chance to leave their rooftop live positions, from where they end up delivering fairly cramped commentaries based on fairly skimpy experiences.

Watch any news channel these days and it will not be long before it serves up a promotional video boasting of its vast global reach and ability to respond to breaking news in an instant. Doubtless, you will be familiar with the genre: the fast-paced jump cuts, the global landmarks, the behind-the-scenes footage of gesticulating reporters, and the on-camera assurances from correspondents promising to fix news whenever it breaks – and from all four corners of the planet.

Yet there is a gulf of difference between the round-the-clock, round-the-world ability to broadcast and nuanced foreign coverage. Indeed, the very thing that news organisations now trumpet, which is to say their speedy reaction times to breaking events, is often a bar to understanding. Commonly, correspondents are summoned to their live positions to tell the rest of the world what is going on without being given sufficient time to find out properly for themselves. The BBC, which has always prided itself on giving correspondents the space and time in which to operate, knows this and tries hard to manage the demand from London. Still, reporters are being asked to do more for less, when foreign news should truly live by the maxim 'less is more'.

The one-click-away availability of information on the internet has also altered the balance of power between correspondents on the ground and editors in London. Google, Twitter, Wikipedia, YouTube and, to a lesser extent, Facebook have greatly empowered editors by giving them access to a vast quantity of up-to-the-second information. Yet information is not the same as journalism, and the process that turns one into the other has traditionally been where experienced correspondents have earned their spurs. Even the most self-regarding of foreign hacks would never be so presumptuous as to suggest they have a monopoly on understanding, but the act of being stationed for years in a foreign country, of reading its history and literature, of talking to its people, of poring over its newspapers every day and of sifting through its flotsam and jetsam does give them an edge. The view from our window generally offers a better vantage point than the view from the newsdesk in London, however many computer terminals or plasma screens it might boast.

A larger danger is one of abdication: that continuous-news channels and online news sites allow others to set the agenda more than we do. So urgent and unrelenting is the demand for fresh headlines, angles, soundbites and real-time news events that there is a tendency to co-opt them from wherever they spring. Here, governments are the most gushing fountainheads, and spin doctors – those skilled practitioners of message management – have become expert at controlling the flow. They start with a leak to a newspaper that generates a friendly overnight headline. They follow up on the breakfast shows with another headline-making interview. Then they stage a pseudo news event, such as a visit to a military base, school or hospital, which they know the news channels will broadcast live and unexpurgated, and that will yield the additional benefit of providing friendly footage for the evening news.

Editors are neither idiots nor supplicants and do not simply cede airtime to propagandists. A live speech from a president or prime minister, say, will usually be followed by the counter-argument from opponents and some quick critical analysis from a correspondent or relevant expert. But they perform the secondary role of responding to the story rather than driving it.

A supplementary problem is that reaction is often mistaken for scrutiny, and they are rarely equivalent. Reaction is instant. Scrutiny, like patient observation, requires time. There is a paradox here. Continuous-news channels have acres of airtime to fill, and some of it could easily be devoted to programmes and segments that offer more thoughtful inspection and analysis. But the format that almost every news organisation has seized upon is all about the fleeting, breathless and occasionally exhilarating sensation of being in the moment and up to the second. Though there is no shortage of time, the newsfeed does not stop for seasoned reflection. It has become a medium of pulsating, audience-pulling graphics that read 'BREAKING NEWS' rather than 'THOUGHTFUL ANALYSIS'.

This partly explains one of journalism's greatest failings after 9/11, a mega-news event that not only perfectly suited the televisual requirements of continuous news but that also coincided with the proliferation of round-the-clock channels and online news. In its aftermath, too many news outlets, especially in America, let others set the agenda, from the adoption of the Bush administration's war-on-terror nomenclature to the framing of the post-9/11 debate as a battle between good and evil.

Never was this more so in Washington than in the run-up to the war in Iraq, where a typical day might see US news channels switching from the White House briefing to the Pentagon press conference, from an Oval Office fireside sitdown, where President Bush would make the case for war or rail against the coalition of the unwilling, to a pep rally at an army base where the commander-in-chief would appear in a leather flight jacket to the cheers of whooping GIs. With the drumbeat for war an ever-building crescendo, so much American airtime was appropriated by pro-war news events that dissenting voices were not just drowned out but also crowded out.

There were other sins of omission, for the industry tended to follow a very narrow terror-centric agenda. When I arrived in South Asia, I was convinced that my biggest story would be the hunt for Osama bin Laden and the al-Qaeda leader's eventual capture. But the war on terror was little more than an abstraction for many of the residents of the region, for whom there were far more pressing local issues.

For countless South Asian shanty dwellers, whether in Mumbai, Kathmandu, Dhaka or Kabul, it was the daily scramble for food and shelter. To an Indian farmer in Andra Pradesh, drought loomed the largest. For a teenage girl in an impoverished Nepali village, sex trafficking posed the gravest threat. For an infant in the Afghan border region, it was the danger from discarded landmines. Violent Islam was irrelevant to a Tamil Tiger rebel railing against Sinhalese discrimination, or the family of a Colombo police officer killed by a female suicide bomber. Nor did it mean anything to young Nepali revolutionaries reared on the teachings of Mao. Pakistani leaders were preoccupied still with India, while India was increasingly preoccupied with China.

We heard from these people and put their stories to air, but it was rare that they grabbed the headlines and took precedence over what was coming out of Washington. Again, there is a paradox here. In the age of continuous news, when technological advances made it much easier to report from far more places, we had both more time and the kind of extended global reach that enabled us to cover a much more expansive menu of stories. Alas, the post-9/11 news agenda tended to get narrower, with the White House and its war on terror the myopic focus.

A corrective is needed here, for I do not want to paint too pessimistic a picture. Nor do I want these last words to be overly gloomy. Money and time is being invested still in lengthy assignments, especially in countries such as Afghanistan and China, where a correspondent and cameraman have the twin luxuries of escaping their live positions and roving faraway.

For all the job and budget cuts – and they have been savage

– the BBC abounds with quite exceptional journalists, whether in the foreign bureaux or at the mothership back in London. The decade has produced countless examples of brave and brilliant journalism. There are times still, as in Tahrir Square in Cairo, when rolling news doubles as rolling history.

Though foreign correspondents face far longer days, far greater dangers and far heftier workloads, the great H. L. Mencken's journalistic homily still holds true: 'I find myself more and more convinced that I had more fun doing news reporting than in any other enterprise. It is really the life of kings.' But I wonder how many foreign correspondents can look back on the past ten years with a sense of unblemished pride at our efforts in navigating an ever more turbulent world. On both sides of the news industry, I suspect, this was a decade of unaccomplished missions.

Postscript

The first time I recall seeing the press working en masse was when reporters descended on a small terraced house in an inner-city back street of my home town, Bristol, just down the road from the church I attended as a child. It was the home of Louise Brown, or the 'Superbabe' as the local paper christened her in its banner headline that evening, the world's first test-tube baby.

As a proud Bristolian, I was rather pleased with this fact, never thinking that 30 years on my wife, Fleur, and I would come to rely on the same *in vitro* fertilisation technology. At first, we thought my years on the road as a foreign correspondent might be to blame for our difficulties in conceiving, and especially the time spent in South Asia. Male fertility is an indicator of general well-being, and I was badly rundown and horribly unhealthy when I came to Australia.

In India, I had drunk way too many beers with droplets of glycerine floating at the top of the bottle, and consumed far too many curries swimming in ghee. After months of detoxification, a period of abstinence from alcohol and the nutritional benefits of Australian fresh produce, the problem was quickly remedied. But not, alas, our infertility as a couple. Still unable to fall pregnant, we feared the cause might be a more serious issue and, after a further year of trying, were told by a surgeon, in an uncomfortably matter-of-fact manner, that it would be impossible for us to conceive naturally. IVF was our only option.

In these situations, news has a habit of intruding at the most unhelpful of moments. Needing to test my virility – as with Clinton's impeachment, I am struggling here for euphemisms – I had booked in at a fertility clinic in Sydney where, such was the demand from 30-something couples, it took months to secure an appointment. When I was finally offered a slot, however, the Victorian bush fires were still aflame, which raised the spectre of having to race from the fire zone, catch a flight to Sydney, perform the necessary and then return to Melbourne in time for the breakfast-news shows in London.

On the morning that Fleur started her IVF injections – a blend of powerful drugs that first tricks the body into thinking it is menopausal and then hyper-stimulates the ovaries into producing a welter of eggs – I had to be in Canberra to interview the prime minister, one of the few assignments near impossible to turn down.

These problems aside, we soon got into the rhythm of the daily injections and the dawn visits to a clinic in the Sydney CBD where couples waited in hopeful silence for blood tests and progress reports on the production of eggs. Our first IVF cycle showed signs of real promise. Though we harvested a relatively small number of eggs, they were healthy and strong. After being fertilised, they combined to produce robust-looking blastocysts, the small bundle of cells that provides the first flowering of human life.

The transfer stage, when the embryo is implanted through the cervix into the uterus through a thin plastic catheter, also went smoothly. By now, we had fallen into the trap that commonly ensnares IVF first-timers, which is to say we were incautiously optimistic. Then our letdown came on the cruellest of days: New Year's Eve. But we limped into the New Year determined to have another go.

This time, we were far more pessimistic, even though our egg harvest had gone better; and during the dreaded two-week wait – the time between the insertion of the fertilised egg and the pregnancy test – Fleur was convinced we would come up with another negative result. Not patient enough to wait until our official blood test, we freelanced and bought a cheap pregnancy-test kit from the chemist's.

As Fleur handed me the plastic stick, I saw that it registered just one bold blue line. Failure. We had been through this agonising process on countless occasions before, but this time I lingered before throwing the stick away. There was now the pale hint of azure. Within a second, it had become a firmer shade of powder blue. Then light blue. Seconds later, it was bright and definitive: a lustrous shade of baby blue. False negatives are more common than false positives, so we were confident but still unsure. It would require a blood test at the clinic, which later that morning confirmed the certainty of pregnancy.

Given a November due date, I rather hoped that our newborn would arrive on Melbourne Cup day, thinking it might confer special powers like those imagined by Salman Rushdie at the midnight unfurling of the Indian tricolour. Presumably, the closer an Australian baby is born to three o'clock on the first Tuesday of every November, the better their tipping skills, bringing both enormous riches in later life and a mantelpiece buckling under the weight of invitations to cup-day luncheons.

Alas, the race that has such an immobilising impact on the nation had much the same effect on our baby, who waited another week before making his move. By then, my wife and I were fully primed, having spent a happy weekend in the countryside learning various calm-birthing techniques and having completed our prenatal classes in Sydney. Here, I resisted the temptation to attend the 'Beer and Bub' course, where advice comes with a few ice-cold libations, and relied instead on a delightful Melbournian woman who plied us with home-made fruitcake and called us 'possums' and 'darls' throughout. Her 40-minute simulation of the second stage of labour will live long in the memory both as an object lesson in natural birthing and as a journey into the lesser-known reaches of the Antipodean vernacular that would make an Australian slip fielder blush. Certainly, we will never look upon the frill-neck lizard in the same light again.

There were times when waiting for the start of labour felt a little like waiting for the start of the Gulf War. Shock and awe was imminent, but we did not quite know when. Here, you will have to forgive me for lapsing again into foreign-correspondent speak, but it exposes the occupational hazard of equating everything that happens to a news event, large or small.

Still, as we were soon to discover, the wonder of the birthing suite defies comparison. Taking more than 50 hours from first contraction to first breath, it was a long, agonising labour, complicated by the fact that our baby had assumed the proportions of his father and decided to spend the final hours of gestation luxuriating on his back in the posterior position. It meant that the contractions, rather than being metronomic and building to a rousing crescendo, had more of a syncopated rhythm, like improvisational jazz. Because backbone was grating against backbone, they were also unbearably painful.

In the face of this pain, however, my Australian wife was resolutely Amazonian – she resisted the temptation of numbing drugs – and a labour that started in the early hours of Wednesday morning finally came to happy fruition late on Friday afternoon. From the periphery of news, I could report back to Britain the most consequential story of our lives, and one that Fleur and I will never tire in telling and updating: the birth of a 10lb 9oz boy. Bonny and smiling, Billy Bryant seemed the perfect name.

With the family over from Britain, our first Christmas could not have been happier, and so was the run-up to the New Year. Truly, the present was golden and the future brighter still. But on Christmas Day, I had made the mistake of listening to the early-morning news bulletin – a rookie error – and heard that a monsoonal trough had crossed the coast from the Coral Sea and was threatening widespread flooding in Queensland.

Immediately, I turned down the volume and made sure not to pick up a paper or turn on the television news for the rest of the week. But from that moment on, I had that unsettling feeling that my holiday would eventually be interrupted by a trip north of the border to the sunshine state.

All foreign correspondents reach the point, I suspect, when the very thing that once made the job so exciting and fun, which is to say its unpredictability, becomes its biggest drawback. Mine had actually come midway through the year of the disasters in South Asia, when a bomb went off in the pilgrimage town of Varanasi on the night before I was due to go on a holiday planned as a respite from bloodshed and suffering. Now, I felt the sensation more powerfully than ever before, as I took the inevitable call from London asking me to get on the next flight to Queensland and to leave my family behind.

The plane left in only a few hours, and the usual mad drop-everything-and-go scramble to the airport was followed, not long after we landed, by the usual mad rush to get a piece to air before our competitors. Then came the 21-hour work days – on major stories, we tend to work double days: the Australian day, followed, without rest, by the British day – the never-ending demands of our continuous-news channels, the usual pinched deadlines, and the familiar logistical challenges of severed roads, hotels without power, and in this instance a satellite that freakishly caught fire in the middle of a live cross to the Ten O'Clock News, our flagship programme.

In Rockhampton and Brisbane, we witnessed the slow inundation of properties and businesses, a ruination of homes and livelihoods that is always sad to witness. But it was the small towns of the Lockyer Valley, such as Grantham, that were clearly the epicentre of this disaster. When phrases came to be used such as 'walls of water' and 'inland tsunamis', I thought they had the ring of journalistic hyperbole. Then I flew into Grantham and saw the devastation myself.

Though on a smaller scale than the wreckage I had seen in Galle, Nagapattinam and Mullaitivu, the waters had nonetheless left behind a tsunami-like wake of destruction. Entire homes had been lifted from their foundations. Cars had been tossed miles further down the valley. This kind of destruction is always hard to look at, and the testimony of survivors and rescuers always harrowing. But these stories were even harder to bear as a new father.

Along with the instant reordering of priorities, parenthood had also made me much more risk averse. It was not as if we were in any great danger in the flood zone, but I was far more hesitant about wading through muddy waters that had venomous snakes zigzagging on the surface, and even felt slight foreboding when zipping over the tops of hill ranges in helicopters to reach the stranded communities – something I have done on countless occasions in far more hostile environments. We did what we had to do, and London was pleased with the coverage, but throughout the month-long crisis I just wanted to go home.

Christchurch was harder still, since major earthquakes are always more brutal to cover than floods or cyclones. Aside from the logistics and occasional aftershocks, the hardest tests were confronting death and ruin on such a large scale. Not since 9/11 had I witnessed such destruction in a First World city. Nor so much bereavement.

Cathedrals with wrecked facades and toppled steeples stood as landmarks to the destruction. So, too, did the parish churches, many of Victorian gothic splendour, with fallen roofs and wrecked naves. Some destroyed office blocks looked like concrete houses of cards, while at others, like the CTV building, which had once housed a community-television station, the devastation was almost complete. Had our pictures been broadcast in black and white, viewers could easily have mistaken them as wreckage from the Blitz.

Just as South Asia had experienced a year of disasters, the Antipodes were living through a summer of calamities. And, as with Queensland, I got out as quickly as London would let me. Here, I suspect another threshold had been crossed: the moment of return and reunion was a far more exhilarating prospect than the point of departure – another massive sea change from the early days of my career.

One of the more affecting sights in Christchurch had come at the airport, outside the perimeter of the downtown disaster cordon, where we had gone to film the arrival of a British urban search-and-rescue team. Greeting it at the gate was a welcome party that included the British High Commissioner, her press man, a couple of relief workers and local journalists. As we walked into the terminal to join them, I noticed off to the side a sad-faced Japanese man dressed in a slate-grey suit who had arrived from Tokyo and been greeted by no one. The bodies of more than a dozen Japanese students were buried still in the wreckage of the CTV building – along with the television station, it also housed a foreign-language school – and he had come to retrieve the remains of his son or daughter, a horrendous journey that he had undertaken with enormous dignity and a minimum of fuss.

Even in the biggest disasters, often it is the small acts of humanity, courage and kindness that set me off, and this poor old man moved me to tears partly because he seemed so determined not to break down himself. The incongruity of the scene made it all the more tragic: a Japanese man landing in a country he probably thought he would never set foot in, who by now had doubtless seen the pictures of the flattened CTV building and knew his child could not have survived.

Hours earlier, we had filmed a Japanese search-and-rescue team sifting through the colourless rubble of the CTV building in their bright-orange overalls. These teams remained in the city to help find and repatriate the dead students. Then, just two weeks later, they hurried back to their homeland, after a quake 8000 times as powerful as the seismic shock that devastated Christchurch struck off the north-east coast of Japan.

As soon as the first aerial pictures came through of the tsunami wave, which were broadcast almost in real-time, it was obvious that Japan was confronting its worst crisis since the war. Again, had the pictures of the worst-affected coastal communities been rendered in black and white, we could have been looking at Hiroshima or Nagasaki.

As ever in these situations, the first death toll was virtually meaningless, for it registered that just five people had been killed. Given the 'end of days' feel to this disaster, footage that resembled the latest in three-dimensional computer animation and the added horror of nuclear reactors overheating to the point of partial meltdown, it was clear early on that the dead would be counted in the tens of thousands.

That Friday night, I had finished up work and was getting ready to join Fleur on a business trip to New York, where I planned to play Mr Mum for a week. Then the call from London came through, asking me to head to Japan. This time, I said no, and I explained my reasons to an old hand in the newsroom who had sent me on countless assignments in the past. 'Don't worry, it's only your first wife,' he deadpanned – a joke I had heard him deliver so many times down various crackly mobile-phone lines that it had become his catchphrase.

Just as I could not have let Fleur down, I would honestly have struggled to cope with such a massive disaster – not that I told him that. In response to a major tragedy, I had said no only once before, when an earthquake struck off the coast of Chile in 2010 just as Fleur and I were in the midst of an IVF round. Under the drop-everything-and-go laws of Correspondentland, it is not a word that comes to be uttered that often. Another threshold had been crossed.

Walking the streets of New York with a four-month-old strapped to my chest was enormous fun, and I found that the city took on an entirely different character when confronted by a newborn. Passers-by smiled. People stopped to stay hello in the street. Weirder still, they allowed me to grab the next available cab.

While I was waiting to meet a former colleague in the lobby of a downtown radio station, a man who seemed vaguely familiar came up to us cooing and aaahing with great Big Apple aplomb. No wonder, it was Kiefer Sutherland, taking a break from planetary-protection duties, who happily chatted away while we waited to be taken upstairs. Impressed by the dimensions of our baby boy, he assumed that my wife must have ingested a tranche of drugs to deliver him. So when I explained that she had let nature run its course, he was ashen-faced. 'Christ, I need a cigarette,' he said, and with that he was off.

For all our fun, as the city prepared to mark the tenth anniversary of 9/11, there were regular reminders of that more fretful period in the aftermath of the attacks when New York was nowhere near as welcoming: the National Guardsmen at Penn Station; the bronze memorials on the walls of every downtown firehouse; the ongoing construction work at Ground Zero; a skyline unrepaired.

Still it was impossible to hear the wailing doppler of a passing police car, or the burps and belches of a fire engine responding to an emergency call, without wondering, however fleetingly, if New York had come under renewed assault.

Then there was the unfinished business from the founding mission of the Bush administration's war on terror: the hunt for the man who had masterminded the attacks. The anniversary loomed as an emotional deadline for his capture, when no doubt he would taunt America with another videotaped message.

Returning home I signed up belatedly, and somewhat reluctantly, to Twitter, which for journalists is not just an outlet for digitally documenting every five seconds of our lives, but also a boutique wire service. On one of my first outings I noticed a stream of chatter, more high-pitched by the second, emanating from Washington. The gossip, which soon hardened into a hashtag, was of an unusual late Sunday-night speech from the president. In the ceremonial East Room, no less. White House correspondents, who only the night before had seen Barack Obama mercilessly lampoon Donald Trump at their annual black-tie dinner, were told this was not an event they would want to miss. Former colleagues received cryptic messages from their contacts within the Obama administration, simply noting, 'Go to work.'

Needless to say, presidents rarely address the nation at such short notice, and never at such a late hour on a Sunday night. When word leaked from the West Wing that the statement concerned national security but had nothing to do with Libya or Muammar Gaddafi – America's latest target – it could mean but one thing.

As on election night in 2000, Fox News raced out of the traps. By strange coincidence, Geraldo Rivera, who had purchased that gun in the hope of killing Osama bin Laden himself, was on anchoring duties. 'Can it be, ladies and gentlemen?' he asked, after receiving word from a Fox News producer working his contacts on Capitol Hill. 'Could it be?' Then he looked down at his computer terminal. 'Hold it, hold it, hold it, hold it, hold it,' he said, as he stared, transfixed, at the one-line message on the screen. 'Bin Laden is dead. Bin Laden is dead. Confirmed. Urgent. Confirmed. Bin Laden is dead.' With that, he gripped the hand of the white-haired general seated alongside him on set in celebration. 'Happy days. Happy days, everybody. This is the greatest night of my career. The bum is dead.'

Even before President Obama addressed the nation, a huge crowd had amassed outside the White House, similar in magnitude and mood to the one that gathered on the night of his election in 2008 – one that mixed celebration with vengeance. In New York, too, chants of 'USA, USA' were soon ringing out at Ground Zero and Times Square, which tapped the same groundswell of ultra-patriotism we had witnessed in the emotional wake of the attacks. The scenes of unabashed celebration also produced one of the ringing images of the night: firemen from Ladder 4 sitting atop their rig watching a news ticker announce the death of bin Laden and punching the air with muscly delight – a blue-collar rendering almost of Alfred Eisenstaedt's iconic portrait from V-J Day in 1945 of an American sailor kissing a swooning nurse.

In Washington, the White House started to weave a narrative that did not always marry with the facts – something correspondents had become familiar with during the post-9/11 years. The incriminating claim that bin Laden's wife had been used as a human shield, with all the insinuations of unmanliness that flowed from it, turned out to be false. So, too, the suggestion that the al-Qaeda leader had been armed. Still, Barack Obama was at pains to eschew the triumphalism of a 'Mission Accomplished' moment, even if the crowds pressing up against the railings of the North Lawn were not in the mood for circumspection.

In any case, it was hardly as if the president needed a victory banner, because the bumper sticker was already in the works: 'Obama got Osama' – although anchors and reporters would repeatedly fluff their lines that week as they tried to differentiate between the two.

That the al-Qaeda leader had been hunted down in the cantonment city of Abbottabad came as a genuine surprise, but not the notion that his compound fell within the gaze of the Pakistani military and, by extension, the ISI. This time, however, the Pakistan leadership, which had been kept in the dark about the mission, was not given the chance to play its double game. In the days after, Pakistan's political and military leadership claimed repeatedly that they had no knowledge of bin Laden's presence on their soil – another staple. They also expressed outrage at the violation of their sovereignty. But was it confected rage? Part of the Pakistani Government's double game with its own people?

That whole week, it felt like the 9/11 years were flashing before our eyes. Barack Obama made a pilgrimage to Ground Zero, with a much more timeworn Rudy Giuliani at his shoulder. Baseball games took on the feel of patriotic rallies, as they had done that September. The more strident scenes of rejoicing, criticised in many quarters as jingoistic excess, even brought back that moment in Firdos Square, when a marine briefly draped the still-erect statue of Saddam Hussein with the Stars and Stripes. On a more sober note, there were the heightened fears of reprisal attacks on American soil, and elsewhere. There was also the suggestion that some of the intelligence used in tracking down bin Laden's courier might have been gleaned from using waterboarding torture techniques at Guantanamo Bay, giving a share of the credit, it was argued, to George W. Bush.

The comedian Bill Maher, who had been taken off air after 9/11, pilloried the Bush administration for losing its seven-year game of hide-and-seek with bin Laden and joked that it had required a black gangsta president to do the job. All week, the usual procession of uninformed talking heads made the short journey into the cable studios of Washington, talking up the political dividend for Obama, their Beltway preoccupation, but having little of interest to say about Pakistan. Alas, the pundit who could have peered much further into the distance was absent from the screen. Captive then in Tumourtown, Christopher Hitchens was losing what he called his freedom of speech. The voice of the British tabloids, however, had not yet been muted. 'Bin Bagged,' crowed The Sun.

Bob Woodward proved he was still the most well-connected Washington reporter by producing the first fly-on-the-wall account of the raid. It included a delicious detail from a White House meeting when the head of the National Counterterrorism Center predicted there was only a 40 per cent chance that bin Laden would be found in the Abbottabad compound. That sounded like a low probability of success, someone chimed in. 'Yes, but what we've got is 38 per cent better than we have ever had before,' he replied, instantly lending weight to what US military chiefs in Afghanistan had told us down the years.

Once the satellite trucks had set up shop, there came a glut of pictures from outside bin Laden's compound, where he had been hiding in plain view. They featured the usual ball-scratchers from the Pakistani Army and young boys, dressed in their shalwar kameezes, picking up fragments of the SEAL team's downed helicopter that would doubtless immediately come to be used as cricket stumps.

Having taken down bin Laden, the Obama administration now sought to snuff out his image. As the week drew to a close, the administration released footage that was as demystifying as the photographic stills of Saddam Hussein having his mouth probed with a wooden spatula. It showed a frail-looking bin Laden flicking through home videos of his days as a warrior in Afghanistan, like some arthritic bantamweight wistfully watching reruns of his title bouts.

For those of us who had covered his hunt, there were feelings that week both of professional exhilaration and of anticlimax. And although the capture of bin Laden opened up all sorts of new lines of inquiry and raised a welter of questions, I suspect most of us felt a sense of journalistic closure, a banality that seems, in this instance, almost unavoidable. At the outset of the 9/11 years, we had made such an effort to find apposite words. Now, we ended them with the laziest of thoughts: that an era had drawn to a close. But mentally it had.

By the time the tenth anniversary commemorations came around, I had retreated further from frontline news, and gone part-time with the BBC. Looking for even more restorative balance in my life, the aim was to spend more time with the family, which I am delighted to report grew unexpectedly in size, with the addition of a beautiful little girl. Leaping briefly from the hamster wheel, which in the age of 140 character news cycles hurtles at an ever more frightening velocity, was a further attraction. For even if my sojourn in Australia had often felt like a lifestyle sabbatical, an escape from the sapping relentlessness of the 9/11 beat, it was time for a proper break.

—

Yet Correspondentland is a near impossible place to abandon entirely, even if for a while you manage to flee its borders. As I pen these final words, then, my newly expanded family is set to embark upon a fresh departure so that I can take up a full-time posting as the BBC's man in New York. Just as Hotel Kabul seemed like a usefully metaphoric starting off point for these chronicles, NYC seems an apt place to draw them to a close. It is, after all, the city that never sleeps, and the modern-day news media is now just as restless.

Acknowledgements

The news industry can be a little like the grand-prix world of Formula One, in that a travelling circus flies from country to country and from continent to continent investing an extraordinary amount of work, energy and ingenuity in order to keep one person ahead of the competition. Apart from the occasional use of flameproof underwear, there – alas – the comparison almost ends. But correspondents often end up scooping the awards and receiving the herograms – just as drivers end up popping the champagne corks – when it is truly our cameramen, producers, picture editors, assignment editors, drivers, local fixers and translators who are more deserving of the plaudits. My great fortune since joining the BBC has been to work with the best of them.

In Washington, what would I have done if the pit lane had not included Dorry Gundy, Joni Mazer Field, Jeanette Thomas, Beth Miller, Karina Rozentals, Linda Seeley Kirkpatrick, Sara Halfpenny, Ron Skeans, Chuck Tayman, Lou Kerslake, Jon Jones, Mark Orchard, Sanjay Singhal, Philippa Tarrant, Rob Magee, Mark Rabbage, Allen McGreevy, John McPherson, Fiona Anderson, Marc Allard, Andrew Roy, Martin Turner and Bill McKenna, the pinball wizard. And what about the staff at the Port of Piraeus cafe underneath the bureau, the purveyors of the famed Delaware Destroyer breakfast sub that kept me going throughout impeachment. Neither should we forget Kerry Meyer and his delightful wife, Misa Rosetti-Meyer, who ran the rooftop television position overlooking the White House and who gave the appearance, at least, of never tiring of my customary voice-level check: 'I'll be talking like this, I'll be talking like this, I'll be talking like this . . .'

Over the years, I shared that backless tent with some of the BBC's smartest correspondents: my dear friends, the husband and wife duo Philippa Thomas and Richard Lister, the great Paul Reynolds, Rob Watson, Matt Frei, Justin Webb, Jonny Dymond and the human megaphone himself, Stephen Sackur.

After Washington, I was lucky to head to Delhi, another fabulously close-knit bureau, where I enjoyed the camaraderie and friendship of Navidip Dhariwal, Nik Millard, Vivek Raj, Paul Danahar, Ravi Lekhi, India's finest home-grown news cameraman, Phil Goodwin, Shilpa Kannan, Sanjeev Srivastava, Adam Mynott, Soutik Biswas and Niraj Nirash. Nik and Phil also provided many of the still photographs from Afghanistan and beyond, offering even more proof of their talent.

Elsewhere in South Asia, I could not have functioned without Ali Faisal Zaidi, our Islamabad cameraman and a two-letter-word fiend at Scrabble, or Bilal Sarwary, our Kabul Mr Fix-It. Shelley Thakral deserves double thanks, for working with me in both Washington and South Asia. Then there are Matt Leiper and Andrew Kilrain in Sydney.

Our foreign duty editors who man the newsdesk in London morning, noon and night are rarely anything other than a delight. The same is true of the traffic managers, who record our dispatches, and the assignments team, who tell us where to go, led with such aplomb by the likes of Jonathan Chapman, Malcolm Downing and Jonathan Paterson. My World News editors, Jonathan Baker and Jon Williams, have shown great forbearance towards a correspondent who kept on going east after Delhi when he was probably meant to go west. Two senior BBC News executives, Stephen Mitchell and Mark Byford, have also been kind over the years.

I could not end my BBC vote of thanks without mentioning Geoff Morley, my first tutor, who at least tried to straighten out my grammar, and Mark Sandell, who first came up with the idea of breaking into Piers Morgan's office and who then packed me off to Jerusalem. Rik Morris was not only the first person to send me to Australia but he also vouched for my professional competency when Washington was looking to bolster its numbers. Then there is our happy band of BBC news trainees: Gavin Allen, Terry Stiastny, Amelia Newsom-Davies, Jasmin Buttar, Sarah Fradgley and my dear friend James Helm, who was also good enough to perform best-man duties in Galle.

To the colleagues and friends kind enough to read chapters of the book – Soutik Biswas, Shilpa Kannan, Vivek Raj, Angus Paull, Richard Lister, Daniel Zammit and Nick Glozier – I owe a particular debt of gratitude, not least for saving my blushes on a number of occasions. Malcolm Balen, the BBC's editorial tsar, was a real pleasure to work with and nowhere near as stern or censorious as his unofficial job title suggests.

My thanks to Random House Australia. Mark Lewis, my publisher, not only saw in my sketchy proposal the seeds of a book but also took the trouble to read all 600-plus pages of my first tome, *The Bystander: John F. Kennedy and the Struggle for Black*

Acknowledgements

Equality. Hopefully, Mark's *Boy's Own* enthusiasm, to deploy a cliché that he himself would try to purge from the script, comes through in its pages. Kevin O'Brien had the unenviable task of editing them and learnt early on that, although the BBC had spent almost a year trying to straighten out my grammar and syntax, it needed considerably more time to fully complete the job. I felt in very safe hands. In Peri Wilson, I could not have hoped for a savvier publicist. I am indebted to the publishing team at Oneworld, led by Mike Harpley. My thanks, as well, to the sharp-eyed Kathleen McCully for anglicizing the manuscript, and to Rachel Beaumont for publicising *Correspondentland* in my homeland.

Had it not been for my agent, the indefatigable Pippa Masson, I would never even have been introduced to Random House. Something of a family mascot, Pippa has managed to get not only my wife into print but my sister-in-law as well. Pippa also suggested that I should overcome both my British and BBC inhibitions to write about my adventures as a correspondent, which was something initially I was reluctant to do. Gordon Wise, my agent in London, was also a source of tremendous encouragement, and helped find a home for *Correspondentland* in the UK and the US.

Where would I be without Paul Kalra, my best friend from college, who introduced me to the lovely Madhu Chawla, who in turn introduced me to the Aussie knicker lady? Not in the Antipodes, for sure.

Perhaps I should even thank my lucky stars that the story related in the final paragraphs of the postscript unfolded before my book was sent off to the printers rather than in the weeks following.

At the end of my first book, I thanked Sarah and Rod Selkirk, my sister and brother-in-law, for their legendary hospitality. Since then, it has become even more lavish and generous, for which thanks again. Ellie, Katie, Millie and Rory are even more of a joy than they were the first time around.

Were I to thank my parents, Colin and Janet Bryant, for everything, this book would require a whole new chapter. So all I will do here is express my gratitude for imbuing me with a sense of curiosity and for never seeking to limit where it might take me. It is not an exaggeration to say that my journalistic training began in the home, with a running seminar from my parents on fairness, integrity and decency.

My darling wife, Fleur Wood, met me at a time when I was in danger of venturing so far into Correspondentland that I ran the risk of being trapped permanently within its borders. And although I realised fairly early on in my career that there was much more to life than two and a half minutes on the evening news, Fleur helped show me precisely what it was. Together, we stand in happy defiance of that Indian proverb: nothing grows under a banyan tree.

As well as her love and a completely new wardrobe, Fleur has given us Billy. The most beautiful of babies – here, confessedly, I deviate from the BBC's normal rules of impartiality – it is a measure of his congeniality and all-round calmness that in the early months of his life I lost far more sleep to news than to him. Dear Billy will soon come to realise, I hope, that his father is not attached umbilically to a MacBook Pro, despite appearances to the contrary during his first six months.

So I complete this book a contented man; and in what has been a life of great abundance, as well as great adventure, Fleur and Billy have been the greatest gifts of all: my family.